THE WANDERERS AND CRITICAL REALISM IN NINETEENTH-CENTURY RUSSIAN PAINTING

MANCHESTER 1824

Manchester University Press

CRITICAL PERSPECTIVES IN ART HISTORY

The Wanderers and critical realism in nineteenth-century Russian painting

DAVID JACKSON

Manchester University Press

Published by Manchester University Press
Altrincham Street, Manchester M1 7JA
www.manchesteruniversitypress.co.uk

British Library Cataloguing-in-Publication Data
A catalogue record for this book is available from the British Library

ISBN 978 0 7190 6434 0 hardback
ISBN 978 0 7190 6435 7 paperback

First published in hardback 2006
First published in paperback 2011

Typeset in Garamond Premier by
Koinonia, Manchester

For Irina Prehn
(1907–1999)

Contents

	List of abbreviations	*page* ix
	List of illustrations	xi
	Acknowledgements	xiii
	Introduction	1
1	Academic autocracy and the artist's burden	6
2	The challenge to the Academy and formation of the Wanderers	21
3	The lower depths: images of the rural and urban peasantry	34
4	The revolutionary's tale: political themes	57
5	Meritocracy: portraiture	78
6	History painting: sedition and tradition	97
7	Landscape painting: styles and ideologies	119
8	The Slavic Revival	133
9	Adapted allegiances	150
	Conclusion	166
	Notes	172
	Select bibliography	185
	Index	193

Abbreviations

The following standard abbreviations are used throughout:

GTG State Tretyakov Gallery, Moscow
Государственная Третьяковская галерея

GRM State Russian Museum, St Petersburg
Государственный Русский музей

Illustrations

Colour plates

1 Ilya Repin, *Religious Procession in the Province of Kursk*, 1880–83, 175 x 280 cm, GTG.
2 Ilya Repin, *They Did Not Expect Him* (*Ne zhdali*), 1884; 1888, 160.5 x 167.5 cm, GTG.
3 Ivan Kramskoy, *Peasant Holding a Bridle* (*Mina Moiseyev*), 1883, 125 x 93 cm, Kiev Museum of Russian Art.
4 Vasily Surikov, *The Boyarina Morozova*, 1887, 304 x 587.5 cm, GTG.
5 Aleksei Savrasov, *The Rooks Have Returned*, 1871, 62 x 48.5 cm, GTG.
6 Ivan Shishkin, *The Thicket*, 1881, 142 x 93 cm, GTG.
7 Isaak Levitan, *Spring Flood*, 1897, 64.2 x 57.5 cm, GTG.
8 Mikhail Nesterov, *The Vision of the Boy Bartholomew*, 1889–90, 160 x 211 cm, GTG.

Colour plates appear between pages 98 and 99

Figures

1 Vasily Perov, *Easter Procession*, 1861, 71.5 x 89 cm, GTG. *page* 25
2 Valery Yakobi, *The Prisoners' Halt*, 1861, 98.6 x 143.5 cm, GTG. 26
3 Ilya Repin, *Barge-haulers on the Volga*, 1870–73, 131.5 x 281 cm, GRM. 32
4 Grigory Myasoedov, *The Zemstvo Dines*, 1872, 74 x 125 cm, GTG. 42
5 Vasily Maksimov, *The Sick Husband*, 1881, 70.8 x 88.6 cm, GTG. 46
6 Sergei Ivanov, *Death of a Migrant Peasant*, 1889, 71 x 122 cm, GTG. 47
7 Nikolai Kasatkin, *Poor People Collecting Coal in an Abandoned Pit*, 1894, 80.3 x 107 cm, GRM. 49
8 Nikolai Yaroshenko, *The Stoker*, 1878, 124 x 89 cm, GTG. 50
9 Nikolai Yaroshenko, *Dismissed. At the Station*, 1883, 141 x 75 cm, State Museum of Fine Art of Uzbekistan, Tashkent. 51
10 Vladimir Makovsky, *Vecherinka (Evening Gathering)*, 1875–97, 108.5 x 144 cm, GTG. 60
11 Vladimir Makovsky, *Sentenced*, 1879, 76.5 x 113 cm, GRM. 61
12 Ilya Repin, *Arrest of a Propagandist*, 1880–92, oil on wood, 34.8 x 54.6 cm, GTG. 63
13 Ilya Repin, *Spurning Confession*, 1879–85, 48 x 59 cm, GTG. 65
14 Ivan Kramskoy, *Christ in the Wilderness*, 1872, 180 x 210 cm, GTG. 66
15 Nikolai Yaroshenko, *Kursistka*, 1883, 134 x 83 cm, Kiev Museum of Russian Art. 72

16 Nikolai Yaroshenko, *At the Litovsky Fortress*, sketch, pencil on paper, 1881, 21.6 x 30 cm, Kiev Museum of Russian Art. 73
17 Vasily Perov, *Portrait of Fedor Dostoevsky*, 1872, 99 x 80.5 cm, GTG. 79
18 Ilya Repin, *The Archdeacon*, 1877, 124 x 96 cm, GTG. 82
19 Ilya Repin, *Portrait of Modest Musorgsky*, 1881, 69 x 57 cm, GTG. 84
20 Ilya Repin, *Leo Tolstoy Barefoot*, 1901, 207 x 73 cm, GRM. 88
21 Ivan Kramskoy, *Portrait of Sofya Kramskoya, the artist's daughter*, 1882, 118 x 70 cm, GRM. 93
22 Ilya Repin, *Portrait of Aleksandra Tolstoy*, 1892, pencil on paper, 40 x 27 cm, Private Collection. 94
23 Nikolai Ge, *Peter the Great Interrogating Tsarevich Aleksei at Peterhof*, 1871, 135.7 x 173 cm, GTG. 99
24 Sergei Korovin, *Before Punishment in the Volost Administration*, 1884, location unknown. 105
25 Ilya Repin, *Ivan the Terrible and His Son Ivan. 16 November, 1581*, 1885, 199.5 x 254 cm, GTG. 106
26 Vasily Surikov, *The Morning of the Execution of the Streltsy*, 1881, 218 x 379 cm, GTG. 109
27 Ilya Repin, *The Zaparozhye Cossacks Writing a Mocking Letter to the Turkish Sultan,* 1880–91, 203 x 358 cm, GRM. 114
28 Petr Sukhodolsky, *Midday in the Countryside*, 1861, 101.5 x 142 cm, GRM. 121
29 Fedor Vasilev, *Morning*, 1872–73, 58 x 96.5 cm, GRM. 126
30 Arkhip Kuindzhi, *After the Storm*, 1879, 102 x 159 cm, GTG. 129
31 The Mamontov house, Abramtsevo, built c.1790. 135
32 Vasily Polenov & Viktor Vasnetsov, *Church of the Saviour*, Abramtsevo, 1880–82. 138
33 Viktor Vasnetsov, *Warrior at the Crossroads*, 1883, 167 x 299 cm, GRM. 142
34 Viktor Vasnetsov, *The Mother of God with the Infant Christ*, apse of St Vladimir's Cathedral, Kiev, 1895. 145
35 Ilya Repin, *Aleksandr III Receives the District Headmen in the Courtyard of the Petrovsky Palace in Moscow*, 1886, 293 x 490 cm, GTG. 151
36Valentin Serov, *Girl with Peaches*, 1887, 91 x 85 cm, GTG. 153
37 Ilya Repin and his pupils at the Academy of Arts, photograph, 1898. 157
38 Vasily Baksheyev, *The Prose of Life*, 1892–93, 68 x 73 cm, GTG. 160
39 Abram Arkhipov, *Before Mass*, 1892, 58 x 114 cm, GRM. 161
40 Sergei Ivanov, *Massacre*, 1905, 70 x 80 cm, The Museum of the Revolution, Moscow. 169

Acknowledgements

A pleasure of any research is to be reminded that a list of acknowledgements is not merely a literary convention but an opportunity to record a debt of gratitude to the many individuals who have generously contributed their knowledge, efforts or simply enthusiasm for the project in hand.

Of the many curators and art historians who provided information and assistance in person and in writing I must make special mention of a few. In Russia I am most grateful to Valentin Rodionov, Director General of the State Tretyakov Gallery in Moscow and to his staff: Vice-Director Ivan Karlov, Galina Andreeva, Ana Grigorieva, Ella Paston for her unfailing assistance and Galina Churak, head of the department dealing with works of the second half of the nineteenth to the early twentieth centuries, who generously negotiated the free use of images from this institution and frequently gave me the benefit of her immense knowledge of this subject.

I am indebted to Deputy Director Evgenia Petrova at the State Russian Museum, St Petersburg, and from the department dealing with works of the second half of the nineteenth to early twentieth centuries, Senior Curator Irina Shuvalova and especially Ekaterina Shilova and Olga Lozovskaya, who assisted with illustrative materials. Mr Yury Vakulenko, Director of the Kiev Museum of Russian Art, was also most generous in allowing reproduction of images from his institution, as were N.I. Ibrahimova, Director of the State Museum of Fine Art of Uzbekistan, Tashkent, and S. Manasyan.

Over many years I have also been assisted in a variety of ways by Elena Kirillina and Galina Pribulskaya to whom I owe much gratitude. All of my Russian colleagues have been exceptionally helpful in facilitating my research, from allowing me to see works not on public display, to locating textual materials, answering my numerous queries and locating illustrative material. Without their cooperation and that of many anonymous officials on whose generosity this project is built, the present publication would have been impossible.

My search for individual canvases led me to many foreign institutions and though I cannot account for them all I wish particularly to thank the staff at the Ateneum, Helsinki, especially Helmiriitta Sariola and Heikki Malme. I wish also to thank those private collectors who gave of their time and enthusiasm but who have preferred to remain anonymous. In particular my publisher and I would like to thank Christie's for their generous help towards the cost of reproducing the colour plates.

As the current volume is the result of many years' research and teaching I wish to record my special gratitude to Professor Dennis Ward, who first encouraged and guided my research in these fields, and to my many students, who have enriched my perspective on the Wanderers through their enthusiastic engagement with the topic. Of many Western scholars who assisted me I wish to make special mention of Dr Rosalind Blakesley of Pembroke College, Cambridge, and Elizabeth Valkenier of Columbia University, New York.

At Manchester University Press I have been greatly assisted by the patient and understanding backing of my editors Alison Welsby and Jonathan Bevan, both of whom have been supportive and patient throughout this book's prolonged production. My research assistant for parts of this project, Elena Kashina, was also a source of diligent and reliable collaboration.

On a personal note I would like to thank Patty Wageman, Deputy Director at the Groninger Museum, Holland, for assisting with illustrative materials and for sharing her opinions and enthusiasm for Russian art, Tamsin Wragg for the use of her peaceful Leeds apartment in which most of this work was written, and my wife Sarah and family for enduring my many absences during its writing.

Throughout the long course of my research into Russian art it was a great honour to find a friend in Mrs Irina Prehn. An eyewitness to the Revolution of 1917 and a personal acquaintance of many significant Russian painters, she inspired my endeavours and guided me to useful source materials which would otherwise have escaped my attention. Her unassuming but extensive knowledge of the culture of her native country was of inestimable value on a wide range of interrelated topics which would be impossible to acknowledge at each turn, but which I enjoyed nevertheless. This book is dedicated to her memory.

Introduction

> Readers can find it easy to criticise, looking down from their comfortable corner on the heights from which the whole horizon lies open at everything that is taking place below, where man can only see the object nearest to him. And in the universal chronicle of mankind there are many centuries which he could apparently cross out and suppress as unnecessary. Many errors have been made in the world which today, it seems, even a child would not have made ... The present generation sees everything clearly, it is amazed at the errors and laughs at the folly of its ancestors, unaware that this chronicle is shot through with heavenly fires, that every letter in it cries out aloud to them, that from everywhere, from every direction an accusing finger is pointed at it, the present generation; but the present generation laughs and proudly and self-confidently enters on a series of fresh errors at which their descendants will laugh again later on.[1]

The rationale of this book started as a simple one; to accommodate within the problematic bodies of knowledge that coalesce around the contestable heading of 'art history' the society of Russian realist painters known as the Wanderers. Throughout the second half of the nineteenth century this important and fascinating circle of artists chronicled the life, land and history of their nation, addressing contentious issues in a critical manner and frequently giving voice to progressive aspirations that expanded participation in cultural and social debate. And yet, in the West at least, this important, fascinating and genuinely popular art movement has suffered a profound and inexplicable neglect.

Gogol's castigation of flawed pretensions perhaps provides a starting point from which to redress this imbalance. In one sense it seems uncannily to map the self-confidence of the canonical avant-garde as it progressed headlong to the future happily consigning to the dustbin of moribund cultures all forms of narrative and figurative art (in essence the whole of the nineteenth century). In time new perspectives in the scrutiny of visual cultures found Modernism's preoccupation with the autonomous 'quality' of art at best restrictive, at worst risible. But if from our privileged perspective much of what once passed for art history appears ill-conceived, misinformed, perniciously motivated or at times simply ludicrous, Gogol's caveat also cautions against the iconoclasm which pervades much contemporary discourse. Belated wisdom and tardy reintegrations, especially if motivated by disdain for past errors, run the risk of leading us into an intellectual cul-de-sac as we too contemplate our own cultural chimeras. Whilst seeking new critical perspectives and progressive analyses, rationally and interrogatively demolishing outmoded models of hierarchical and received wisdom, we must also guard against falling foul of our own certainties.

In this respect the current volume is conceived in a spirit of conscious but altruistic revisionism, to place a neglected body of knowledge in the public arena as part of the now long-lived project of intellectual pluralism that rightly regards all forms of cultural manifestation as legitimate subjects of intellectual scrutiny, rather than seeking to impose or define what constitutes 'good' or 'bad' art. But as I attempt to give what I perceive as overdue exposure to the Wanderers my task is problematised by the fact that this project cannot be a reintegration or a revival in any sense, as this is not an aspect of art history that has been dismissed or marginalised (perhaps beyond the general marginalisation of the nineteenth century) but one which has been simply ignored. Despite the best efforts of a few intrepid commentators it remains, largely, a cultural *terra incognita*. As an undergraduate first becoming interested in Russian realist art of the nineteenth century I was told unequivocally by my tutors in art history that it did not exist. There were icons (boring) and the avant-garde (unimpeachably good) but nothing in between (and by inference nothing after – Soviet Socialist Realism, of course, was not 'art' under any rubric).

In part, of course, this was the result of the classic canon of art history, which found no room for the Wanderers any more than the myriad of disenfranchised, disregarded or marginalised 'others' who fell outside of its narrow and partial exclusivity. But whilst this once impregnable edifice has been much interrogated and undermined by the one-time 'new' art history and its subsequent progeny, the paradigm is surprisingly resilient and it is still the exceptionally rare publication that indexes the word 'Russian' in a nineteenth-century context. Look for 'Wanderers' and the search becomes almost futile.[2] That an entire school, so intimately enmeshed with the socio-political pulse of its times, can somehow be 'overlooked' is perhaps indicative that most narratives of art have little to do with 'history' and more to do with a culturally mediated criticism that gives insight into recent and contemporary tastes, fashions and aesthetics. In turn this privileges the cultural agenda so that certain periods, places, individuals or areas of conceptual enquiry are disregarded, or worse, not even identified. Perhaps it is unavoidable that we select from the past that which has significant resonances for us, but where aspects of frequently remarkable cultural activity become invisible through neglect or ignorance, their lack of appreciation becomes a self-perpetuating blindness; we cannot begin to appreciate that which remains concealed.

In seeking to remedy this myopia I have structured the material around the Wanderers' major themes, ranging from the radical to the seemingly conformist.

By this method I hope to analyse the consistencies and contradictions within their oeuvre and to seek an evaluation of the Society's significance within the tenets of realism as a movement and a philosophy. I have opted for a methodology that seems best suited to this project by focussing primarily on non-pictorial societal and political factors as agents shaping visual culture, rather than privileging formal innovation or experimentation – though these aspects have not been ignored. This model seems tailor-made for the Wanderers since an engagement with modern Russian society primarily informs their subject matter, whilst the images produced are conditioned by the rigid and censorial Tsarist regime. This is not to suggest, as have some commentators, that efforts to gain a degree of freedom or creative autonomy within that system are necessarily anti-tsarist stirrings, but rather that all images produced at this time are unavoidably and explicitly mediated by these socio-political factors. As the leading artist Ilya Repin noted: 'It was a tendentious time: everything had to be based on an idea; without an idea, a picture would be considered worthless, both by critics, and even by other artists, fearful of acquiring a reputation for being ignorant. A picture without an idea exposed the artist as reprehensibly stupid and insignificant.'[3]

A secondary but important element of addressing this project has been the polarisation of source materials – left and right, East and West – which have been key agents in the cultural marginalisation of the Wanderers. This is manifestly so of a reliance on Soviet sources and their inherent historiography which insists on art being read 'through' Stalinist interpretations (frequently called Marxist though bearing little resemblance to such) that subsume all beneath the familiar model of Soviet bowdlerisation and cynical distortion. That said, the reverse is no more palatable. In as much as the Wanderers are beginning to come under more scrutiny in the West, the desire to shed the politicised mantle forced upon them by Soviet art history has witnessed an illogical volte-face wherein the realists of the Russian school are scrutinised for the slightest nascent signs of Impressionism or viewed through the prism of aesthetic autonomy that robs these socially engaged painters of their context. Unpalatable as it sometimes seems, Soviet historiography is often astute, pertinent and incisively perceptive about its own culture, and a careful sifting of source materials beyond its (mercifully very naked) biases is frequently rewarding. Though they should rightly be treated with the utmost scepticism these disparaged commentaries contain many penetrative insights, perhaps precisely because they approach their materials from, to us, so fundamentally divergent a perspective.

I have chosen then to view the Wanderers not only in the broadest social context, as palpably a product of their time and place, but also as a politicised entity. This is not to impute to the Society a political agenda or even consistent evidence of a communal political awareness, but to acknowledge that the restrictions and proscriptions of Tsarist Russia frequently rendered the tamest of actions, the most modest aspirations and the mildest of visual images highly problematic or subject to seemingly disproportionate reactions on the part of the state and loyalist commentators. Alternative readings and methodologies would, of course, yield different and no less compelling results, and the field of Russian nineteenth-century art remains a fertile and largely uncharted territory for research activity. Aspects of class, race and gender have found their way into my interpretations, but have not been my primary methodological tools since none of these varied approaches seemed singularly apposite for attempting to introduce a large and varied school of unknown practitioners to a Western readership.

I have, therefore, concentrated on viewing the Wanderers within the milieu of Russian culture, consistent I believe with their self-imaging as an essentially national school of art. Aspects of European thought and production have been addressed contextually where these seemed pertinent, either as comparisons or contrasts to the Russian experience, but the main thrust of this book has been to endeavour to address the essential 'Russianness' of what constituted the Wanderers without, hopefully, falling into a cultural constriction. The book is in this respect a conscious addition to the growing body of literature offering critical alternatives to the Francophile bias of modern art histories. Whether what results is an unwitting attempt to integrate the Russian realist school into the already crowded canon under the heading 'neglected' or 'interesting case study in the aberrant', or whether greater exposure of the Wanderers might prove the catalyst to fresh perspectives that develop beyond the specifics of place or period remains to be seen. Certain aspects, hopefully, incline towards the latter. Although many artists feature in this study, apart from the pre-eminent role enjoyed by Repin the Wanderers spawned few 'famous names' that might be added to the roll-call of nineteenth-century greats, thereby augmenting rather than questioning the biographical imperative of traditional art history which is still alive and well. In large part the fascination of the Russian realist school is that without seeking to it resulted in a partial 'death of the author', whereby personal interests were frequently subsumed by communal aspirations and where engagement with innovative subject matter overshadowed questions of formal development. That these characteristics also became defining features of Stalinist art is regrettable for the Wanderers, but not coincidental.

If all of the above sounds like a pre-emptive apology, that is a unfortunate reflection on the obscurity of the subject which this work specifically sets out to redress, but also the cultural misunderstandings that surround Russia, at once alien and exotic, familiar but unknown, neither a wholly Western nor Eastern society but fascinating in its paradoxical ambiguities. During production of this book my writing was halted temporarily to help mount the exhibition *Russian Landscape*, which was opened in December 2003 by Mikhail Gorbachov in Groningen, Holland, before moving on to London's National Gallery in June 2004. This large, ground-breaking show, primarily of the best works of the Wanderers, was greeted with critical praise and surprise (where had these artists been hiding?), and attendance figures and catalogue sales in both countries exceeded all expectations. However (and it would be unfair to single out any one author), despite a few criticisms from predictably traditionalist publications even the glowing panegyrics of 'friendly' reviewers frequently grafted the Western experience and its cultural models onto these Russian images to produce curiously incongruous readings or, with hindsight, to observe the menacing shadow of Stalinist art marching towards the future.

Working against these cultural misconceptions this book attempts the first full critical analysis of the Wanderers' output from an art-historical perspective. As with anybody working in this field I am deeply indebted to Elizabeth Valkenier's pioneering work *Russian Realist Art. The State and Society. The Peredvizhniki and Their Tradition*, the structure of which has been exceptionally helpful in framing much of my contextual material. Whilst I frequently diverge from her opinions and at times reach conflicting conclusions, Valkenier's seminal work provides a wealth of factual data which is invaluable to any study of the Wanderers and I have endeavoured to acknowledge this wherever relevant. At the same time I have tried to bear in mind that revisionism holds the danger of dumping current and localized belief-systems onto other cultures and coming up with incongruous conclusions. This publication will, hopefully, provide a discursive and socially informed introduction to the art of the Wanderers that will equip the reader to make independently informed judgements concerning the Society's aims and objectives, successes or failures, its significance or lack of it, rather than the 'series of fresh errors' of which Gogol so rightly warns.

1

Academic autocracy and the artist's burden

On 28 November 1871 in St Petersburg the inaugural exhibition of a newly formed artistic society, The Society of Travelling Art Exhibits, opened its doors to a curious public. A modest affair (it showed only 47 paintings compared to the Imperial Academy of Arts' 400) consisting mainly of innocuous landscapes, it nevertheless caught the public imagination and occasioned the painter Nikolai Ge, one of its prime movers, to record:

> It was a frightening thing for many. Each of us must have sensed that what was happening was not at all simple; each must have wondered, in his conscience, 'can I see this through?' On the day of the opening, several members withdrew. The position of those remaining was risky.[1]

Defining this moment of transition from dominant academic monopoly to unprecedented plurality, Ge's apprehensions were shaped by experience. The advent of the group of painters who would become known as the Wanderers was rooted in a long and arduous cultural evolution towards artistic autonomy, an evolution frustrated and conditioned by the specifics of the imperial Russian political scene which had shaped, moulded and perverted the nation's arts. Though artists, writers, composers and their like had rarely been allied to the furtherance of social or political thought, and even then perhaps tenuously at best, the creative mind in Tsarist Russia found itself drawn without choice into a culture of repressive restriction where the twin constituents of coercion and threat were deployed by the state to safeguard its comprehensive control over the dissemination of ideas within the empire.

Ge's fears, which throw up connotations of incendiary political radicalism on the eve of revolution, may seem curiously inappropriate when related to an exhibition of contemporary art by an undistinguished gathering of variable young talent. But as a leading intellectual force behind the novel venture of a secessionist association of artists, free of academic restriction and Court control, seeking to carve out economic independence within new markets of patronage, he was keenly aware that this incident embodied the culminating riposte to decades of cultural inertia or failed initiatives, which in turn threw a truly historic responsibility on the success or failure of this bold enterprise.

The events and thought processes which led to this singular occurrence had been long anticipated in intellectual circles, though the visual arts were not necessarily the ground on which this battle had been foreseen. Artists were not then regarded as legitimate members of Russia's celebrated intelligentsia, which operated predominantly in literary and political spheres. The visual arts were felt to be too steeped in the academic tradition and too closely tied to state enterprise to be regarded as fertile ground for dissent. And yet, for reasons which are not always coherent or explicable beyond the Society's pursuance of creative freedom, the Wanderers were to be associated with a critical and radical ethos throughout the majority of their half-century of existence.

The simplistic polarisation, that the Wanderers were the socialistic free-thinking alternative to the restrictive hegemony of the Imperial Academy of Arts, has a broad if crude appeal. Despite many similarities and cross-fertilisations (the first Wanderers exhibition actually opened in the halls of the Academy), despite close ties and personal affiliations being maintained between various representatives of both institutions, this rough cultural sketch largely holds true. The Academy was the past: conservative, stagnant, monolithically powerful and in thrall to the Court. The Wanderers presaged future hope: outsiders, insecure, fledgling, but with ambitions to transform cultural torpor into creative diversity. Their very nickname, from the Russian *Peredvizhniki*, 'those who travel about' (sometimes translated as the Itinerants), sprung from the Society's desire to tour their brand of accessible realism beyond the capital or Moscow, and to reach hitherto neglected provincial audiences.

In one sense their history is no different from that of any other secessionist school; youthful innovation confronting tired tradition, new markets superseding old, fresh talent and ideas replacing hack work, vivacity ousting moribund custom. But in a broader context the opening of this small exhibition in the Russian winter of 1871, and the subsequent vicissitudes of the Society, are symptomatic of the complex cultural nexus of Imperial Russia; not merely the role of the visual arts under the Tsars, but the fundamental nature of art's development, of what constituted 'art', and of how the arts were structured and interpreted within the highly organised specifics and the arbitrary idiosyncrasies of this most autocratic of states.

Russian 'art' in development

The first thing that strikes the student of Russian art is its eccentric roots and lack of development. From Russia's conversion to Orthodox Christianity in 988,[2] until the reign of Peter the Great (1682–1725), 'art' on Russian soil was essentially an importation of ecclesiastical models, chiefly icons (for many still the very symbol of Russia) derived from the Byzantine tradition, a sacred and hieratic form of visual culture, undesirous of change and painted to strict prescription in terms of style and subjects. The merit of iconic art resided chiefly in its function (something to which the Wanderers did fall heir) as an integral part of religious devotion, for which aesthetic merit, acknowledgement of authorship, or development of style were unimportant. The icon by its very nature sought a timeless and unworldly quality, for which unchanging models served successfully. Not until the early twentieth century, particularly the 1913 Exhibition of Early Russian Art in Moscow, when newly cleaned and restored artefacts were greeted with great acclaim, were icons addressed as 'art' in a modern, secular sense.

This is not to deny that over the centuries, despite fierce resistance on the part of the Church, modifications of tradition did result in stylistic developments, and certain practitioners received authoritative status. By the early seventeenth century the infiltration of European and secular influences can also be seen in the use of perspective for architectural forms as well as expressively individualised portraits, but these are minor modulations that barely disturb nearly seven hundred years of dominance by theocratic models. To the untutored eye visual culture in Russia between the turn of the millennium and the late seventeenth century simply ossifies – or attains its unchanging perfection, a true embodiment of Platonic ideal form.

The catalyst to propelling Russian 'art', forcibly, from the native, religious tradition of the icon, to a secular, wholesale adoption of the Western academic tradition was Peter the Great. By officially proclaiming an end to the Church's stylistic monopoly a major cultural shift was enacted in line with the Tsar's sweeping political and social reforms, aimed at aligning Russia with the ideals of the Western enlightenment, and transforming it from an isolated and backward state to a major world power. Russia effectively by-passed the Renaissance and was launched into the European academic tradition at the behest of the Tsar, as a matter of state policy. Foreign architects, painters and sculptors were imported to build and decorate the modern capital, St Petersburg, symbol of the new and progressive Russia. At the same time promising young Russians were sent abroad to complete their studies. Within little more than a single generation Russian art leapt from the iconic tradition and the first stirrings of simple natural treatment, to a refined professional competence. By the late eighteenth century Russian artists had assimilated the styles, subjects and techniques of the West, no better or worse than the standard European academic fare.

Peter's imposition of Western cultural models is an important point of fracture within the history of Russia's development as a modern European nation, the repercussions of which were to inform wide-ranging political and social debates during the nineteenth century. Discontent with Peter's legacy found vent in the 'Slavophile–Westerner' question which dogged the Wanderers. In essence this divided the intelligentsia between those who regarded Peter's reforms as desirable and saw Russia's future in continuing to follow Western models, especially where political reforms were concerned, and those who regarded his reign as calamitous and who saw Russia's destiny in a reassertion of indigenous, pre-Petrine values.

Peter's immediate successors, however, were like-minded and continued his work. The Empress Elizabeth (1741–61) established Russia's first official Imperial Academy of Arts in 1757, opened by Catherine the Great (1762–96) in 1764, and which inculcated a thorough technical training, aimed at producing proficient and well-educated artists who would be a credit to the nation. Though not synonymous with state servants, artists found themselves inhibited by the usual academic restrictions on style and subject matter. Emphasis was placed on biblical, historical and classical subjects as the apogee of artistic ambition and the full, gruelling term of academic study comprised a daunting fifteen years.

Perhaps the most telling aspect of academic study at this early stage was that it included an all-round education in the humanities, an enlightened step that acknowledged that the general level of education and literacy amongst artists was very low. The curious demographics of Russia, as well as the low esteem in which the visual arts were then held, meant that a disproportionate number of native artists were drawn from the lowest of Russia's social caste system, including serfs (individuals lacking freedom and remaining in bondage). Within the social hierarchy of post-Petrine Russia it was not only important to know one's place, but one's place was quantifiable, set in a Table of Ranks instituted in 1722 which ran through society labelling and pigeon-holing large sections of society, effectively bureaucratising most walks of life. On graduation an artist received the fourteenth and lowest of the rankings, though in theory this facilitated social progression through merit, rather than privilege. For those at the lower end of the social scale, graduation from the Academy therefore conferred not merely honour or prestige, but the vital necessity of freedom. This too would be a crucial issue in shaping the early realist school in Russia and defining the liberal intellectual ethos of many of the artists within the Wanderers.

The formation and power of the Academy under Nicholas I (1825–55)

Whilst the development of art on Russian soil during the early nineteenth century was professional, capable but generally unexceptional when compared with the standard European academic 'product', the accession of Tsar Nicholas I in 1825 was to prove a cultural reactant. Despite the intransigent climate in the political, social and artistic life of the nation at the time, the roots of most modern developments in the Russian arts are nevertheless traceable to Nicholas' interventions and restrictions, and to the frustrated ambitions that found an early testing ground in his conservative reign.

The luminaries of this period espoused the fashion for huge academic historical and religious canvases, facilitated by increased state patronage. Karl Bryullov gained an international reputation for his heady mix of melodrama, morbidity and archaeological authenticity *The Last Day of Pompeii* (1830–33, GTG). Fedor

Bruni specialised in complicated historical melodramas in the mould of David and Gericault, such as *The Brazen Serpent* (1826–41, GRM). An unlikely subversion of canon was provided by Aleksandr Ivanov who worked for over twenty-five years on his enormous canvas *Christ Appearing to the People* (1832–57, GTG), for which he adopted an experimental attitude towards the direct recording of natural phenomena, and is frequently credited with being the first Russian artist of an essentially realistic outlook.

Bryullov, Bruni and Ivanov are considered now the greatest of the early nineteenth-century artists who, whilst retaining much academic influence, nevertheless imbued their works with elements of individual temperament.[3] But these were bright spots on an otherwise darkened landscape. During the first half of the century the state retained a powerful hold on the propagation of the visual arts in Russia and in so doing laid the foundations of discontent. This would wait until the 1860s to be manifested in an open defiance of academic authority, but its first stirrings would be felt within Nicholas' reign and from surprisingly modest quarters.

Nicholas' reign was characterised by an ethos of militarism and bureaucracy encapsulated under the catchphrase of the regime: 'Orthodoxy, Autocracy and Nationality' – hardly a slogan to foster experimentation. An accomplished engineering draughtsman and a man of strictly neoclassical tastes, Nicholas regarded himself as a connoisseur and took a keen interest in cultural matters. On a day-to-day basis the administration of the Academy was in the hands of its President, the Governing Council, and its Conference Secretary, but in reality power was vested in the Tsar, who effectively hired and fired them all. Nicholas certainly energised the Academy and was most generous in funding student grants for travel abroad, but this fostered a climate of creative allegiance which constricted artists to the role of state servants set on a structured career path in pursuit of lucrative state commissions. Beyond that little was possible. Conflating the various spheres of public life Nicholas regarded all opposition as tantamount to political protest, and in a thorough overhaul of the Academy's statutes in 1840 he set about widening its scope and authority to create a more autocratic and exclusive power base than any other comparable European institution.

On the most basic level Nicholas bureaucratised the Academy in line with the civil service and military. Originally artists had graduated with the fourteenth and lowest social ranking inaugurated by Peter the Great's civil reforms, and with the title 'Artist', which entitled the holder to work throughout the Empire. Beyond this an artistic career was delimited by the tenth social ranking and the purely honorific title 'Academician'. Nicholas expanded these to produce a hierarchical career ladder of ranks and titles earned through promotion and examination. Discipline at the Academy was strict and, in moves aimed at maintaining a quiescent student body, the amendments allowed for degrees of punishment up to and including induction into the military for a period of twenty-five years. This alone might be thought sufficient inducement to deter student dissent but, coupled with the innovation of a policeman to the Academy's staff, to ensure rigid military discipline, and the ubiquitous presence of the state censor, we have a telling commentary on how autocracy perceived the role of the artist. This is a crucial badge of 'difference' that should contextualise attempts to make meaningful comparisons between the imperial Russian art scene and that of other European powers.

The complexity of Nicholas' honours system, which remained a keynote of frustration for later secessionists, can be illustrated with reference to the student experience. Like many academic pupils they followed a laborious programme. It was in three stages: drawing from plaster fragments, from entire casts, and from life. Those who finished this course and won a gold medal at examination were awarded the fourteenth civil-service rank of 'Class Artist, 1st Grade'. Lesser achievers received a silver medal and the title of 'Class Artist, 2nd Grade', and might claim their civic rank when they attained a government appointment. Those who graduated with no distinction became 'Non-class' artists and were forced to resubmit their work at a later date. Similarly with the teaching staff, the titles of Academician and Professor were divisively graded, entitling the holders to civil-service ranks equivalent to an army major or a naval captain; indeed on the studio floor an academic professor in his smart uniform, epaulettes and decorations of office and preferment would have been indistinguishable from his military counterpart.

These moves at least allowed for a greater degree of social mobility than previous glass ceilings, but this was a by-product not of Nicholas' beneficence, but his desire to promote a culture of ambitious advancement which rewarded the career-minded and threatened those who fell outside of this artistic regimentation. The same ethos permeated the competition medals and would later prove the breaking point for a group of beleaguered students who challenged the Academy's monopoly. The 1st class, or Grand Gold Medal, competition – which carried a six-year scholarship for foreign travel, and to which all serious students aspired – was a strictly regimented affair. A subject was assigned to the students, who, within twenty-four hours, would then have to work up an initial sketch under close, solitary supervision. Once completed, this 'blueprint' could not be deviated from during the year or two that completion of the competition required. Allowing for no development or modification of the initial vision, this severe constraint to artistic freedom was resented by many, more so even than the usual requirement of antique or outmoded subject matter.

This rigid state of affairs was bolstered in parts by complementary spheres of governmental control, and exacerbated in others by various cultural absences. Court control over the Academy in time became dominant. Not merely was the Tsar its figurehead, but in time the Presidency passed to the Imperial family regardless of the individual's competence. In 1850 the Ministry of the Imperial Household arrogated administration of the Academy from the Ministry of Education and in 1852 Grand Duchess Maria, Nicholas' daughter, succeeded her husband to the post and in the process became the holder of enormous influence in staff appointments and the conferment of titles and prizes. Nicholas' reign also saw the extension of the Academy's powers throughout Russia as from 1832 the supervision of secondary art schools, as well as the right to grant titles and medals, had passed to the Academy, creating a nationwide programme of central supervision and producing an asphyxiating hegemony over the visual arts.[4]

Compounding these assertive manoeuvres, Russia had few pedagogic alternatives. Nicholas did not encourage provincial art schools due to his desire for rigid centralisation. A school was established at Arzamas, East of Moscow, in the first half of the nineteenth century by A.V. Stupin, an icon painter with an academic education, but when after seven years he reported to the Academy on his efforts to disseminate art throughout the provinces he was rewarded with the title of Academician and the 'honour' of having his school taken under the Academy's aegis (in effect it made him an offer he couldn't refuse). Other schools that were established by former academic pupils were quickly brought under Imperial 'protection'.

The Moscow School of Arts remained a unique but only partially independent exception, extravagantly described by the artist Aleksandr Benois as a place where 'absolute freedom, at times degenerating into confusion and looseness, reigned supreme'.[5] Established in 1833 as an informal venue for art classes, it passed to academic control in 1843 as the price for being granted the status of an official training centre and remained a subordinate institution, conferring only the lowest rank upon its graduates: all else, including medals and prizes, remained the Academy's privilege. Notwithstanding, the school was regarded as being less restrictive and therefore attractive to many students who sought a more liberal environment at a geographical remove from the capital.

The only other venue for artistic tutelage, and notably the only one that offered students the possibility of studying abroad, in this case Italy, was the Society for the Encouragement of Artists, established in St Petersburg in 1820 by three wealthy patrons (in 1882 it significantly changed its title from 'Artists' to 'Art'). But this too was fraught with limitations. In essence the Society offered a preparation for entrance to the Academy via its drawing school and it too adhered to the classical traditions and scepticism towards artistic innovation. As early as 1822 it was receiving state finance and in 1833 it was auspiciously renamed as the 'Imperial' Society for the Encouragement of Artists. From 1852 it too was headed by Grand Duchess Maria.

The problem of patronage made the artist's dilemma more acute and the state's power-hold more secure. Notwithstanding a general disinclination on the part of the aristocracy to patronise native art, the odds were stacked heavily against its development. In an inferior condition of industrial development, the population was long divided between the peasantry and nobility, with little in between. The educated population was very small, perhaps no more than 1.5 per cent by the 1830s, and it is estimated that 75 per cent of the small estates owned by the gentry were in debt, hence even the bulk of this class did not actively patronise the arts. Some estimates have placed the 'active' number of patrons at no more than 3,500 for the entire Empire, a pitiful figure by any standards. With less than 10 per cent of the entire population urbanised by 1850 patronage resided chiefly in the provinces where tastes seldom went beyond icons and family portraits, painted by often highly competent serfs on the rural estates.[6] Despite the few exceptions of early mercantile patronage that will be looked at in the following chapter, a curiosity of the Russian scene is that until the serfs were emancipated in 1861 there was almost no labour market for free artists. Why buy paintings when one could own a painter?

This situation was also instrumental in restricting the influence of the ascendant wealth of the industrialised middle-class, crucial to the transition from aristocratic to bourgeois tastes. In Russia this long remained in embryo, though a recent study has suggested that it was wider spread and more sophisticated in taste than has previously been credited.[7] As a class, however, the Russian merchants were generally excluded from a high-level public life by virtue of their lack of social rank, and although the next generation achieved greater prominence in the nation's cultural life, they were long stigmatised as conservative, religiously ultra-Orthodox and scornful of cultural affectation and urban foreign manners. This patronage would later become crucially influential with the erosion of aristocratic taste and the acceptability of Russian subject matter, but for now it serviced a tiny minority of artists and so the largesse distributed by the Court and the Academy remained the primary source of patronage, which aspiring and established artists could not afford to ignore.

As context then to the advent of the first stirrings of a realist and critical tendency in Russian art, an art which privileged indigenous and contemporary subjects, the first half of the nineteenth century is a crucial but inauspicious breeding ground. As Nicholas' reign came to a close in 1855 the power of the Academy seemed unassailable as it propagated a conservative, neoclassical style and a restricted range of subjects through its omnipotent control. It was, virtually, the sole arbiter of tastes. Only the peasantry was perhaps immune from its aesthetic ideals.

The precursors of Realism[8]

The paradox, however, was that where Russian art was seen to develop tentatively towards modern, national subjects treated with greater veracity, its proponents were frequently of low social rank, often from the peasantry itself. Mikhail Shibanov's *Celebrating the Marriage Contract* (1777, GTG), showing a joyous and festive scene with close attention to authentic representation of dress and setting, and Ivan Argunov's *Portrait of a Russian Woman in Peasant Costume* (1784, GTG) are variously cited as the first 'true' Russian subjects by native artists. Both were born serfs, Shibanov to the powerful Prince Potemkin, Argunov to the wealthy Sheremetev family, and both illustrate the curious role and status of the artist in Imperial Russia. Whilst little is known of Shibanov's life, both he and Argunov clearly trained as painters, and we know that Argunov was additionally obliged to act as superintendent of the properties owned by his masters.[9]

Though unconventional in terms of subject, both worked in a conventional academic manner. They mark the early stirrings of native motifs, but provide a harbinger of how the development of Russian art would be characterised more by subject than by style. Shibanov's work is important in this respect as he sets his subjects convincingly in their environment and treats them less as picturesque or decorative emblems of their class, but with a warmth and dignity as befits an image painted by one of their own kind.

Up to the liberation of the serfs in 1861, and even beyond, the Russian 'artist' can be forgiven a high degree of identity crisis. Not merely was his low birth and lack of professional status a psychological stigma, but frequently, like Argunov, he was required to fulfil several roles and a diverse range of functions. Vasily Tropinin, one of the earliest and most gifted of genre painters who specialised in portraits of professional 'types' surrounded by the accessories of their trade – lacemakers, embroiderers, washerwomen, peasant boys – utilised a still-life fidelity with sharp characterisation to produce a fascinating gallery of Russian subjects observed from life. And yet this significant body of work was produced under the most trying circumstances. Tropinin remained a serf until his release aged forty-eight, and only then was he allowed to qualify at the Academy. He had come to his Ukrainian master as part of a wedding dowry and managed to study painting on a part-time basis in St Petersburg when sent to the capital, aged twenty-two, to train as a confectioner. In 1804 he was recalled by his master and until his release fulfilled the functions of cook, gardener and valet. And artist.[10]

Following his release, Tropinin's career indicates both his tenacity and the limitations that many painters faced. He settled in Moscow and taught occasionally at the School of Painting and Sculpture, eventually becoming a sought-after portraitist for the middle-ranking nobility and foreigners in Moscow, a significant achievement for this provincially born piece of human property. Yet he failed to find patronage with the Russian 'high' aristocracy or the Court, who favoured foreign artists as a mark of distinction. Tropinin's works, however, were certainly influential. They provided exempla of non-aggrandising subjects, intimate and gentle images of Russian social types, and were key to granting Russian genre a respectability and popularity which later artists built upon.

It should nevertheless be noted that Russian subjects in painting were generally not favoured and remained the exception rather than the norm. A fascinating aberration in this respect are the little-known works of Ivan Ermenev, who in the 1770s remarkably produced a series of watercolours (GRM) that rank as the earliest examples of critical realism. With descriptive works such as *Beggars* and *Blind Men Singing* Ermenev sharply delineated the social hardships suffered by rural and urban peasants, who are depicted as ragged individuals living in poverty and squalor, frequently set against bleak landscapes.[11] This experiment would not be repeated for nearly seventy years, with Pavel Fedotov's sharp social satires of the 1840s, but by the early nineteenth century Russian genre painting had gained a certain legitimacy, particularly during the period 1820–40, spurred on by the works of Aleksei Venetsianov and his 'school'.

Originally a civil servant in St Petersburg, a draughtsman and surveyor, Venetsianov took up copying Italian and Dutch masters in his spare time at the Hermitage. Eventually, in 1810, he entered the Academy, becoming a product of an individual and academic training. An insular figure, he didn't travel abroad, but was much influenced by Dutch genre painting – De Hooch, Vermeer and David Teniers – and by two French contemporaries particularly: Chardin and François-Marius Granet. The French influence inclined him to drop academic rhetoric and attempt to compose his figures and effects of lighting with greater naturalism, utilising more unassuming subjects. In 1818 Venetsianov retired to a modest country estate in Tver where, except for winters in St Petersburg, he spent the rest of his life. Here he found his métier, painting contemporary themes, chiefly peasant life, which he portrayed idyllically if unconventionally: serene and gentle images of landowners and peasants living and working harmoniously, with each other and with Nature.

His treatment of figures and landscapes reveal an academic training; classically composed and arranged in eye-pleasing formations. But his subjects – bathed in soft, diffused lighting and epitomised by such titles as *The Threshing Floor* (1822–23) and *Sleeping Shepherd Boy* (1824–25, both GRM) – reveal unorthodox experiments in naturalism, images of the Russian peasantry at work and rest against a backdrop of untainted agrarian simplicity.

Venetsianov's professed intention was 'to represent nothing at variance with nature'.[12] His figures are authentically dressed and the 'data' of the scene is recorded with a dispassionate eye. Much of what we might regard as archaically picturesque – dress, location, rusticity – would have struck a contemporary eye as quite the opposite. And if his peasants appear clean, well-fed and seemingly contented, his output importantly cut away at the pomposity of 'grand art', combining elements of prose and poetry in an unpretentious manner that was at odds with official strictures and current fashions. His many portraits of peasant types would also become highly influential for future generations. Small, often of an unfinished and uneventful nature, they conceptualise art as formed from mundane contemporary subjects. Treating the peasantry as subjects in their own right, rather than as components of genre painting, Venetsianov quietly broke new ground that was to be taken up afresh by the Wanderers half a century later.

This innovative aspect of Venetsianov's career also characterised his pedagogic outlook. As early as 1818 he had taught art under the auspices of the liberal Society for the Foundation of Schools of Reciprocal Training, which aimed to spread literacy amongst peasant and working-class children (he instructed history through the use of portraits and biographies of prominent Russians). On his estate he also taught reading, writing and various trades to the serf children and sometimes adults. He even acted as their doctor. Maybe his painted peasants were indeed contented and not idealised; few masters were as liberal-minded.

Convinced that his method of working from nature was more relevant than academic traditions, Venetsianov opened a modest provincial school that took in poor but talented artists, sons of peasants and tradesmen, and thrived between about 1820 and 1850. Students paid no fees and lived free on the estate. Venetsianov strove to liberate those who were serfs, persuading owners to free them, collecting donations from wealthy philanthropists, even organising lotteries to raise money to buy their freedom. They studied in his apartments in St Petersburg during the winter, and on the estate in summer, always, unconventionally, working from nature. However, he was not an iconoclast but insisted on the 'grammar' of art, particularly perspective, and considered it beneficial for the students to copy from Old Masters, to learn from them rather than imitate them.

This was by any standards a singular experiment and a bold venture, the problematic nature of which is embodied in the 'career' of the school's most gifted pupil, Grigory Soroka, who, despite Venetsianov's best efforts, failed to gain his freedom from a less genial master. Trapped in this painful impasse Soroka took to drink, and though he was eventually freed by the emancipation of 1861 quarrelled violently with his former owner over his conditions of release. Sentenced to a public flogging (a punishment reserved for the lower orders) he hanged himself rather than face such humiliation.[13]

Venetsianov's school had limited success but its importance to the realist legacy resides in his breaking new ground in the naturalistic treatment of his 'unworthy' subjects drawn from nature rather than precept. In retrospect he can be credited with eroding the academic hierarchy of genres by introducing and legitimising peasant subjects at a time when, as one nineteenth-century writer put it, 'the Russian peasant was sold like a beast, and the poor, rough, and dirty devil had no picturesque costume of his own'.[14] This was to have a significant influence on succeeding generations and become a stock in trade of Wanderers' art. His works were a progressive step towards the democratisation of subject matter, but they conveyed no sense of ill-being in Russia, far less of protest.

These aspects were brought to the fore by Pavel Fedotov, an army officer from Moscow who became the unlikely forerunner of critical sentiment in painting.[15] Like Venetsianov, he trained by copying the Old Masters. During his spare time he frequented the Hermitage, copying principally from Dutch and Flemish examples, as well as being a devoted admirer of Hogarth, from which he derived a love of anecdote, descriptive gesture and a passion for verisimilitude which found outlet in rendition of the fine detail of everyday living.[16] He studied only briefly at the Academy as an auditor, and was not allowed officially to enter on the grounds of being too old, but his influence was sizable.

Essentially a gifted amateur, Fedotov was nevertheless friendly with the grand academician Karl Bryullov, though his small, often squalidly scabrous contemporary urban comedies were the antithesis of Bryullov's illustrious romantic dramas. Consciously unsubtle in their comedic content, Fedotov's works nevertheless introduced a new cutting edge to art, a discernibly critical note, filling his brief career with scenes satirising the foibles of the urban bourgeoisie and the rampant abuses of bureaucracy. His works were daring for his time and fell foul of the official censor.

In works such as *A Newly Decorated Knight* (1846, GTG), showing a pompous subordinate official who has just received his first decoration, or *The Major's Courtship* (1848, GTG), which exposes the venality of a wealthy merchant family arranging a match for their daughter to an impoverished, middle-aged, but noble suitor, Fedotov delivered the caustic humour that characterised his work. Though the target of Fedotov's humour was obviously the vainglory of the petty official, *A Newly Decorated Knight* created a sensation at exhibition where large crowds flocked to see its open mockery of imperial distinctions. It was refused permission to be reproduced as a lithograph (an important income stream) until Fedotov removed the offending medal and retitled the work *After the Party*. As we shall see, Russian art is strewn with examples where the 'naming' can appear less problematic than what is depicted.

It would be wrong to suggest that Fedotov was an artistic rebel or a cultural iconoclast with a social conscience tuned towards protest. Despite his critical content, he, like all artists, remained dependent on the state, the Academy, for the conferment of titles, pensions, even in later life his hospital bills. Consequently compromises of this sort were frequently affected. *The Major's Courtship*, though a riotous commentary on the vulgarity of human manners, was a work which earned the artist the title and social rank of Academician, suggesting that his output was not necessarily regarded as a challenge to the academic canon.[17] An added irony is the consideration that Fedotov's patrons, the wealthy merchant classes for whom he provided small, domestic-sized canvases of contemporary mores, were also the butt of much of his satire. Production and reception is seldom coherent.

In retrospect Fedotov's paintings seem hardly dangerous but gentle even in their castigation of human frailties. In the context of an autocratic and militaristic setting, however, their irreverence could be regarded as having an unhealthily undermining influence. In the fine arts such open jeering was unprecedented and critical uproar surrounded the appearance of his mature oil works. Unfortunately for Fedotov his best works were done around or soon after 1848, when in the wake of European political unrest the censorship laws were made still tighter. His tenuous association with the trial of a group of revolutionaries, the Petrashevsky circle, which included the writer Dostoevsky, further encumbered his career. His patronage dried up and the censor repeatedly refused publication of his works. He began slowly to lose his senses, and eventually became violent and had to be straitjacketed, dying in an insane asylum at the age of thirty-seven.

A literary painter, like Hogarth and Wilkie, both of whom Fedotov admired, his output can be seen as a pendant to the literary works of Gogol and the plays of Ostrovsky, but within a fresh sphere. More than any other artist Fedotov most firmly established the legitimacy of genre in Russian art, and with a more overtly critical flavour, even if, wisely, he tempered it with humour. In Russia he is regarded as the first critical artist, one who studied and exposed the contradictions, absurdities and vices of society and who, in so doing, paved the way for the tougher brand of realism during the 1860s, which fed into the Wanderers' oeuvre. We should also observe that his art was contemporary, as opposed to the classicising exemplars towards which 'serious' artists were encouraged to aspire.

At the point then that Russian art moves into an avowedly 'realist' phase, it carries forward the encumbering political, social and cultural baggage which in various ways will delimit and define it, but the early part of the century had provided fertile ground for development. The emergence of genre, of contemporary native subject matter, of a greater degree of naturalism in the face of academic rhetoric, and of a discernible strain of critical subject matter were all factors that would assist the maturing realist school of the 1860s, the challenge to the Imperial Academy and the formation of the Wanderers.

The status of the artist

The changes wrought by these developments were such that by 1859 genre painting, if still regarded as inferior, was accepted for minor and later major academic competition themes, though not without controversy. In general, art seems to map its developments to those in the literary sphere and to social and political thought, moving by degrees towards a liberal, sometimes critical appraisal of contemporary subject matter. But the visual arts tended to follow or shadow these, subject as they were to different pressures and restrictions, different modes of production and reception, as well, it should be noted, as a different range of aspirations.[18]

The omnipotent nature of the Imperial Academy, especially under Nicholas I, proved the biggest hindrance to the liberalisation of the fine arts, but to this traditional story of art's slow secession from state hegemony, the cultural scene in Russia by turns ossified and progressed under a series of singular circumstances. Some of these, such as the rise of mercantile patronage and issues surrounding national identity, were familiarly played out on an international stage, whilst others, particularly the status of the artist, the fiercely competitive intellectual climate, and the tensions between Slavophile and Westernising tendencies that were further entangled in current political events, combined to produce a remarkable cultural firmament from which the Wanderers emerged. These influences firmly shaped the aims and ethos of the realist school, but at other times art made its interventions to question or reinforce a variety of agenda.

And at all times the presence of the official state censor was felt. This factor alone should give serious concern when seeking to analyse any aspect of cultural production within Imperial Russia, since at all times there existed a power which could circumvent debate and intellectual exchange without recourse to appeal, thereby imposing a swift closure on the development and dissemination of free (and not necessarily dissident) thought. The dilemma of the artist, as opposed to the literary feuilletonist or the seditious pamphleteer, was that protest had to take place in public spaces, though in a strategy encompassing confrontation and retreat the visual arts consistently tested the boundaries of acceptability and the perimeters of official tolerance. When individual works incurred state displeasure their impact was consistently more dramatic, and if this happened infrequently Russian painters nevertheless showed themselves adept at tackling a range of uneasy subject matter which seems remarkable given the climate of its manufacture.

Remarkable too is the inferior social status of artists, particularly those of the first generation of the Wanderers. With few exceptions the majority of artists were drawn either from the peasantry, or *meshchanstvo*, a word which unsatisfactorily translates as *petit bourgeoisie.* That art was practised chiefly by the two lowest classes in Russia is indicative of the low standing of that profession, still more associated with the artisan than the intellectual. For the peasant artist prior to emancipation life was at best a capricious affair as a portion of another's property. Even after the liberation of the serfs in 1861 this class was subject to a variety of civic obligations such as restriction of movement and residence via an internal passport system. Taxation was arbitrary and the obligation to civic duties during periods of emergency was also levied. Corporal punishment, as we saw in the case of Soroka, was another privilege particular to this class.

Until the 1870s military conscription of up to twenty-five years was also a threat for the two lowest estates and might be invoked at any time. A specific case of this and of the artist's dilemma is provided by the young landscape painter Fedor Vasilev. He was arrested in 1871 en route to the Crimea – presumably it was thought that he was attempting to dodge the military draft, whereas in reality he was seeking to ameliorate his tuberculosis. Despite concerted efforts by his fellow artists to have Vasilev granted the graduate title 'Artist' which would release him from his civic obligations, he was still awaiting a response from the neolithic academic bureaucracy two years later when he died, aged twenty-three. Ivan Kramskoy, one of the Wanderers' leading mentors, made it plain that he considered that the inequalities resulting from Vasilev's low social standing were the root cause of his death.[19]

Ilya Repin, perhaps the great realist talent of the school, who as a student already had a reputation for artistic dissent, took a calculated decision not to join the Wanderers until he had completed his academic course. As a peasant born into a military settlement, in effect a piece of state property, a social grading, even the lowest, was the only way he could escape the poverty which was his life's experience. During his first four years as a student Repin did not return home for fear of the military draft but worked assiduously wherever he found employment. 'In order not to starve', he recalled, 'I took to all kinds of work, decorating the iron roofs of houses, carriages, even iron buckets'[20] In search of a sponsor to assist his studies, Repin was introduced to a wealthy St Petersburg General. When the man agreed to become Repin's benefactor the tearful young student instinctively fell to his knees, kissing the hem of the general's satin dressing gown before noting on his way back up that he had never seen hands so smooth and soft.[21] One could hardly want for a more graphic example of the social gulf which existed between the majority of artists and the class which governed the artistic establishments.

To be sure, not all artists came from these lowest social rungs, but for many this was a common story. The pre-eminent landscape artist Isaak Levitan was exempted from fees by the Moscow School of Arts in 1873 on the grounds of 'extreme poverty'. As a student he was orphaned, homeless, and led a hand-to-mouth existence, occasionally sleeping in the hut of the school's night-watchman, more often in the empty classrooms. On one occasion the School's Board of Teachers, appreciative of his talents, even bought him paints and brushes, such was his dire need. It is small wonder then that artists from these backgrounds found themselves poorly equipped to assert their independence, although their humble roots perhaps mark a distinctive quality of Russian realist art, that its 'vision' was shaped by those who were perfectly placed to document contemporary Russia.

2

The challenge to the Academy and formation of the Wanderers

The intelligentsia

The desire by a generation of artists to escape the irrelevance of academic subject matter, to paint what they knew, and to choose freely their subjects, were factors in the rise of realism. Perhaps more important, if less easy to quantify, was the pressure brought to bear on artists from Russia's celebrated literary intelligentsia as, aware of the cerebral gulf which separated them, artists frequently allowed the agenda to be dictated by these university-educated thinkers. It is, however, highly debatable as to how much influence artists imbibed from here, even if it seems reasonable to suggest they could hardly have been oblivious of the broad trends in intellectual developments.

The chief preoccupation of intellectual thought throughout the nineteenth century was the drive to define or recapture a national identity which Peter the Great's 'Westernisation' of Russia had effectively eradicated. Whilst both the Westernisers and Slavophiles argued the respective merits of European or Slavic modes of culture, governance or social structures, there was unanimity on the need for a national school of art; one that would express a Russian spirit and character, instead of merely aping Western traditions. The medium by which this would be achieved seemed fixed; the academic style was sufficiently ingrained to be regarded as desirable by all sides.[1] The 'how' of achieving the goal was more contentious and nebulous. Westernising factions wanted a critical, contemporary, socio-political content; the more conservative Slavophiles, the majority of whom upheld the autocracy, wanted a panegyric celebration of what was quintessentially Russian and were uneasy about art and criticism mixing.

Critical pressure on artists increased steadily over the decades but initially the call was simply to fill a cultural vacuum. In 1836 Petr Chaadaev set the ball rolling in damning fashion in an open letter signed 'from the Necropolis', pointing out Russia's total lack of original thought.

> Isolated in the world, we have given nothing to the world, we have taken nothing from the world; we have not added a single idea to the mass of human ideas; we have contributed nothing to the progress of the human spirit ... not one useful thought has sprouted in the sterile soil of our country; not a single great truth has sprung from our midst ... whatever anyone says, we mark a void in the intellectual sphere.[2]

Reaction was swift. The journal in which the letter appeared was banned, its editor exiled, the censor reprimanded, Chaadaev declared insane and put under house arrest. The Russia of Nicholas I was not open to question.

Vissarion Belinsky, one of the greatest of Russian liberal thinkers, took up the challenge more positively, charging art with the duty to defend civilisation, enlighten the human spirit, resist autocracy and obscurantism, and to formulate a national character. In particular he opposed the notion of art as an exclusive amusement but was exceptional in insisting on aesthetic standards rather than bald propaganda, stating: 'art must first of all be art, and only then may it be an expression of the spirit and direction of society ... Whatever the beautiful thoughts that fill a poem ... if it has no poetry it can have neither beautiful thoughts nor problems, and all one may note in it is good intention, badly fulfilled.'[3]

The beneficially didactic potential of art was not a novel concept. In the earlier part of the century Venetsianov pre-empted Belinsky in stating: 'the art of drawing and painting itself are nothing other than a weapon serving literature and, as a result, the enlightenment of the people'.[4] But the heyday of liberal progressive thought did not mature until the late 1850s to 1860s, the period preceding the formation of the Wanderers and encompassing the 1863 student secession. Its leaders were commonly styled as *Shestidesyatniki* or 'Men of the Sixties', though the word is genderless and might be more properly translated as 'People of the Sixties'. Adherents of such thought were also called *Raznochinets*, signifying an educated person of non-noble birth. Nikolai Chernyshevsky and Nikolai Dobrolyubov for instance, were sons of priests, educated at seminaries and then university. Debarred from other classes by birth they sought to question such anomalies. Their style was brash and contemptuous of accepted conventions and their agenda sought a radical renewal of a society where serfdom was regarded to have permeated all levels. Women, for instance, were viewed as an extension of the father's estate and therefore subjugated as surely as the peasantry. In a heady mix of utopian sentiment and utilitarian practicality, followers attempted to live by new and radical values that encompassed communal living, equality of the sexes, and economic freedom for women.

On the more extreme side of utilitarianism were thinkers such as Dobrolyubov and Dmitry Pisarev. In essence they regarded art and culture as an elitist irrelevance and agitated for their subordination as tools of social and political change. In a recipe that might have encapsulated some of the most doctrinaire products of Stalin's Soviet Union, Dobrolyubov identified the priorities: 'what exalts art the most = the description of a babbling brook and the contrast of hill and dale, or the presentation of the course of human life and the conflicts of different principles and social interests?'[5]

Even the title of Pisarev's most famous work, *The Destruction of Aesthetics* (1865), sums up his programme for the arts; utility and durability. Utility was art's ability to convey radical thought, and durability the survival of only the most robust modes of popular artistic practice. The latter was codified under the aphorism 'what can be smashed should be smashed'. If it could not survive it was not worthy. Such thinkers considered even critical genre painting as timorous and looked to art to overthrow the state, not to reform it. Their preoccupation with materialist convictions, assessing art by its usefulness to society, found its conservative nemesis in Dostoevsky, who frequently parodied what he viewed as the innate philistinism of the *Raznochintsy*. In his 1871 novel *The Devils* the respective merits of a jug, a pencil and Raphael's *Sistine Madonna* are debated to the detriment of the painting, which has no practical use. Similarly the aestheticism of Shakespeare and Raphael are found inferior to the utility of petroleum and rubber boots.[6]

The chief influence through the 1860s, however, was Chernyshevsky, a radical left-wing thinker who wrote widely and with conviction on social, economic and cultural problems. Of seminal importance for Russian thought was his doctoral dissertation of 1855, later published as a book, *The Aesthetic Relationship of Art to Reality*. In addition he also scandalised society with his tendentious utopian novel of 1863, *What Is to Be Done?* Amongst other things this promoted equality of the sexes, the abolition of marriage and the establishment of a co-operative economy. How it passed the censor is still a matter of some conjecture.

The Aesthetic Relationship of Art to Reality posed a less vitriolic stance than Pisarev and Dobrolyubov but was more uncompromising than Belinsky. Chernyshevsky intellectualised the educative role of the arts and sought self-censorship through a persuasive dialectic with his reader. He argued rationally but resolutely against the academic aesthetic which placed Beauty as the overriding goal of high art. Real life, he argued, was more important than Beauty, and more important than art. It followed therefore that art, inferior to life, should serve humanity rather than being a branch of an elitist entertainment industry: this might have been sloganised as 'Art for Mankind's sake'. Chernyshevsky's bottom line was that art should assist society by helping to understand and explain life, and inevitably by passing judgement on it.

> In the events of real life ... there is not that one-sided, narrow view from which all the works of man suffer. As instruction, as learning, life is fuller, truer and even more artistic than all the works of scholars and poets. But life does not think to explain its phenomena. This is done in the works of science and art ... Science and art are a handbook for those who are beginning to study life; their purpose is to prepare the student for reading the original sources and later to serve as reference books from time to time ... aesthetics alone persists in asserting that art is higher than real life.[7]

But who would decide which parts of life should come under scrutiny and from what perspective? Whose critical agenda should prevail? For Chernyshevsky there was insufficient time to expand his manifesto. In 1862 he was sentenced to fourteen years' hard labour and life exile to Siberia, though this was later commuted to two years' imprisonment followed by twenty years' exile, a questionable act of mercy preceded by the public entertainment of a 'civil execution'. The writer was made to stand on a scaffold with a sign around his neck declaring his traitorous nature and, surrounded by armed guards with sabres drawn, the flat of a sword was broken across his head as he was officially declared to be a 'non-person'. So far as the tsarist authorities were concerned he had ceased to exist.

Such was the reward for espousing democratic and radical political convictions, and Chernyshevsky's example doubtlessly loomed large in the minds of his followers and those who supported the cause of 'progress' in its many forms. For artists the intellectual legacy was more generally dispersed. With few exceptions they followed a broadly liberal agenda; Westernisers in their desire to democratise Russia, but patriotic in their promotion of a Russian school of art utilising native subject matter. As such, a Slavophile tendency, a nostalgic romanticism for pre-Petrine culture, was always present in Russian realism. Later in the century, as aestheticism in the arts challenged the realist school, Repin summed up his rejection of art for art's sake by invoking the critical ethos of this period:

> I am a man of the sixties; I am a backward person for whom the ideals of Gogol, Belinsky, Turgenev, Tolstoy and other idealists, are not as yet dead. With all my meagre strength I strive to embody my ideas in truth; contemporary life affects me deeply, it gives me no peace, it demands to be represented on canvas.[8]

The spirit of the 'Men of the Sixties', and of the first phase of Russian realism, was therefore consciously unconcerned with aesthetic problems, though individual artists were not insensitive to them. In general it was felt that political and social matters in autocratic, censorial Russia, where the vast majority of the population were peasants, and where free expression was banned, demanded their attention. Russian realism established itself 'at a time when the ulcers on the body of Russian society were becoming all too visible'.[9] Neutrality was the cardinal sin with Chernyshevsky stating that the artist who did not address the problems of Russian society proclaimed his support for the status quo. The visual culture that developed was therefore frequently and consciously tendentious, but most consistently in a liberal and reformist spirit. Repin again summed it up: 'The pictures of those days made the viewer blush, to shiver and look carefully into himself ... They upset the public and directed it onto the path of humanness'.[10]

The artists' *Artel*

When in 1863 a body of fourteen students dramatically seceded from the Imperial Academy it seemed likely that intellectual pressures played a part. On the eve of the revolt, a strong stimulus appeared in the shape of an article by I. Dmitryev, a follower of Dobrolyubov, which fiercely attacked the servility of artists, likening their thraldom to obligatory competition themes as akin to creative serfdom.[11]

Considering the low birth of many artists and their general lack of education it is questionable whether such an opinion directly influenced their actions, but they could hardly have been ignorant of the spirit of the times or its critical pressures.

Innovation in terms of critical content indeed flowered in the 1860s. In a series of hard-hitting canvases, Vasily Perov depicted such controversial issues as poverty, hunger, drunkenness, prostitution and death, and attacked official abuses with unprecedented gusto. His most celebrated work, *Easter Procession* (figure 1), a detailed depiction of rural poverty and a drunken priesthood, caused great offence and was withdrawn from exhibition. Amongst other artists of the mid-nineteenth century, pushing forward the limits of acceptable subject matter whilst, covertly or otherwise, weaving strains of social discord into their narratives, was Valery Yakobi, who painted a wretched and bedraggled group of Siberian-bound political convicts in *The Prisoners' Halt* (figure 2) causing a predictable uproar. Vasily Pukirev's *The Unequal Marriage* (1862, GTG) portraying the wedding of an aged wealthy groom to his young and impoverished bride, reputedly shamed a number of real-life generals out of marrying in similar circumstances, and whilst not taking Chernyshevsky's line in advocating the abolition of marriage he nevertheless exposed it as an exploitative institution.[12]

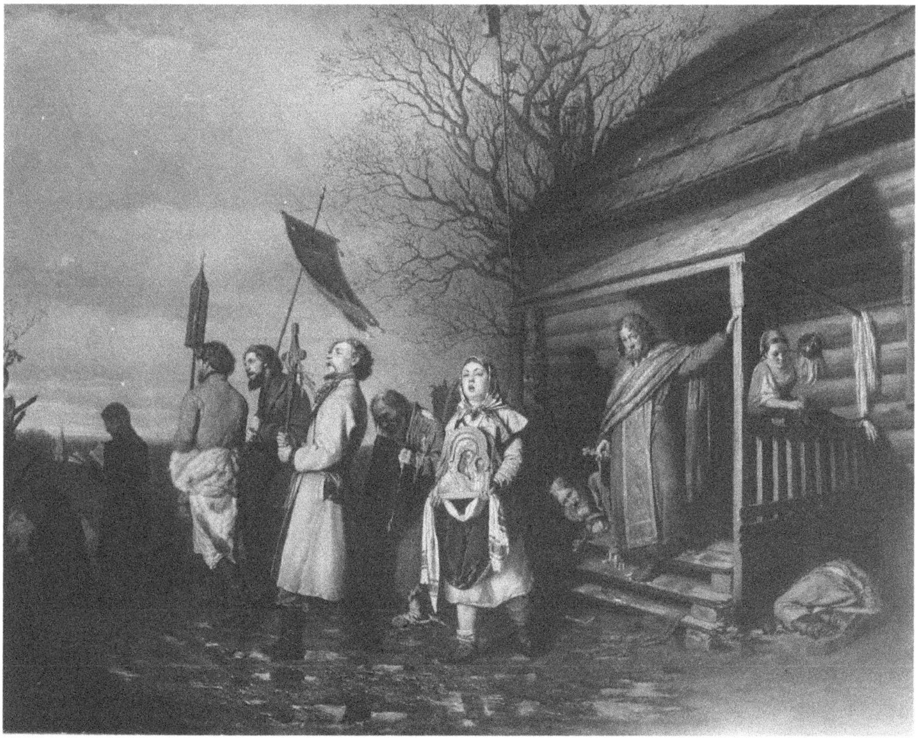

1 Vasily Perov, *Easter Procession*, 1861, 71.5 x 89 cm

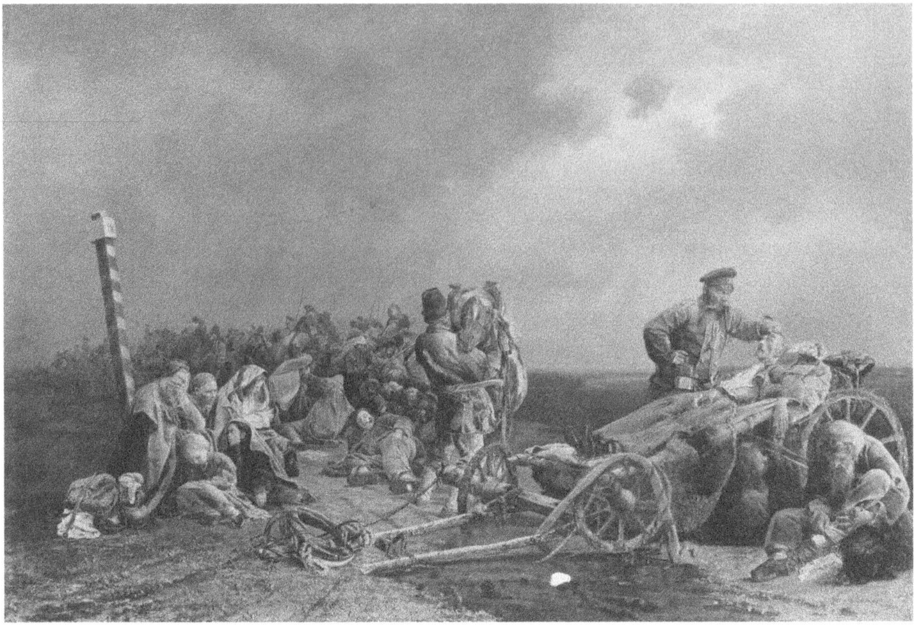

2 Valery Yakobi, *The Prisoners' Halt*, 1861, 98.6 x 143.5 cm

The secession may be viewed therefore as the culmination of various pressures and restrictions that were already under siege. A month before the scheduled date for the Grand Gold Medal the competing students petitioned the Academic Council for the right to select their own subject matter. Receiving no reply they rejected the officially chosen theme and asked to be awarded diplomas and the lowest graduating rank of 'Artist'.[13] A negative reaction was predictable since all forms of striving towards freedom and individuality were regarded as subversive. The dissenting students were certainly viewed as such, not merely because they chose to defy an august institution with imperial connections, but because the gesture was one which required great personal sacrifice, the Academy being the sole guarantor of a livelihood in a country where private patronage was scant.

Surprisingly though, Kramskoy's writings suggest that the fourteen had little more in mind than the need for freedom of expression. The debate was not about style, and only in part about subject matter; the sticking point was the denial of freedom of choice.[14] In line with events in industry, and with Chernyshevsky's *What Is to Be Done?*, an artists' *Artel*, or co-operative, was formed by thirteen of the dissidents, capitalising themselves by dedicating 10 per cent of private income and 25 per cent of all commissions received through the *Artel*. Financial survival was precarious and various types of routine work, such as painting portraits from photos, or retouching photos, supplemented their income. Works produced by the *Artel* are few, doubtless due to the constraints of money, but were primarily contemporary genre scenes suggesting an inclination towards liberally minded reform movements of the 1860s, rather than the acidic polemics of writers such as Dobrolyubov, to whom they are sometimes mistakenly tied.

The relationship between the *Artel* and the Academy is a complex and often misunderstood one. The brave gesture of the dissenters was certainly a slap in the face for the Academy and for some years to come *Artel* members were subject to police surveillance and interrogation. Yet ties with the Academy were never fully severed: in 1869 Kramskoy received the rank of Academician and the Wanderers' inaugural exhibition of 1871 even took place within the Academy's halls. Members of the *Artel* had a vested interest in keeping alive their ties with the Academy since the preferment of rank and the distribution of commissions were things from which they simply could not afford to divorce themselves fully. But why the Academy should take such an apparently easy-going attitude towards them is a matter which points to an intricacy of agenda that should discourage portrayals of the *Artel* members as subversive followers of radical politics hell-bent on smashing this detested symbol of tsarist artistic repression.

The only point which might be made in favour of the Academy is that the restriction on competition themes was regarded as the only means of providing objective criteria of assessment. The practice was designed with good intentions but had deteriorated into an uncompromising state of siege mentality. The Academy is sometimes credited with conceding ground to calls for more socially relevant subject matter, since in 1863 the students who seceded could have tackled the Gold Medal subject in the less prestigious genre section *The Liberation of the Serfs*. To this extent it has been suggested that discontent with the Academy was not the sole cause of the revolt.[15] This fails to take stock of two salient facts: firstly, that the professors who set this theme more likely had in mind a grandiloquent portrayal of Imperial largesse than a depiction of the wretched masses receiving their birthright and, secondly, that the issue, as Kramskoy had indicated, was freedom, for which concessions were a poor substitute.

The Wanderers

The student secession became, in time, the precedent and catalyst for the formation of the Wanderers, an event with far-reaching implications for Russian art. They enjoyed little commercial success but their brave act of creative independence showed that the Academy could be questioned, and in 1871 the formation of The Society of Travelling Art Exhibits realised Kramskoy's dream of an independent artistic organisation which, unlike the *Artel*, was professionally administered and attracted mass popularity. The impetus came from Moscow, largely from the painters Grigory Myasoedov and Nikolai Ge, to whom were added Vasily Perov, Aleksei Savrasov, Illarion Pryanishnikov and Lev Kamenev. As a well-educated member of the gentry and the intellectual community who had made contact with the radical thinker Aleksandr Herzen during his time in Italy, Ge played a key role in establishing the Society's position and was perfectly suited to bridge the intellectual gap between the artistic and literary communities.

In November 1869 the Moscow artists signed draft statutes for the Society, based on the need for their art to be freed from bureaucratic controls and to be circulated amongst a wider public. These, surprisingly, received a tepid reception from the *Artel* and only four members joined. Others wished not to further antagonise the Academy, a point of view on which Myasoedov poured scorn.[16] Kramskoy, however, was enthusiastic, urging his colleagues that union with the Muscovite artists could only strengthen their position. The statutes received official approval from the Ministry of Internal Affairs in November 1870 and the inaugural exhibition opened on 28 November 1871 in the halls of the Imperial Academy. This initial benevolence, repealed in early 1875, appears to have been an aberration since for fifteen years from 1873 onwards the Academy adopted a hostile attitude: students were prohibited from exhibiting with the Society upon pain of debarment from the Grand Gold Medal competition; rights to exhibition space were restricted and attempts made to stem the flow of patronage. An unsuccessful attempt at pressurising Ge and Kramskoy to merge with the Academy was bravely faced down in 1874 in an audience with Grand Duke Vladimir Aleksandrovich, President of the Academy (and incidentally the Tsar's brother). The Academy even set up a rival Society of Art Exhibits in 1875 specifically to lure Wanderers back to the fold, and began its own travelling exhibitions with a reduced entrance fee. None of these measures reduced the popular strength of the Wanderers, though the school struggled financially. Patronage was initially hard to come by; ticket receipts provided some income, but true to their democratic ethos Society members survived by making cuts, taking second-class travel to exhibitions and touting for free exhibition space. The Wanderers, however, unlike the *Artel*, were not open to all comers. New members were elected annually by the existing members, who also acted as a selection panel, voting on which works could be included in the exhibitions.

The aims set out in the Wanderers' statutes included widening the financial market for artists and circulating exhibits to the provinces to 'broaden the circle of art-lovers'. The Society spread a socially engaged brand of art to provincial centres hitherto considered cultural backwaters, creating artistic debate and spurring the local intelligentsia to the formation of provincial art schools and galleries. In turn artists donated works to the galleries, completing the circle of intellectual reciprocity. Otherwise the document concerned itself with administrational formalities and characterises the Wanderers as essentially an exhibiting society, a supportive affiliation of disparate practitioners whose common aim was freedom from the constraints of the bureaucratic Imperial Academy.[17] Though in temperament and ideological outlook the artists were of the liberal, reform-minded generation of the 1860s, the principal aim of the Society was a simple one: artistic autonomy.

Critic and patron

Where, crucially, the Wanderers succeeded beyond the *Artel's* limited aspirations and promoted themselves as a viable alternative to the Academy (it held forty-eight exhibitions between 1871 and 1923) this was due principally to able business administration, powerful literary support and a substantial economic base. In these areas two influential figures were of crucial importance: the critic Vladimir Stasov and the merchant collector Pavel Tretyakov.

Stasov, who also held the position of Head of the Art Division at the St Petersburg Public Library from 1856 to 1906, was from the 1850s an untiring opponent of academic art, classical content and conservative forces, agitating for a socially involved, national school in music and art. A follower of Chernyshevsky and an admirer of Proudhon and Courbet, he held firmly that art must be contemporary and socially relevant. Stasov's vastly influential voice and uncompromising tenacity made him the preeminent critic of his day. Dogmatic to a fault, he was something of a cultural terrorist for whom the ends justified the means. He was not above bowdlerising his sources, and after Kramskoy's death carefully edited the painter's diaries and letters to promote him as a committed democratic-nationalist. Stasov notably shaped the career of the young Repin and continued to promote his protégé along a national-critical path. When in France in 1873–76 it seemed that Repin was wavering in his commitment as he began an urban Parisian scene, *A Parisian Café* (1875, Private Collection), and, even worse, making receptive noises about Manet and the Impressionists, Stasov took action by publishing in Russia an edited version of the artist's letters from Italy and Paris portraying him as a boorish, ardent nationalist, contemptuous of all things Western. This damaged Repin's standing with the liberal Russian intelligentsia who regarded with horror such jingoism and uncouth provincialism, but it kept him where Stasov wanted him, on a short lead.[18]

In Stasov's favour, however, were his bravery and commitment. With Chernyshevsky's example in mind, potentially the greatest casualty of aggressive polemics would be Stasov himself. The sculptor Mark Antokolsky became one of the few artists to consciously escape Stasov's baleful influence, but it seems characteristic of the critic's eccentric loyalties that when in 1893 Antokolsky became the target of anti-Semitic press attacks Stasov most publicly and unflinchingly took up his cause. Stasov had a truly missionary zeal for the Russian arts and from his ecstatic reception of the first Wanderers' exhibition, through the Society's heyday and decline, he was an outspoken supporter during periods of great political repression. Nor was he a sentimentalist infatuated with popular culture, native traditions and the innate wisdom of the common people, all of which he found symbolic of Russia's backwardness and cultural isolation. His vision for the arts was avowedly civic-minded, to instruct and enlighten, to critique the social and political inequalities of modern Russia. In this respect he was a valued and at times incontrovertible force for progress, but how closely artists shared his vision or were brow-beaten into submission by his pugnacious authority remains uncertain. To a large extent he created the Wanderers' public image and whilst he seized the role without asking, he was generally accepted as their spokesman.

The other significant force driving the success of the Wanderers was its patronage. A curiosity of the Russian scene is the ability to pinpoint almost to the day the inception of what elsewhere in Europe is a general rise of middle-class patronage, since before the emancipation of the serfs in 1861 the lack of a free labour market restricted such economic development. The crude division of society hitherto had been one of an overwhelming serf population and a small aristocracy with little between. Entrepreneurship was not unknown and pockets of collecting and patronage existed, but in the broader context it required the establishment of a wage-earning labour force to create the capitalist base, notably in Moscow, from which the new wealth and patronage could flow. This made itself known most forcefully from the 1850s as the leading merchant businessmen began to develop an interest in the indigenous arts. As was common throughout Europe, mercantile and bourgeois patronage sought a role in national cultural life through a rejection of the academic classicism preferred by aristocratic collecting activity, turning instead to contemporary naturalistic art. Regarded socially as inferiors, the term 'merchant' carried the miasma of an uncultured retrogressiveness, even from artists who were not always appreciative of their uninformed interventions, something the new patrons had to fight strongly against.[19]

Leading Moscow collectors included Gerasim Khliudov, Kozma Soldatenkov, Vasily Kokorev and Fedor Pryanishnikov. Overshadowing all, however, was the textile magnate Pavel Tretyakov. The largest of his rivals' collections ran to no more than a few hundred works, most of which were dispersed on their owners' deaths or swallowed up by Tretyakov, whose collection numbered 1,757 when it was donated to the city of Moscow in 1893. A shrewd business man and devout Orthodox believer, Tretyakov espoused traditional and loyalist sentiment, collected contemporary Russian art with chauvinistic zeal, but modernised his mills with the latest Western technology, doubling his family's already considerable fortune.

Tretyakov also had an eye on posterity, opening in 1874 the first public Russian art museum, which still bears his name. Not until 1898 did the Russian Museum of Emperor Aleksandr III (now the State Russian Museum) eventually follow Tretyakov's lead in establishing a Russian collection, as did the Tereshchenko family in Kiev. Between the first Wanderers exhibition in 1871 and his death in 1897, Tretyakov expended vast sums of money on modern Russian painting and as an alternative to Court patronage was wooed even by left-wing followers. This resulted in some anomalous acquisitions and some acrimonious disputes with critics and artists concerning individual works. Tolstoy, for instance, attempting to convince Tretyakov to purchase Nikolai Ge's biblical canvas *What is Truth?* (1890, GTG) accused him of indiscriminate buying, likening his collection to 'a heap of dung' and Ge's painting to a pearl that had been overlooked.[20]

But Tretyakov's commitment to Russian art was broad. He also collected icons, eighteenth-century works, and canvases by early ninetheenth-century masters such as Bryullov whom Stasov excoriated. As the Wanderers evolved into a national school of art, Tretyakov's part in guiding it away from progressive and tendentious themes was considerable, though hardly, it seems, programmatic. His innate preference was for contemporary indigenous subject matter celebrating his homeland and for aesthetic quality but, as we shall see, in the process he acquired some of the most radical and controversial canvases addressing the most inflammatory of themes.

Alien influences

Whilst the Wanderers were originally marketed in terms of their 'Russianness', their devotion to national themes, and were hailed as presaging a national school, chiefly by Stasov, the crucial issue of a relationship with the West became problematised and the attitudes and reactions of Russian artists towards European painting took on an aspect not merely of personal taste but also of ideological outlook. The responses of young, impressionable students, confronted by the artistic wonders and treasure-houses of the West, became the touchstone for sifting the dissenters from the traditionalists, the innovators from the conservatives, and, naturally, the Slavophiles from the Westernisers. The terms Slavophile and Westerniser were applied broadly, often crudely. By advocating social renovation and identifying with the liberal intelligentsia, the artists of the 1860s were akin to the pro-Western would-be enlighteners. In the case of painters, however, native subject matter was too easily convertible to insular nationalism. So, artists who exhibited a preference for native subjects might be labelled Slavophiles in that their concern was primarily inward looking, yet those conversant with new trends in European art might be dubbed Westernisers simply because their horizons extended beyond national boundaries. Polarisation of debate saw little room and negligible inclination to accommodate artists who found much to admire on both sides.

Throughout the first half of the nineteenth century, Rome, Munich and Paris were the important centres of artistic education, but by the second half of the century Paris was challenging strongly for the role of the artistic capital and increasing numbers of painters sought an education there. The generation which matured under the age of reform was consistently harangued to review their artistic position in an ideological and utilitarian light. Under such pressures Russian painters abroad for the first time, even if well disposed towards Western painting, frequently felt that the problems and issues closer to home were more pressing and therefore more deserving of attention. In effect, and to the detriment of wider recognition abroad, the focus of most artists from the late 1850s right up to the close of the century was set strongly on a national rather than international path. Vasily Perov, for instance, served only two years of a six-year scholarship abroad during 1862–64, at which time he showed no awareness of the establishment of the *Salon des Refusés*. Perov summed up his dilemma:

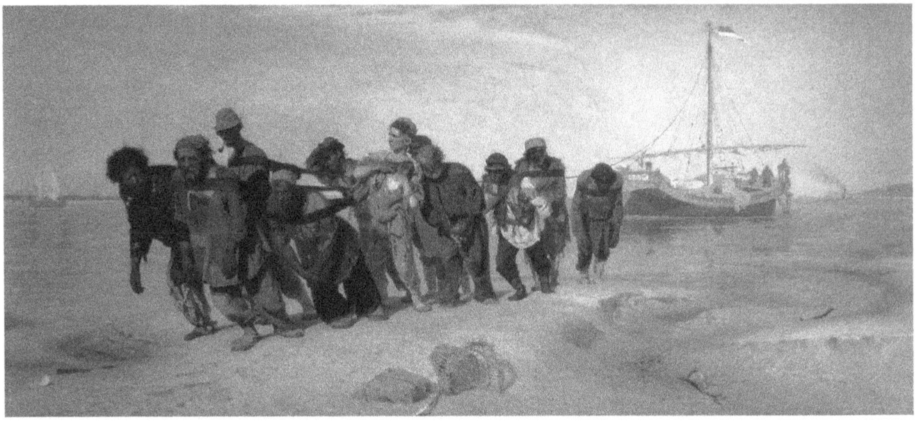

3 Ilya Repin, *Barge-haulers on the Volga*, 1870–73, 131.5 x 281 cm

> To my mind, rather than devote several years of my life to the study of a foreign country, it would be far more worthwhile to make use of the immeasurably rich subjects from urban and rural life in our country. I have in mind some subjects drawn from Russian life and hope to have more success with these than with subjects from a people I hardly know.[21]

The landscape painter Ivan Shishkin postponed for three years his scholarship for foreign travel awarded in 1860, devoting himself instead to native scenes, and once abroad, in an unnatural *milieu*, supposedly begged to be reunited with the Motherland. Repin too postponed his foreign scholarship, awarded in 1871 for *Christ Raising Jairus's Daughter from the Dead* (1871, GRM). By retaining the classification of a genre painter he was able to spend three out of the six years conferred by the Grand Gold Medal at home, instead of abroad. This gave him time to complete work on the *Barge-haulers on the Volga* (figure 3) and possibly too much ideological sentiment should not be read into the delay. The prospect of foreign travel and a closer acquaintance with the art of the West was nevertheless not so great an attraction as to draw him away from the completion of an important (and very Russian) painting.

It would be misleading to infer from the experiences of Perov and Shishkin that a generation of painters rejected, or felt innately hostile towards, Western art *per se*. Repin's experiment with *A Parisian Café* shows an artist adapting to new trends and cognisant of continental modernity, though in general memoirs of the period show a predilection for the established 'stars' of the artistic firmament. The sculptor Mark Antokolsky recalled his and fellow students' admiration for Gérôme, Meissonnier and Delaroche, whilst Kramskoy, who was in Paris during 1869, though just as ignorant of current events as was Perov, exhibited no hard prejudices, eagerly accepting his first opportunity for foreign travel.[22] Russian artists were provided with excellent examples of Western painting prior to travelling abroad.

The Hermitage, with its magnificent collections of European art, chiefly Dutch, Flemish and Renaissance, was supplemented by the mainly French collection of Prince Kushelëv-Bezborodko, donated to the Academy in 1866 to form the core of its study collection, which included works by Delacroix, Millet, Corot, Rousseau and Courbet.[23]

That these attitudes eventually hardened towards a more insular nationalism was due to the critical and separatist agendas of conservative and liberal camps, but it was not an inevitable concomitant of the development of a national school. The more bellicose statements of pro-Russianness are not to be found at the Society's inception, though it is true to say that few Russian painters found the European experience ultimately rewarding. Returning in 1876 from his first period in France, Repin mournfully concluded: 'I long ago decided I would never do anything worthwhile abroad and so I would have been amazed, yes, incredulous, if something of mine had succeeded. Everything I have done here has been insipid or barren; well enough of that, I must be away home'[24]

In like vein a generation of Russian artists settled to the task of documenting, recording, critiquing and celebrating their homeland in a variety of genres that ranged from the radical and controversial to the noncontentious and the seemingly conservative-traditionalist. In the process, however, the Wanderers proclaimed both their arrival and their credentials as the school that firmly established the 'Russian' within contemporary visual culture, and with this consolidated a position of the most successful and genuinely popular movement in Russian art history.

3

The lower depths: images of the rural and urban peasantry

The realist credo of contemporaneity, which usurped the primacy of academic history painting, was early summed up by Courbet:

> Historical art is, by its very essence, contemporary. Every age should have its artists, who will express it and depict it for the future. An age that has not been able to express itself through its own artists, does not have the right to be expressed by outside artists. This would be falsifying history ... The true artists are those who take up their epoch at exactly the point to which it has been carried by preceding ages. To retreat is to do nothing, is to work without result, is to have neither understood nor profited from the lessons of the past.[1]

Though Courbet dismissed all titles imposed upon his art, even that of 'realist', he was adamant as to how the artist should address his task:

> I also believe that painting is an essentially CONCRETE art and can only consist of the representation of REAL AND EXISTING objects. It is a completely physical language that has as words all visible objects, and an ABSTRACT object, invisible, and non-existent, is not part of paintings' domain.[2]

In France the updating and democratisation of history painting was strengthened by the Revolution of 1848. For a while politics and art united in espousing the dignity of labour, and the common man, a central support of the new régime, was considered as a worthy, independent subject. This new-found respect for the labourer, especially the agrarian peasant, was most fully expressed in the impassive works of Courbet – whose *Burial at Ornans* (1849, Musée d'Orsay, Paris) audaciously treated the mundaneness of peasant life on a scale hitherto reserved for momentous historical events – and in the humane, emotive paintings of Millet, whose monumental *Man with a Hoe* (1859–62, Private Collection) is at once both brutal yet noble. In van Gogh's view it was Millet, not Manet, who epitomised 'the very core of modern art'.[3]

In Russia there was no social catalyst on the scale of the European revolutions of 1848, and the integration of the lower classes into genre painting by artists such as Ermenev, and more fully by Venetsianov, was a slower, later and more variable process. The peasant genre became increasingly prominent during the first half of the nineteenth century as native subjects became more popular and acceptable, but did not come into its own fully until the 1860s, developing a critical edge and greater veracity, boosted by intellectual pressures. As we have seen, the political awareness of art students during the 1860s is questionable, but they were not oblivious to the critical pressures coming to bear on them. The political reforms of the 1860s, especially the liberation of the serfs in 1861, galvanised radical critics to demand that the genre of social exposé – reflected in art by depictions of drunken fathers, impoverished widows and hubristic petty officials – needed to sharpen its cutting edge. Whilst artists did not respond to the extreme views of writers who wanted art to assist in the destruction of the autocratic order, the reform-minded social genre of the 1860s was injected with a greater degree of urgency, tackling contemporary themes on a larger scale and with greater candour.

Vasily Perov led the way with a series of uncompromisingly bleak paintings which addressed the deprivations of both the rural and urban peasantry. Works such as the funereal *The Last Journey* (1865) the desolate *Drowned Woman* (1867) and *The Last Inn by the Town Gate* (1868, all GTG) showed the wretched consequences of poverty: hard work, degeneration and death.[4] And these were only a few of many. In *Troika* (1866, GTG) Perov depicted a group of small children hauling heavy water vats in a dark winter townscape. The title, meaning a cart pulled by three horses, suggests the animal nature of their work whilst overtly addressing the issue of child labour. Peasants, especially children, were frequently cheaper to use than horses since they required no capital outlay and incurred no responsibility to the hirer.

Easter Procession (figure 1) is a summation of Perov's critical daring which caused sufficient offence to occasion its removal from exhibition. It shows the rural masses as poor and ignorant, and their clergy no better. The procession leaves the house of a prosperous peasant, a merchant perhaps, as its members, who have been drinking heavily, stagger into the street. At the head of the procession two figures chat impiously, whilst at its centre a woman carries her icon mindlessly, without spiritual involvement. A bent and tattered old man next to her carries his upside-down. The priest, holding insecurely to the porch is clearly the worse for drink whilst a deacon falls to the floor. The host, hung over the porch, is doused in an effort to revive him from his stupor, whilst another participant has crawled under the steps to sleep it off, literally 'legless'. The whole is a muddy, unidealised, drunk and disorderly view of rural Russia, showing scant respect for the clergy whose mission should be to lead by example. If one considers the critical kudos attaching to Courbet's *Return from the Conference* (1863), a milder work painted under a less draconian regime, which hints at the priest's drunkenness via comic ridicule, the force and daring of Perov's painting is remarkable. His forthright depictions of peasant hardships and stoical endurance marked a new, robust tone within the genre, lacking idealisation or picturesque qualities and seldom resorting to humour except of the blackest kind.

'The peasant is the judge now'

The principle of modernity to which Stasov adhered, and to which he and liberal critics urged the Wanderers, was in some manner similar to French realism. Stasov was a great admirer of Proudhon and Courbet and demanded that art be a concrete depiction of existing and observed subjects. However, the objective pretension of French realism, the quasi-scientific, dispassionate observation of life's phenomena was never espoused in Russia. Under an autocratic, bureaucratic and censorial regime, the critical (and therefore subjective) element of artistic creation was regarded as essential and desirable. The only debating points were how overtly, with what severity, and to what end the criticisms were shaped. Chernyshevsky, writing as early as 1855, pre-empted Courbet's insistence that art be concrete, non-abstract and based in reality, but went further, insisting it pass judgement:

> if a man, whose mental activity is powerfully stimulated by the problems that are aroused in his mind by his observation of life, is gifted with artistic talent, he will, in his works, consciously or unconsciously, express the striving to pronounce judgment on the phenomena that interested him ... In such a case, the artist becomes a thinker, the works of art, while remaining in the sphere of art, acquire a scientific significance.[5]

In industrialising France artists initially treated contemporaneity largely in terms of agrarian hardships, it being essentially a rural culture with a predominantly peasant population. In Russia the situation was even more marked. A country of overwhelmingly rural composition, inferior technical development, populated almost entirely by the peasant class, only recently rid of serfdom, and lacking a developed middle class, the artistic focus was firmly on the rural lower orders.[6] The Wanderers depicted both the sufferings and the integrity of the peasant, or *muzhik*, in a sympathetic but hard-hitting manner. Their works differed from those of artists of the 1860s in being generally more constructive and less overtly pessimistic or crudely critical. The tone is empathetic, granting their subjects a respect and dignity; the Russian *muzhik* is seen as real, suffering, but decent and stoical. Unflattering depictions are uncommon and humour is used rarely. At the same time idealised or pastoral views are totally missing: the public was well aware that life in the countryside was menacing – peasant revolts were not uncommon and well documented. In general portrayals of peasant life are hard, but the people admirably enduring. Seldom does an artist depict an 'up beat' mode of life.

Behind the transformation of the peasant genre from a subject with picturesque possibilities to one of serious social concern were a series of developments that subverted the popular conception of the masses, chiefly the intervention of Populism. Awareness that the reforms of the 1860s had been largely ineffectual led many to question the paternalistic role of the intelligentsia's mission to structure political and social solutions in a 'top-down' fashion. In seeking a new impetus, attention and respect were increasingly turned to the common people, the *narod*. These might be regarded as the true Russians, uncorrupted by the moral laxity of the Westernised lifestyles of the Court and nobility (who mostly spoke French); pious, long-suffering Orthodox believers, a source of innate wisdom, people whose hard lives were not built upon the exploitation of others. As the composer Musorgsky, himself of peasant birth, and who introduced the common people into Russian opera, wrote: 'Only the masses, huge, unenhanced and unadorned, have true integrity.'[7]

Under the banner of Populism, which had its cultural and political aspects, a shift towards studying the peasantry and its customs saw the Wanderers' intellectual stock rise considerably. Since many artists shared this peasant heritage they were increasingly recognised as worthy contributors to the grass roots enlightenment of Russia, the authentic voice of the *narod*. Simultaneously their peasant origins were turning from a source of insecurity to one of pride, and whilst many artists felt uncomfortable with the idealising tendencies of populist philosophy born of the intelligentsia's insecurities, they reaped the benefits of the peasants' enhanced standing as an object of cultural veneration.[8]

Concurrent with the rise of Populism in the social sphere, the Russo-Turkish War of 1877–78 engendered bellicose patriotic sentiments that fudged previously divisive issues and engendered a spirit of national unity. Journals on the left and right of political opinion soon found themselves united in nationalist support for a war of liberation, fought in support of the ethnic Balkan Slavs who rose against their Turkish masters, a humanitarian fight shared by the Wanderers who individually donated works to the cause, and in some cases even enlisted in the army. A few voices were raised against these dual influences. Stasov was scornful of populist sentimentality about the *narod*, whilst both the critic Mikhail Saltykov-Shchedrin and the writer Vsevolod Garshin saw the war as a distraction to internal problems. However, neither the critic's voice nor the writer's pacifist stories found acceptance in the heady atmosphere of a war which was eventually concluded on terms favourable to Russia.

Between the war and the populist cause, the gradual process of disassociating the Wanderers from radical sentiments took root. As the society became more frequently associated with 'Russianness', in large part due to the intelligentsia's shift towards populism, their art was increasingly regarded as seeking to encapsulate and celebrate the national heritage, a banner under which all sides, in some measure, could unite.[9] But this was a slow and incomplete process: protest, questioning, radicalism – all remained facets of the Wanderers' output even if not characterising the school. The peasant genre was a major influence in consolidating the Wanderers' reputation as documentors of their native land and its provincial customs, but at the same time it addressed serious and contentious issues in a manner that unsettled many. In a famous aphorism which set the tone for much of the Wanderers' art, Repin identified the burning question which seriously minded, socially committed artists could not ignore and indeed had a duty to address – the world as it appeared to the overwhelming majority of Russians: 'The peasant is the judge now, and we must reproduce his interests.'[10]

Barge-haulers on the Volga

These interests were represented at the first Wanderers exhibition of 1871 in works by Perov and Kramskoy, and more forcibly by Illarion Pryanishnikov, a fellow pupil of Perov's and later a teacher at the Moscow School of Arts: *Burned Out* (1871, GTG) a desperate prospect of a mother and children amidst the charred ruins of their small shack, and *Peasants Driving Home* (1872, GTG) a scene of harsh winter discomfort.[11] These early works have a literary, almost pedagogic attitude, as if seeking to instruct the viewer of the peasants' daily reality, but are conceived in a laconic and therefore more persuasive manner.

The benchmark for peasant painting was set the following year by Repin's large and imposing canvas *Barge-haulers on the Volga* or *Burlaki* as it is popularly known (figure 3, p. 32). It became recognised as a major artistic breakthrough that foreshadowed how artistic debates of the next two decades would divide between liberal and conservative camps, aesthetics being ignored in favour of divining ideological intent. In its time, and since, it has been greeted as a denunciation of autocratic injustice, though ironically it is the product of a student of the Imperial Academy, and whilst it seems to embody the ethos of the Wanderers and was of seminal importance to the Russian realist school, it was produced outside of the society.

As a student Repin had taken to outdoor sketching and painting trips, something discouraged by the Academy. His first sight of the wretchedly dressed haulers, victims of the ill-framed reforms of the 1860s, forced into this dehumanising work by necessity, was a shock even for him. Repin saw the haulers toiling amidst a group of prosperous picnickers and conceived a painting with a social parallel, expressing his indignation.[12] However, during the summer of 1870, when he and some fellow students chartered a boat down the Volga, proximity to the haulers convinced him that he should paint them for their own sakes, an example of the growing maturity of realist art which no longer relied on crude juxtapositions. The canvas went through a variety of mutations before it was exhibited at the Academy in March 1873, having been commissioned by its President, Grand Duke Vladimir. It had, however, been an essentially personal project at variance with academic practices.

The work broke new ground in treating a seemingly unsavoury theme on so large a scale, imbuing it with an importance reserved for the profound content of the historical genre, as well as more widely addressing the role of barge-hauler as a social phenomenon (not all of them are necessarily peasants). What further perturbed many was the careful individualisation of each hauler, based on life studies through which Repin was at pains to stress what he considered their objective characteristics, chiefly a collective integrity. He was particularly attached to Kanin, the sagacious fore-figure, a defrocked priest whom he romantically likened to a Greek philosopher educated on Plato, Aristotle, Socrates and Pythagoras and sold into Roman slavery.[13]

Fedor Bruni, under whom Repin studied at the Academy, called it 'a great profanation of art', referring literally to a tendency to treat a sacred thing with irreverence.[14] Stasov assessed the work as role model for his own brand of Russian painting: critical, realist and national. He was at pains to stress the brutally real yet positive portrayal of these human pack-animals, pointing to the central motif, the youth lifting his head, as embodying the will not to be crushed by his labour, presaging a positive future.

> At 28–29 he created the foremost painting of the Russian school. Simple people, working like cattle, peasants brought down to the level of horses, a centuries-old story. Such important and profound concerns had hitherto not been tackled in Russian art. Its appeal was universal ... you will not find another painting in European museums which so depicts the bright sun, hot air and summer's intense heat. And under this same sun, whilst others take refuge at home, in the shade, in shops, chambers and halls, is a whole crowd of unfortunate convicts, but convicts to somebody else's will, voluntary hirelings, trudging their way, dishevelled, along the Volga's banks. And the whole century they have gone this route. A thousand years of such life has brought this terrible *voluntary* state.[15]

Those who shared this interpretation included Musorgsky – who told Stasov: 'I am constantly tortured by the thought of Repin's *Burlaki*' whilst Kramskoy declared that the painting had broken new ground in Russian art: 'Four years ago Perov was ahead of everyone, only four years ago, but after Repin's *Barge-haulers* it seems hardly possible.'[16]

Dostoevsky, a vehement opponent of tendentious art, reviewed the exhibition for the conservative *Grazhdanin*. Though he approached the canvas with fears of its social critique, he found himself unexpectedly pleased with what he regarded as an apolitical set of character studies. Having expanded on what he saw as the ingenuous traits of the haulers – merriment, cunning, deceit, quarrelsomeness, resignation – he concluded with a swipe at Stasov and those on the left:

> And do you know, dear critic, that precisely this humble innocence of thought ... achieves the purpose – your tendentious, liberal purpose – much more effectively than you suspect! ... It is impossible not to start reflecting that one is indebted, actually indebted, to the people ... For this haulers' 'gang' will recur in one's dreams; it will be recalled some fifteen years hence! And had they not been so natural, innocent and simple, they would not have produced such an impression[17]

In effect Dostoevsky saw precisely the same message as did Stasov, they merely disagreed on the artist's approach: Stasov believed it was overt and intentional, Dostoevsky that it was insidious, working independently of the artist's primary intention to depict the haulers' individual traits. Clearly the 'intent' was potentially more seditious than the realisation.

The widely differing interpretations of the haulers, Stasov seeing suffering where Dostoevsky saw life's rich tapestry, were reflected in continental reviews. At the Vienna World Exhibition of 1873 an apoplectic Stasov noted that the German painter Friedrich Pecht wrote rapturously of the 'sun-filled' painting, praising its aestheticism, but contrived not to notice the barge-haulers.[18] Five years later, at the

1878 Paris Universal Exhibition, the French critic Vashon called *Burlaki* 'a staggering scene' and spoke of:

> ordinary people with severe, wild features ... All those unfortunates, stretched out and toiling hard under the scorching sky, burning their chests ... disfigured and exhausted by deprivations ... moral and physical torments. One, with long suffering submissiveness carries his beggarly yoke; another proudly raises his head and stares at the sky in fury with a look of damnation, as if inviting death to end his terrible existence.[19]

Though this constitutes a reading of the picture as a denunciation of a social injustice, the description of the youth is the antithesis of Stasov's symbol of hope. Another French writer, Jules Claresi, described the haulers as 'a mixture of dishevelled and savage animals in human form. All that is most horrifyingly thin and ferociously savage has been gathered here'.[20] Returning to Dostoevsky, it is hard to believe that the two writers are describing the same canvas: 'Nice, familiar figures: the two fore-haulers are almost laughing'.[21]

It is not easy to pin down Repin's motives. His account of the Volga expedition, written late in his life, aware of the turn-of-the-century shift towards aestheticism in the arts, is heavily tinged with claims that the process of painting and the observation of individual idiosyncrasies were paramount, and that the haulers' social standing did not interest him. This is at odds with the clearly humanitarian project first conceived as a contrast between haulers and affluent picnickers.

The painting is certainly selective in several respects. Repin toned down the suffering of the subjects, rejecting a sketch of an emaciated, exhausted young hauler, which would have detracted from the positive portrayal of the central youth. It also required considerably more men than Repin depicts to haul a fully laden barge, as can be seen in studies by Vasily Vereshchagin – who earlier worked on the same theme, *Burlaki* (1866, Kiev Museum of Russian Art) and projected three gangs of haulers, each comprising between twenty and twenty-five men. The figures, by contrast with Repin's, are relatively well attired; Dostoevsky felt Repin's haulers too poorly dressed even for peasants, an element he concluded was designed for pathos. Possibly the theme itself is selective to the point of misrepresentation. Repin's admission that the haulers were a revelation to him in 1868 suggests that such scenes were not typical, and might confirm conservative outrage at the wilful selection of an emotive but unrepresentative scene. The art critic Anton Ledakov complained of this anachronism, stating 'Repin painted this at a time when steamers were already scurrying up and down the Volga and the trade of barge-hauler had been left to legend'.[22] (There is in fact a small steamer travelling against the current, far right of the canvas.)

The strength of Repin's painting, however, is in forcing the viewer to confront the unfortunates as sentient beings, rather than faceless symbols of suffering, for which he necessarily reduced their number, sacrificing objectivity to the greater 'reality' of their condition. It is clear that regardless of treatment, the subject itself was controversial. Class sensitivities and political sensibilities ensured that the barge-haulers, many of whom were victims of the ill-framed reforms of the 1860s and were forced into this seasonal work by land shortages, had become a byword for suffering and a cue for instant guilt complexes amongst the affluent.

An interesting consideration of the painting's reception, however, resides in realist attempts, chiefly by Stasov, to analyse the work as a piece of modern history, of actuality. Whilst claiming that *Burlaki* was a slice of life, much as one could view throughout Russia, and therefore in accordance with the dispassionate objectivity of French realism, Stasov nevertheless dwelt on subjective elements such as the peasants' nobility and the uplifting gesture of the young hauler. This aspect of the work later assumed heroic proportions as Soviet writers claimed that the haulers constituted part of a general striving by Russian artists to find positive prototypes of the *muzhik*. Such an outlook departs from the specific, to regard realist canvases from a wider, more profound viewpoint, resulting in claims that Kanin for instance embodies 'a human ideal, expressing spiritual beauty and rich simplicity'.[23] This notion of heroic idealism is directly contrary to a realist philosophy, having more in common with academic conventions, and again points to the complexity of cultural currents at work in Russia. Whilst it seems clear that Repin was driven by a humanitarian concern and genuine respect for his subjects, as a young man lionised by Russia's intelligentsia, he did not contradict the socially critical readings of his canvas. The significance of the painting proved to be not just its ground-breaking approach to a sensitive subject, but that it was a harbinger of the many controversies and misunderstandings which bedevilled subsequent canvases, as polarisation of debate fell between radical and conservative analyses.

The hard life

Burlaki became a paradigmatic image of Russian realism, and for many the configuration of peasant hardship was a characterising feature of the Wanderers' output, though this too was treated with a variety of agendas and tactics. Grigory Myasoedov's *The Zemstvo Dines* (figure 4) offers a more subdued but didactic commentary than Repin's enigmatic profile of peasant types. A group of peasants sit eating a meagre meal during a sessional break of the local council on which they serve. By a reform of 1864 provision was granted for representatives of all classes to sit on this, the lowest level of provincial administration, although legislation ensured that its powers were weighted in favour of the gentry. The inequality and ineffectualness of the institution is eloquently portrayed in the dejected mien of the men, whilst the difference in social standing between the peasants and the other, unseen participants is expressed through contrast. The peasants, clothed in rags, sit on the courtyard floor eating their paltry meal of black bread and onions in the company of a few chickens, whilst through the window a waiter attends to the porcelain and silverware from which the more prosperous *zemstvo* members will dine.

Seen at the second Wanderers show this was an unexpected offering from an artist who at the inaugural exhibition had showed *The Grandfather of the Russian*

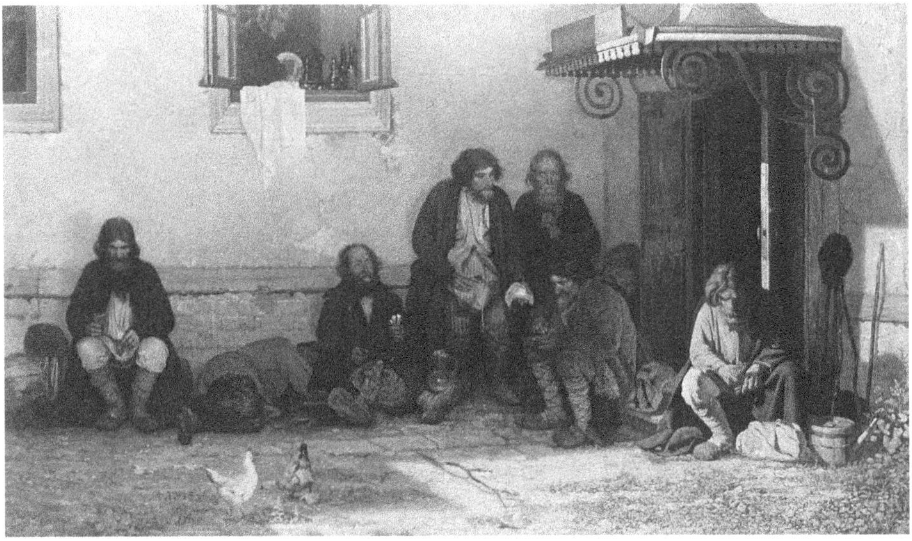

4 Grigory Myasoedov, *The Zemstvo Dines*, 1872, 74 x 125 cm

Navy (1871, State Museum of Fine Art of Uzbekistan, Tashkent) a conventional (if Russian) history painting. In a change of direction typical of many realist painters, Myasoedov switched allegiance to themes addressing social issues, of which *The Zemstvo Dines* was his first major offering. In terms of size and the frieze-like composition, Myasoedov leans heavily on academic convention, but applied to a downmarket contemporary scene. The figures are generally dignified; the peasant on the extreme right serious and pensive, an intelligent, possibly literate individual with the philosophical mien of Repin's Kanin. Aesthetically it is a mature and finely painted piece in terms of colour harmony, treatment of light and authenticity of peasant dress, but it is the 'thought', the unflattering contrast between social positions, suggested only by the trappings of wealth, that predominates. Myasoedov's peasants are out-manoeuvred by political chicanery, held in check by the unfairness of the reform laws.

The following year Myasoedov exhibited *Reading the Emancipation Manifesto* (1873, GTG) depicting a cross-section of peasant types hearing of their own freedom as a small child reads out the proclamation; a comment at least on rising rates of literacy. Its interest resides chiefly, however, in what Stasov christened the 'choral' canvas; one that generalised its subjects into 'types' representative of Russia's social system, rather than the specific individuals of Repin's *Burlaki*.[24] As we shall see, the use of 'type' was much favoured by some left-wing critics, including Belinsky and Chernyshevsky, as a means whereby the specific could be utilised to address broader, more general issues.

This approach was by no means a prerequisite, however. Tougher, more direct views of the peasant–master relationship abounded. Nikolai Kuznetsov's *Inspecting*

His Estate (1879, GTG) addressed the reality of the day-to-day manifestation of the landowner's power by showing a submissive peasant being angrily threatened with his master's whip, their relationship underscored by the peasant's dog, which rolls submissively on the floor as the landowner's dog advances on it aggressively. Well handled such works were powerful and sympathetic, but lesser artists too easily fell into sensationalism. Titles such as Aleksandr Shevchenko's *The Landlord Exchanging Peasants for Dogs* require little elucidation.[25]

In any event, the social hierarchy of rural Russia was not altogether simple. Though the peasant was undoubtedly at the bottom of the pile, there were within this class literate and illiterate peasants, the relatively wealthy and the abjectly poor, with subtle shades between; ownership of livestock might mark a vital distinction in terms of individual fortunes. And though rarely imaged, peasants might be put upon by their own kind as much as the state or nobility. These ambivalences are most fully addressed by Repin's next major work, the largest and most renowned of the 'choral' canvases, *Religious Procession in the Province of Kursk* (colour plate 1). An ambitious project painted over several years, it comprises a panoramic cross-section of life in rural Russia and a model of the Wanderers' ethos.

In its first version, *Religious Procession* (1877, GRM), Repin conceived a simple scene, unlocated in time or place, the emphasis on rural pageantry. But by 1883 this had developed into a harsh record of contemporary life, accommodating more and varied representatives of Russia's social caste system. The setting was transferred to a bleaker terrain and the composition passed from a frieze-like motif to a dusty, human juggernaut, disappearing out of sight at the picture's edges, enforcing the illusion of relentless movement towards and beyond the spectator.

On the right a gilded shrine which houses a miracle-working icon is paraded aloft, decked with votive and supplicatory offerings, by peasants in festive dress. Behind them come two merchant-class women who reverentially carry the icon's empty wooden case, itself a mark of distinction, and a country choir of young boys martialled by an elderly sexton-cum-village-schoolmaster and his young counterpart, their old Russian and modern European ways markedly contrasted in the older man's kaftan and beard, and the younger's frock-coat and shaven cheeks.

The centre of the canvas is held by a priest clad in golden vestments, behind whom the crowd parts to reveal the small, stout figure of a land-owner's wife, the local aristocracy. Dressed in yellow silk and bows and supported by an officious steward, she carries the icon itself – the highest honour – with a look of tired complacency. The left-hand side of this vast canvas is occupied by a teeming herd of cowed, ragged pilgrims, poor peasants trudging in the stifling midday heat and headed by a crippled hunchback, the most positive figure in the painting. He moves resolutely towards the shrine, but is fended off by another *muzhik* who clearly knows his place. The whole scene is presided over by a mounted Cossack militia; to the right one lashes out at a woman in the crowd, his wild staring eye echoed by that of his foaming horse; far left another raises his whip in a menacing gesture.

Even the landscape, barren and parched, giving no shade for the unfortunate crowd, assists the air of despondency and is used to make a social point. Original sketches were verdant, the change prompted by Repin's anger at the wanton deforestation of a once fertile region by avaricious timber contractors seeking to turn a quick profit. The whole might be read as a metaphor for rural mismanagement, an early intervention of 'green' issues.

The controversy engendered by Repin's work resulted in some scathing receptions but drew a huge number of visitors: four thousand in one week alone.[26] The peasants are allowed some dignity. They are grave, long-suffering or religiously fervent. The representatives of class and profession, however, well-fed, well-dressed, are all in some measure presented in an unflattering or risible light, be it the effete, dandified and bored priest, the pietistic timidity of the women carrying the empty icon box, or the stark pomposity of the aristocratic woman and her unctuous staff. Stasov's favourable review of the canvas, which focussed on the inherent violence of the social system embodied in the Cossack police force, saw the journal's editor forced to review the exhibition again in the next issue along with an editorial disassociating the journal from Stasov's views.

Most regarded the canvas as an open attack on all but the lower orders of Russian society, and particularly offensive in flouting the canon of fine art in its use of unattractive, unidealised figures. The painting was savaged in the conservative press, who remarked on: 'the regretful tendentiousness, and unpleasant mendacity of the composition ... especially the intentionally odd selection of ugly, animal-like and idiotic types'.[27] Only Tolstoy, it seems, who thought the work highly accomplished, differed from all else by considering that Repin had taken a neutral stance, whilst one reviewer went beyond the confines of the painting to denounce the undesirables who thronged around it at exhibition, noting a preponderance of liberated women with short haircuts, nihilistic young men, and a strong Jewish element: the chief characters of Imperial xenophobia.[28]

What was lost in these debates was recognition that Repin was considerate of not only subject, but also style and execution. The *Religious Procession* reveals an artist greatly exercised by purely painterly problems and the picture's innate artistry became its saving grace for the next generation of artists, more occupied with formal concerns, who, whilst condemning its social sermonising, wrote rapturously of its *plein air* atmosphere: its brightness, the convincing evocation of summer heat, haze and dust thrown up by the vast crowd.[29]

Tretyakov paid a record price of 10,000 roubles for the picture, but was also unhappy with its content and pressured Repin to replace the women carrying the icon case with a beautiful young girl, exuding spiritual rapture. Repin's refusal to comply gives an insight into the realist approach to art, the demand for integrity and 'truth to life'.

> In a picture you can only leave in the sort of face which fits the general artistic scheme. It is a subtle feeling which cannot be explained by any theory, and intentional

> embellishment would have ruined the picture. It is impossible not to sacrifice details for the sake of vividness and the harmonious truth of the whole ... A picture is a highly complicated and very difficult thing. You can perceive it only through the concentration of all your inner powers into one feeling, and only at such moments will you sense that above everything else stands truth to life[30]

Yet the 'truth to life' here is not that of an objective documentary record. The events and individuals portrayed are not those observed on a specific occasion, but in line with the choral canvases espoused by Stasov are intended as an accurate reflection of the general conditions of Russian society and its class types. The 'details', as Repin calls them, have been sacrificed to a more general but, as he saw it, objective truth of the state of the Russian nation in the 1880s. Repin's 'truth', however, was another person's tendentiousness, as was reflected in the largely hostile critical reactions to the work.

Religious Procession in the Province of Kursk is Wanderers art at its best, an incisive but sympathetic portrayal of the physical harshness and political marginalisation of the life of the Russian peasant, the artist resisting attempts by a wealthy and influential patron to make it conform to conventional or clichéd standards. It is a work risking official censure to make plain on a grand scale its strength of criticism. It is ironic to consider, however, that the unsubtle social contrasts which Repin so successfully avoided with *Burlaki*, here diverted the attention of the critics away from the plight of the suffering masses, to an urgent consideration of the indignity heaped upon the representatives of Russian officialdom.

Repin was far from unique in his depiction of the rural peasants' religious observations, and canvases of processions and pilgrims were not uncommon. Myasoedov exhibited *The Drought* (1878, M.A. Vrubel Museum of Fine Arts, Omsk) depicting a long file of peasants kneeling and standing in supplication at an outdoor altar, the clergy shown praying in unison with the congregation and the emphasis directed more at expressing the plight and piety of the participants. Perov, who painted some uncompromisingly realistic character studies of peasant pilgrims, depicted both the severity of their lives and the worldly excesses of the clergy. In the enigmatically titled *Pilgrim in a Field. On the Way to Eternal Bliss* (1879, Nizhny Novgorod Art Museum) he portrayed the exhausted body of a peasant lying amongst wild grass and flowers, an icon at her side, in stark contrast with the joyous natural scenery. One might presume she has died of her toil, a fact enhanced by the word-play of the title.

The social, class-conscious, critical element of Repin's painting differentiates it from those of his peers. In scope it is most closely matched by a number of paintings by Pryanishnikov, including *The Saviour's Day in the North* (1887, GTG) and *The Procession of the Cross* (1893, GRM), which make use of large, outdoor, processional scenes and imaginative compositions, drawing the viewer into the canvas. Despite superficial similarities of subject and treatment Pryanishnikov's works centre around religious unity devoid of the tension Repin creates by highlighting earthly inequalities.

Closer in its critical approach is Konstantin Savitsky's *Meeting the Icon* (1878, GTG) depicting a crowd of villagers converging on a carriage, from which the miracle-working icon (as in Repin's picture) has already appeared. A corpulent priest follows behind, being assisted from the vehicle by one of his acolytes. The throng of kneeling peasants are well kempt, the men respectfully attired, the women in colourful Sunday best. The treatment of the clergy contains a strong vein of ridicule as the officiating priest emerges from the carriage with great physical effort, like some over-fed eastern potentate – a satirical note more in keeping with the works of Fedotov and Perov.

Vasily Maksimov's *The Sick Husband* (figure 5) provides a bleaker, more uncompromising view of peasant life. A despairing wife prays over the still living body of her husband, stretched out under the icons in a corner of their spartan *izba*. Tension is created by the absence of iconographic symbols suggestive of recovery or regeneration, though a note of solace is perhaps contained in the composure and fortitude of the woman. In terms of addressing the piety and resilience of the peasantry the scene is somewhat reminiscent of Millet's *The Angelus* (1857–59, Musée d'Orsay, Paris). The unity provided by Millet's image is, however, fractured here by the spectre of death, and where the religiosity of Millet's praying figures is underscored by a romantic evening landscape, Maksimov's is subdued but literal,

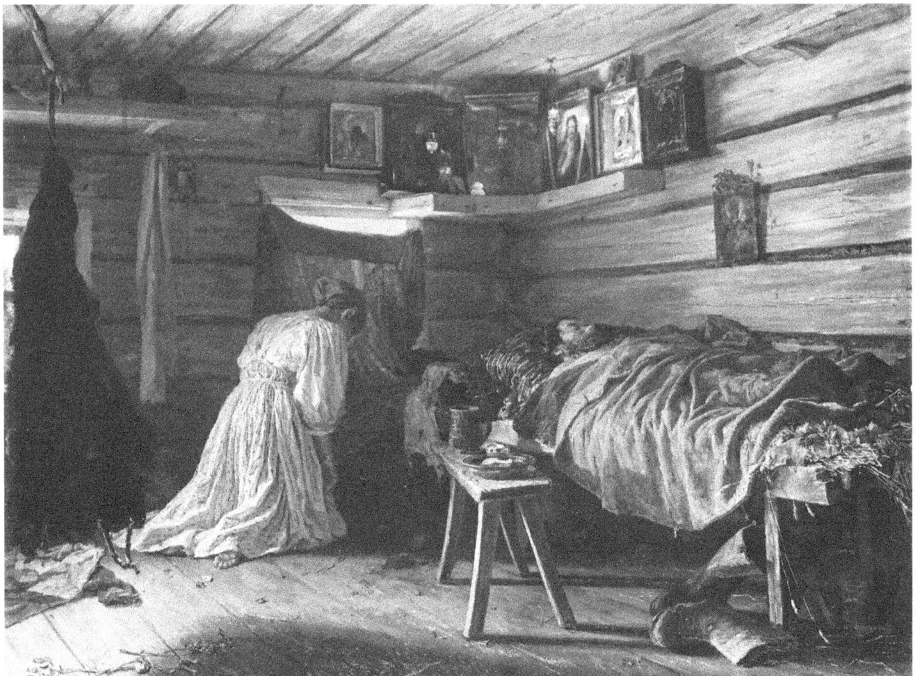

5 Vasily Maksimov, *The Sick Husband*, 1881, 70.8 x 88.6 cm

the icons being merely a realistic part of a genuine contemporary interior. Though artists were willing to depict the hardships of peasant life, in general they avoided pessimism, defeatism, or brutally direct depictions of the crushing hardships and humiliations that most endured. Chekhov noted that the peasants:

> break their backs from morning till night, fall ill from work which is beyond their strength, are all their lives afraid of death and disease, are all their lives looking for remedies for their illnesses, fade early, age early, and die in filth and stench. When they grow up, their children start the same thing all over again; and so centuries pass, and millions of people live worse than beasts, and all for a crust of bread – living in a state of continual fear.[31]

Such sentiments were rarely approached in art and then usually tempered by sympathy, not conceived of an overt anger. By contemporary standards Maksimov's work is a remarkably graphic and pitiful scene, a reminder too of the gender interdependency of peasant life.[32]

Sergei Ivanov's *Death of a Migrant Peasant* (figure 6) takes this theme further. Here the prospect of death has been realised. A particularly unflinching exponent of peasant hardship, Ivanov revived the flagging commitment of Wanderers' canvases during the society's decline with a series of canvases on the dilemma of the migrant peasant, which he observed from experience. The need for land caused by the rural overpopulation of European Russia resulted in many uncertain and hazardous eastwardly migrations. *Death of a Migrant Peasant* – set against a barren, parched landscape which, like Repin's *Burlaki* and *Religious Procession in the Province of Kursk* enhances the human misery – shows the bitter consequences of failure, the collapse of all hope. With even greater severity than Maksimov's painting it exposes

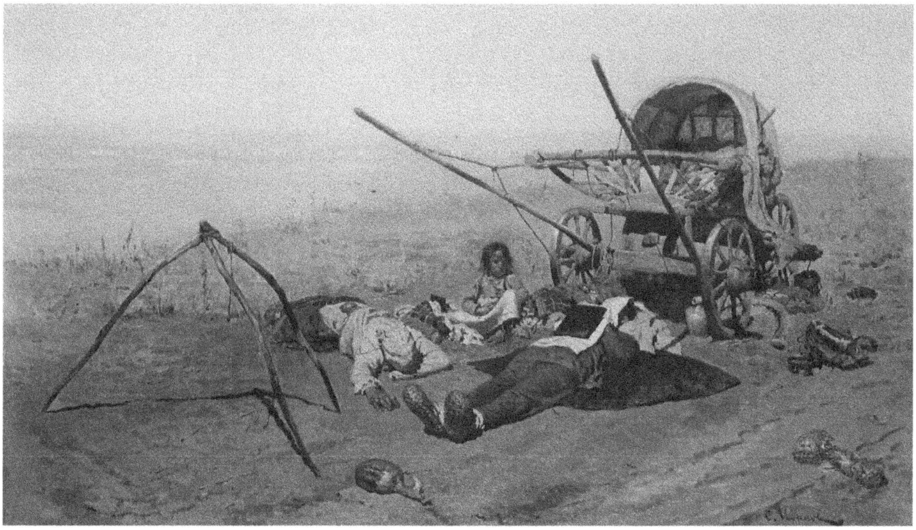

6 Sergei Ivanov, *Death of a Migrant Peasant*, 1889, 71 x 122 cm

the vital interdependency of the peasant family unit, here by imaging its collapse. The utter desolation of the dead man's wife and her as yet uncomprehending child evoke a mood unique in Russian realism, that of pure despair. This is quite literally the end of the line and no comfort can be gleaned from the plight of this family, representative of hundreds more who suffered a similar fate.

Urban and industrial life

Though part of the Wanderers' repertoire, the urban life of the industrial peasant was tackled less often than depictions of the rural peasantry, though little more might be read into this than a statistical balance. Industrialisation began later in Russia than in many other European countries, the heyday of Russian realism coinciding with a period when only a small fraction of the peasant population resided in large conurbations or worked in industry. Precedents abounded nevertheless. Though set in the countryside Konstantin Savitksy's *Repair Work on the Railway* (1874, GTG), another image of heavy labour in unrelenting heat, addresses the then topical issue of the peasant in post-reform Russia as the nation sped up its capitalist industrialisation. Criticised at the time for superficial compositional similarities with Repin's *Burlaki*, it is interesting to speculate that where Repin's canvas was criticised by the conservative press for being anachronistic, Savitsky's is probably the more topical and accurate in its contemporary depiction of industrial incursion into rural Russia.

An intriguing commentary on industrial urban life was offered by a small but unconventional work by Vladimir Makovsky, *On the Boulevard* (1886–87, GTG). This depicted a young worker, his wife and baby sitting on a public bench in autumn, she having travelled from their village to see him, doubtless a long and miserable journey on foot. Whilst she is clearly crushed and dejected by her poverty the drunken husband ignores her presence, unable to disguise his impatience to be rid of her; a pitiful personal tragedy made public by the couple's lack of a private meeting place (he would be living in a worker's hostel). Though not obvious at first sight this is a powerful work that exposes the loutish peasant increasing the burden of his own kind and more widely addresses the misery caused by the disruption of village family life after the emancipation reforms, when the very poorest were forced to migrate to the cities in search of work.

Makovsky returned to this theme with *A Doss-House* (1889, GRM) depicting a prodigiously large and thinly clad crowd of vagrants seeking application to an overnight hostel on a freezing winter's day in Moscow. For many Russians the industrial revolution came as a great shock, and the evil of urban squalor which formed the societal underbelly of Dostoevsky's novels was soon being compared unfavourably to the lesser deprivations of country life. Tolstoy blasted this new form of misery in his great social polemic of 1886 *What Then Must We Do?*[33]

Without doubt the strongest proponent of this genre was Nikolai Kasatkin, a product of the Moscow School of Arts and pupil of Perov, who in the 1890s worked on a cycle of mining pictures which are still quite unique in their forceful, uncompromising depiction of the rigours of working life. Kasatkin's miners are not the politicised proletariat of the early 1900s but the mere depiction of urban workers, new members of the revolutionary pantheon, carried a degree of political charge since of the peasantry they above all were considered politically astute. Kasatkin produced a sequence of paintings which evince a strength of committed political interest and which have lost little of their power in over a hundred years. *Miners. The Shift* (1895, GTG) shows the massed ranks of coal blackened workers leaving the pit-head as their replacements await their turn to descend into this modern-day industrial inferno, their lives an endless cycle of dirt and toil.[34] His most famous mining image, however, ironically contains no miners and is set above ground. *Poor People Collecting Coal in an Abandoned Pit* (figure 7) insinuates grinding drudgery and poverty as a group of ragged women and children seek to supplement their meagre living by scraping for surface coal in an exhausted pit. The mine, high on the horizon, remains in darkness, a brooding presence dominating their lives. Three generations are represented as an indication of the past, present and future round of ceaseless labour, but it is, nevertheless, a seemingly positive depiction of the workers. The central, younger woman, stands at the apex of a heroic, pyramidal composition, similar to that used in academic history painting. She appears grave but strong, a resolute figure, suggestive of a more optimistic future; perhaps she will escape the fate of the frail and bent figure of the elderly woman in front

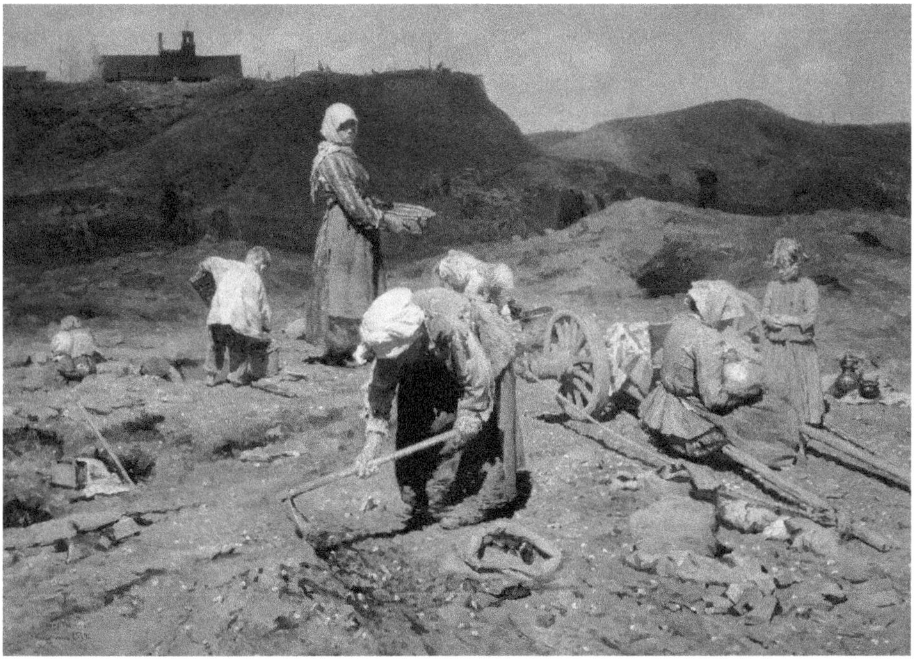

7 Nikolai Kasatkin, *Poor People Collecting Coal in an Abandoned Pit*, 1894, 80.3 x 107 cm

of her. Once more the use of a sun-scorched and desolate landscape increases the misery of the scene, though in this later work by an artist developing a broader, less fussy application of paint, the sunlight sculpts harsh, almost photographic tonal contrasts, which give the painting its acute sense of reality. Kasatkin remained true to his uncompromising treatment of themes containing the urban worker and was one of the few artists who made the transition to Soviet Socialist Realism with ease, being regarded as a founding father, his subject matter tailor-made for a celebration of the proletariat.

The iconographic image of the worker found its most durable incarnation in Nikolai Yaroshenko's *The Stoker* (figure 8) possibly the first and perhaps still the best commentary on the condition of industrial labour. Yaroshenko was an artist with amongst the best revolutionary credentials who assumed the role of the Wanderers' ideological mentor on Kramskoy's death. The stoker's physical appearance is both a testament to and indictment of his back-breaking toil and unbearable working conditions. The huge arms and hands, rough and sinewy, exaggerated in size, his bent stance, all point to the physical deformity occasioned by hard labour. The scene, bathed in red light, is purposely like Hades, the painting a direct reproach to a society which allows such outrages to persist. But again, the spectator cannot deny the stoker his monumental dignity as he fills the canvas and engages us in direct eye contact. The artist's dilemma in such instances was how to evoke sympathy and outrage, to empathise with the stoker, without degrading the

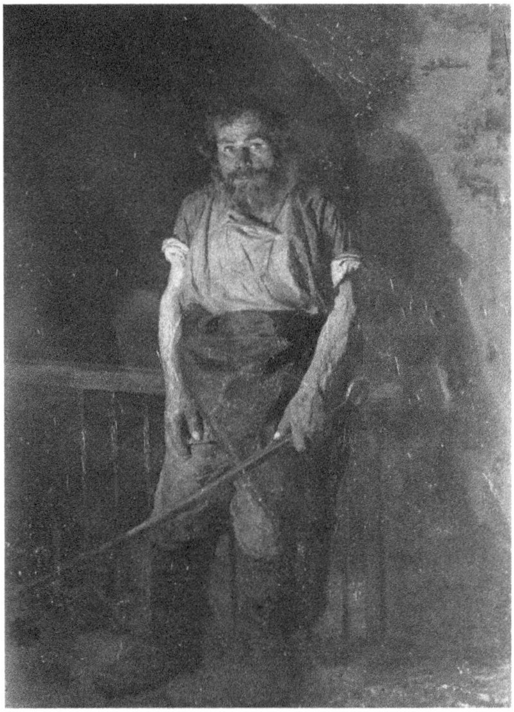

8 Nikolai Yaroshenko, *The Stoker*, 1878, 124 x 89 cm

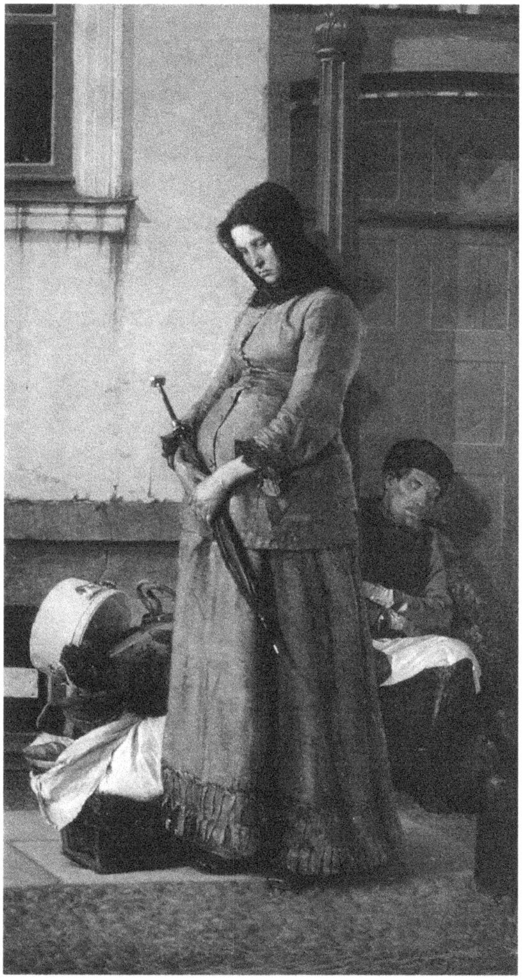

9 Nikolai Yaroshenko, *Dismissed. At the Station*, 1883, 141 x 75 cm

subject or provoking mawkish pity. The writer Garshin was moved by this picture to write his short story 'Artists', parodying in his character Dedov the painter who seeks honours and prizes and who is unmoved by the evils of contemporary life that afflict his tormented realist counterpart Ryabinin. Dedov disdains Repin's *Barge-haulers on the Volga* as being incompatible with 'true art', the role of which is to convey the grace and harmony of natural beauty, something he rapturously applauds in his own, clearly facile landscapes.[35] However, the story is more sentimental than the painting, the stoker being converted to a pitiful boiler-maker, and whilst Garshin is forceful about the crippling nature of industrial labour, Yaroshenko rejected a request to illustrate the story, citing a disinclination to show a working man humiliated by his toil: 'My Stoker is upright and monumental. A worker is not just somebody victimised. A workman is Labour ... a mighty force. My Stoker's chest may be crushed by heavy toil, his head may be jammed between his shoulders, but just you try bending him!'[36] Yaroshenko's forays into hitherto uncharted subject matter are most overt in the theme of revolutionary activity, but as an unorthodox contributor to contemporary issues he showed a rare willingness to tackle subject matter which marked an individuality of approach. Expanding the perimeters of the urban theme, *Dismissed. At the Station* (figure 9) addresses the female worker, here a discharged servant having fallen prey to the sexual appetites of her master or one of his household. Though conceived out of sympathy rather than anger, possibly the only means whereby the artist could be assured of avoiding censorship, the work is clearly an implicit condemnation of common social mores, of the hypocritical double standards of 'respectable' bourgeois society that denies shelter and employment to the single mother and her illegitimate child. Whilst the appeal is generally towards pathos it is nevertheless a bold and singular work; the canon of Western art before the decadence of Klimt is devoid of so literal and prosaic a realisation of a woman in a heavily pregnant condition. Traditional images of female expulsion from the domestic Garden of Eden, or of repentant unmarried mothers seeking domestic forgiveness, are usually couched in more histrionic and psychologically charged terms, such as Richard Redgrave's melodramatic *The Outcast* (1851, Royal Academy of Arts, London). Yaroshenko's inclusion of the sleeping porter provides a subtle antidote, suggesting the ubiquity of the scene, insufficiently remarkable to arouse interest.

This is however a unique image and given that sexual morality could possibly be considered in more execrable taste even than political sedition, it is to the artist's credit that he tackled this and related 'unacceptable' themes. *Nevsky Prospekt at Night* (1875, State Art Museum of Poltava), showing prostitutes plying their trade on a particularly cold, wet and unpromisingly empty street, is further evidence of Yaroshenko's engagement with the margins of contemporary culture. The whole joyless and mundane scene is remarkable too in a total lack of the usual prurient titillation associated with comparable European examples when addressing risqué subject matter.

The invisible peasant

As familiarity lessened the impact of the peasant genre the original critical ethos of the Wanderers was diluted with anecdote and sentiment, or, during the more politicised populist 1870s, saw literary critics espouse a reverence for the *muzhik* which many artists, themselves of peasant stock, found positively maudlin. The 1890s did see a fresh infusion of critical-realist blood in the shape of a second generation of painters such as Nikolai Kasatkin and Sergei Ivanov, but works such as Nikolai Bogdanov-Belsky's *At the School Door* (1897, GRM), showing a picturesque tattered young peasant boy on the threshold of his village class, became increasingly typical of peasant scenes. Similarly Ivan Bogdanov's *The Novice* (1893, GTG), showing a tearful child apprentice being ticked off by his drunken boss, is characteristic of many late nineteenth-century canvases which shifted their focus from the general deprivations of the lower classes to emotional renditions of individual misfortune. Executed in fresh, bright colours, such works are largely anecdotal, devoid of the unsettling elements which marked earlier canvases. In general artists did not fall into themes of despondency, nor dwell on the stark humiliations of the peasants' life except in the most restrained manner. Bogdanov again, in *Reckoning Up* (1890, GTG), painted a humble, apologetic peasant, his head bowed, being rebuked for falling into arrears by a complacent affluent couple seated by their samovar. Whilst addressing the wide social gulf between peasant and masters, the appeal is to sentiment, not the intellect.

But whatever the inclinations of individual artists, shifts in taste or the predilections of patrons, there were always limits of propriety which were simply not transgressable, rendering important areas of the peasant experience invisible so far as the visual arts were concerned. Ultimately artists require buyers and their output is conditioned by this. One searches in vain for a pictorial condemnation of the hideous murders, rapings, burnings and mutilations of the pogroms which were a regular feature of tsarist Russia. Other subjects, less brutal but equally distressing, such as the serious, frequent and widespread instances of famine, were also skirted.

So too the was darker side of the *muzhik*'s life avoided. The social blight of alcoholism which was endemic to peasant society and which had early found outlet in genre works such as Aleksei Korzukhin's *The Drunken Father's Family* (1861) and later in Vladimir Makovsky's *No Entry* (1892, both Kiev Museum of Russian Art), was occasionally aired, as has already been seen in relation to Makovsky's *On the Boulevard* and Bogdanov's *The Novice*. These were generally treated as domestic dramas striking a tragic chord and whilst their approach to so difficult a theme should not be negated, pictorial representations fell woefully short of the brutal reality.

Repin ventured forcibly into this territory but confined it to the less prestigious sphere of graphic art. *The Drunken Father* (1888, GRM) a pencil illustration to a pamphlet by Tolstoy on the evils of drink, depicts the return of a dishevelled peasant to a terrified household of emaciated figures: his wife, an elderly woman, a young boy and a tiny baby. Those who are able make pitiful attempts to hide themselves from the club-wielding apparition whilst the baby, lying naked and vulnerable on top of the stove, increases the awful tension of the scene. Repin also illustrated Chekhov's 'Peasants', a short story about the disillusionment of a *muzhik* in ill-health who returns from Moscow to his native village only to find it a barbaric and fearful place, populated by wild, drunken animals, prey to all manner of vice, cruelty and disease. Chekhov vividly describes the family's dark, crowded and filthy hut, black with soot and flies, and how every occasion is made the excuse for drunken sprees invariably ending in bouts of domestic violence. Repin did a number of studies for the story in pen, ink and watercolour, including *The Drunken Kiryak* (1899, Chekhov Museum, Taganrog) depicting the brother of the central character beating his wife. Chekhov describes the scene:

> Every single child in the hut burst out crying ... There was a drunken coughing, and a tall man with a black beard and a fur cap came into the hut. As his face was not visible in the dim lamplight, he was quite terrifying. It was Kiryak. He went over to his wife, swung his arm and hit her across the face with his fist. She was too stunned to cry out and merely sunk to the ground; the blood immediately gushed from her nose.[37]

This and the previous drawing are of scenes Repin could have often witnessed as a child; stark and disconsolate depictions of violence that expose the darker side of a people who, in his oil works, are the centre of sympathetic concern. Only in the graphic media was he willing to relinquish the representation of the peasant's victimisation, to show instead something of the misery they inflicted upon one another.

Imaging the peasant

Although the images produced by the Wanderers offer a variety of meditations on *muzhik* life, the sole constant in their shaping for public reception the precarious, mundane or deleterious existences of the Russian peasantry is one of approach. Unlike any other European centre of cultural production the Russian experience appears unique in that those producing the images were in the majority of the class depicted. Elsewhere it would be correct to observe that 'The way artists perceived villagers was inevitably conditioned by stereotypical assumptions they had brought with them from urban, bourgeois contexts'.[38] In Russia the reverse was true. Many artists had bitter firsthand experience of the scenes they produced, resulting in an essentially 'insider' view of a life only recently removed from a feudal setting. Inevitably this became mediated by their urban artistic training and exposure to current intellectual trends, and eventually their works were destined for metropolitan consumption (although many Russian provincial centres were hardly more than large towns) but Russian artists were seldom visual tourists in search of rural curiosity or encounters with the picturesque.

But neither were they impartial documenters. The Wanderers did not strive towards a detached, objective depiction of peasant life in post-reform Russia, but consciously imbued their works with a personal, emotional input to produce images of the common people that were broadly humanitarian and sympathetic. Artists' biographies would offer good reason why this should be so; they were not willing to disavow their own people. Whether or not they distorted this image beyond a degree of acceptable subjectivity is debatable. Artists en masse avoided the darker, more sinister side of life at the lowest end of the social scale. Repin's *Religious Procession in the Province of Kursk*, for instance, contains none of the beggars and peasants who congregated at the major religious festivals and shrines to wave their hideous afflictions – running sores, physical mutilations or loathsome diseases – in the faces of likely benefactors.[39]

In general the peasants are seen as victims of circumstance and it is exceedingly rare for artists to expose anything of the misery this class inflicted upon one another.

But this was also rare in literature. Maksim Gorky is an exception, a peasant writer full of anger and 'bitterness' (his pen-name is taken from this Russian adjective). So too is Anton Chekhov, an urbane and educated writer whose seemingly objective depictions of contemporary life angered the aristocratic Tolstoy by what he regarded as their brutal pessimism. As Chekhov observed:

> Who maintains the pubs and keeps the peasant drunk? The peasant. Who embezzles the village school and parish funds and spends it all on drink? The peasant. Who robs his neighbour, sets fire to his house and perjures himself in court for a bottle of vodka? Who is the first to revile the peasant at district council and similar meetings?[40]

Such sentiments were simply not manifested in art, but if the Wanderers did not dwell on the infernal or unseemly side of contemporary life, few were romantic or sentimental about it. Maksimov hated the mawkish sentimentality and intellectual reverence of populist thought: 'Pretty words about the "people" made over a glass of beer in noisy company.'[41] Repin, reared in the brutal atmosphere of a military settlement, clashed angrily with Tolstoy, for whom he otherwise had an exceptionally high regard. He was appalled by the writer's homilies on peasant virtue and his efforts – in writing and in practice on his estate Yasnaya Polyana – to preserve and further their traditional existence, rather than lift them out of the mire of ignorance. Repin regarded his philosophy as romantic, dangerous and retrogressive.

> I cannot accept his negation of culture ... At the sight of the inmates of Yasnaya Polyana, in their black, dirty huts with cockroaches, without light, stagnating in the evenings by a kerosene lamp, giving off nothing but stench and soot, I was pained, and could not imagine the possibility of any bright, joyous mood in this Dante's inferno ... To descend for one minute into this darkness and to say 'I am with you', is hypocrisy. To wallow with them forever is a senseless sacrifice. To elevate them! To elevate them to one's own level, to give life – this is a heroic deed![42]

Whilst Repin's view exposes a certain paternal approach not dissimilar to that of the educated intelligentsia, it nevertheless encapsulates the reformist and instructive nature of much Wanderers art, a feature shared with the Populist movement and the maturation of progressive liberal thought during the period of the society's inception. Though Kramskoy warned of the dangers of painterly messages usurping the artistic animus, the desire for commentary – to 'say something' about contemporary life and, in so doing, to make a difference, to effect change in an educative manner – permeates the society's output.[43]

That many observers, often from opposing critical viewpoints, regarded the majority of the Wanderers' peasant pictures as factual, perhaps too factual for comfort, is evident in the ferocity with which they were praised and vilified from both camps. However we might regard the severity or benignity of individual canvases, in the eyes of contemporary critics, at least, the verisimilitude of many works earned the school a reputation as uncompromising or mischievous documentors of contemporary social ills. Repin's aphorism 'The peasant is the judge now, and we must reproduce his interests', with its proto-revolutionary intimation of subverting the social order, seems to invite a call to arms, an agenda for acutely political, condemnatory canvases to redress the traditional imbalance. The Wanderers' output, however, suggests the phrase would be better understood as a humanitarian statement than a politicising one; that the world of the peasant is henceforth the legitimate Russian perspective. In a restrictive society such as tsarist Russia, however, humanitarian and political intent remained inextricably linked. It would be a very dense or detached spectator who could consider the plight of the barge-hauler independently of the socio-political system that put him there, or, when viewing *Religious Procession in the Province of Kursk*, could refrain from reflecting on what twenty years of 'freedom' had done for the peasant.

4

The revolutionary's tale: political themes

The invitation extended by the intelligentsia, for artists to interrogate and critique society, is most blatantly manifested in works that directly address a political content; the theme of revolutionary activism. That such a genre arose in autocratic Russia seems paradoxical, although it would be true to say that the state treated all expressions of protest as being of a political character and that pictures of a sociological tendency might easily fit under the rubric of political imagery. The *Artel* members, for instance, wanted nothing more than creative freedom but became subject to police surveillance. The treatment of Chaadaev, Chernyshevsky and other liberals was far harsher. In the visual arts Perov's *Easter Procession* (figure 1) was banned from exhibition whilst Repin's *Burlaki* (figure 3) and Kasatkin's mining pictures (figure 7) were considered to carry a seditious polemic. Myasoedov's *The Zemstvo Dines* (figure 4) directly criticises a political institution and the ineffectiveness of political reform. But these were not depictions of political activity, the development of which seemed inescapable. In setting the agenda for contemporary artistic subject matter, the social commentators of the 1860s placed political involvement firmly to the fore. Chernyshevsky invited consideration of all aspects of life, maintaining that art was a moral activity, an instructive and didactic medium encompassing 'everything in reality that is of interest to man – common man'.[1]

The severe lack of political freedoms in Russia, where sincerity might be mistaken for sedition, ensured that the emphasis on 'everything' and 'reality' inevitably conflicted with the state. In tackling previously unconfronted subjects, however, the first tentative forays into this genre were backed by positive and progressive forces. Despite their blatantly materialist convictions, this first generation of *Raznochinets* critics who were influencing the nation's art and thought were far removed from the ends-justifies-the-means school of revolutionaries who evolved into the terrorists of late nineteenth-century Russia. An intense strain of moral indignation coexisted with a constructive ethos, as Dobrolyubov put it: 'to spread in society a bright outlook, truly noble convictions'.[2]

This outlook informed the images of social inequalities that became the

Wanderers' hallmark – something that could be developed, though not without controversy, by honing the cutting edge of the existing satirical and peasant genres, as Perov did. But if literary liberals were having such a rough time from the censor, even to the point of imprisonment, it was a more arduous proposition to translate the convictions of radical journals, still less the seditious contents of printed and handwritten pamphlets which passed amongst the trusted few, into publicly displayed visual material. Consequently the 1860s became a period of experimentation, of testing boundaries and evolving the formula for the 'political' canvas.

A basic requirement for a political work of art was initially an overt confrontation or unflattering comparison involving a representative of the official order, ideally the forces of law and order since ridicule of the Orthodox Church, though potentially subversive, was something of a tradition. The formula was not, however, easily defined. Perov's *The Arrival of a District Police Officer at an Investigation* (1857, GTG) depicting a fettered prisoner being judged by a corpulent, complacent official, is an early work which makes a bold statement. But as with Sergei Korovin's fully fledged realist creation of 1884, *Before Punishment in the Volost Administration* (figure 24) it attacks only rural despotism at the lowest level and, since the prisoner is a peasant, the mistreatment of whom was institutionalised, the impact, though not negligible, is mitigated.

Yakobi's celebrated *The Prisoners' Halt* (figure 2) is evidence of how much further artists were soon willing to commit themselves ideologically. Despite the reassuring figure of the policeman tending an emaciated convict dying from the forced march, this is a bold depiction of dishevelled prisoners and their families resting in a bleak landscape as they trudge towards Siberian exile. Doubtless many in the party would have been convicted of political crimes. The work is characteristic of the new robustness of paintings during the 1860s despite its largely academic conception.

Perhaps the earliest exponent of a purely political theme was the little-known Arseny Shurygin (1841–1873) who died young, leaving a limited body of work. Shurygin had contact with the *Artel* during his student days, and in 1868 sent three canvases to the Academy with the request that he be granted the minimum rank of 'Artist', an action in keeping with the secessionists of 1863. Amongst these works was *Arrest* (1867, Kazan State Museum of Fine Arts) depicting a middle-class revolutionary, his comfortable apartment floor strewn with illicit literature, being separated from his wife and child by two officers. Though the presence of the victim's wife and baby provided a sentimental touch, the portrayal of an educated, well-dressed, middle-class sympathiser turned activist in an affluent setting was a progression in terms of depicting political activity. Due to censorship the painting was exhibited only after the title was changed to *A Contemporary Idealist*,[3] perhaps because it was felt to be more redolent of well meaning but essentially misguided intentions, but the social standing of the central character still suggests the serious social inequalities that would drive a respectable figure to such desperate actions.

The first tentative appearances of the revolutionary on canvas fell far short of what radical critics had sought, and despite assertions that Chernyshevsky and his contemporaries were required reading at the *Artel* gatherings its members failed to address the increasingly unsettled contemporary scene in their paintings. In 1864, for instance, Herzen called in vain for a pictorial denunciation of Chernyshevsky's civil execution, whilst Repin's student sketch of the execution of Dmitry Karakozov, who in 1866 tried to assassinate Tsar Aleksandr II, is a notable exception of political awareness, but it was never developed.[4]

The revolutionary theme

Despite the prominence accorded it in Soviet art history, the theme of the revolutionary was not particularly recurrent, the province of a minority of artists, chiefly Repin, Nikolai Yaroshenko and Vladimir Makovsky. It was, however, a deeply controversial and culturally explosive theme that came to prominence with the society as artists began to find their independence, and was most prevalent during the 1870s–80s, a period of significant political agitation in Russia. Reacting to and influencing current trends, the works align with contemporary political developments, particularly the transition from populism to terrorism. During the early 1870s the beneficent idealism of the Populist movement, with its new-found reverence for the *narod*, witnessed attempts at awaking the revolutionary potential of the masses through the 'movement to the people'. This entailed hundreds of well-intentioned *narodniki*, mostly intellectuals and students, venturing earnestly to the provinces to enlighten and help liberate their peasant 'brothers' through the power of educative propaganda. In 1874 the government reacted in typically draconian fashion, closing universities, censoring publications, and arresting the populists in huge numbers. Crucial to the failure of the movement, however, was that the populists were rudely rejected by the loyalist and conservative-minded *muzhiks*, who often handed them directly to the police, not infrequently after having exacted summary justice with (and some entertainment from) a physical beating. A more virulently revolutionary populism had its roots in these reverses, forcing direct political action underground and increasingly towards acts of terrorism during the late 1870s–80s. This second phase of agitation culminated in the assassination of Aleksandr II, the Tsar Liberator, on 1 March 1881, by a group styling themselves *Narodnaya Volya* – 'The People's Will'.

Aleksandr's death marked a watershed as the first instance of assassination as a strategy for effecting social and political change, the result of a structured terrorist campaign waged by a cohesive organisation of intelligent, educated, idealistic and above all ruthless members, the majority of whom were from privileged backgrounds. Within three years nearly all of *Narodnaya Volya*'s members were captured. Five of its most prominent members were hanged; others were thrown into the Peter and Paul Fortress quite literally to rot. A fiercely reactionary and repressive period followed, characterised by mass trials, executions and severe prison sentences. The mood of intransigence was matched by the revolutionaries, who in turn confronted the authorities with more assassinations and bombings as the spiral of violence raged out of control.

Populism

Most notable of the canvases produced during the populist phase of political activity is Vladimir Makovsky's *Vecherinka* or *Evening Gathering* (figure 10). Makovsky was one of the minority of artists not from humble stock. He was the son of one of the founders of the Moscow School of Arts and one of a notable family of artists that included his brothers Konstantin and Nikolai, as well as a sister, Aleksandra. Vladimir was the most dedicated in terms of civic outlook and with Konstantin had been a founder member of the Wanderers. Konstantin had also been a member of the student *Artel*, but where he later turned to sweet pictures of maidens and mythology, Vladimir remained true to a critical-realist ethos even into the Soviet period.[5] An artist of great integrity and dedication, he began revolutionary themes early in the populist era, culminating in this rare depiction of political comradeship, a scene of intimacy and cordial interaction: a meal is set, the samovar boils and the floor is littered with cigarette butts. Makovsky presents an image of debate and solidarity ranging across divides of class, profession, age and sex, though realistically the participants would have been much younger (of approximately one

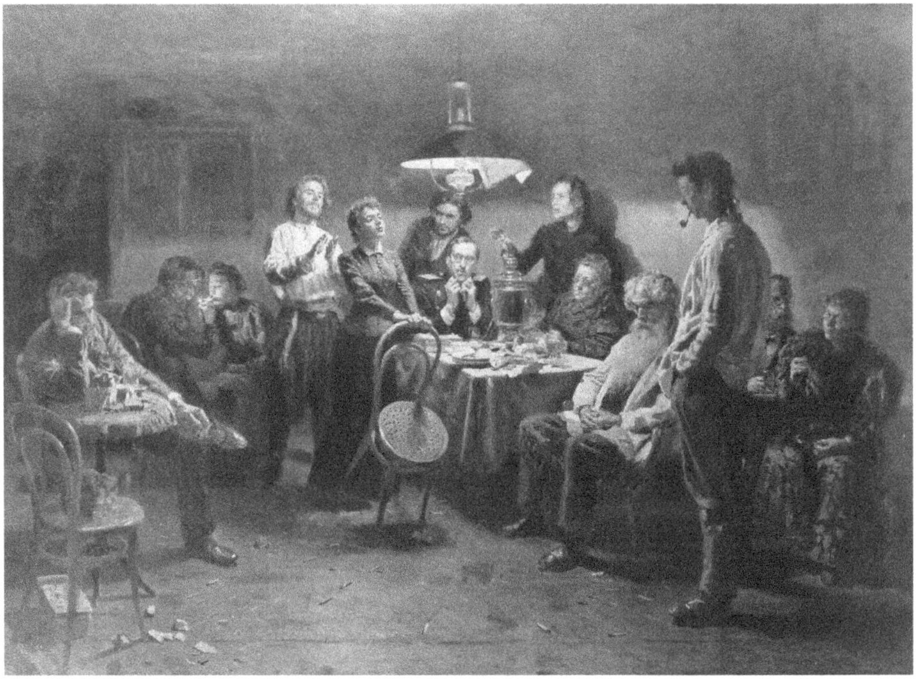

10 Vladimir Makovsky, *Vecherinka (Evening Gathering)*, 1875–1897, 108.5 x 144 cm

thousand arrests in 1874 virtually all were under thirty years of age).[6] However, the whole is a synthetic image full of retrospective wisdom which was worked on into the 1890s, an homage to the Populist movement with its students and intellectuals, young protagonists and elder statesmen and women. At the far left a suitably angst-ridden intellectual grapples with life's larger questions; at the table a uniformed officer, a student of the Military Medical Academy, represents society's disaffected, a convert to the cause; the worker with his pipe embodies the proletariat, whilst the central figure of the female student, short-haired and holding the debate as she is applauded by her male counterpart, is the much vaunted 'progressive' woman, whose incarnation found fullest outlet in Yaroshenko's *Kursistka* (figure 15). The smoking female figure in the rear is also a progressive touch in keeping with then current issues concerning the role and position of women in Russia society – as we shall see in relation to Yaroshenko's work.

Despite the camaraderie of Makovsky's scene his activists are still shown in isolation to the wider society, although in general the work bucks the trend for more tragic depictions of lone individuals as the populist cause began to break up under the pressures of peasant rejection and state persecution. At the end of the 1870s, when the *narodniki* were at their height of activity, Makovsky completed *Sentenced* (figure 11), a charged image of state power and the impotence of the individual as a young man is marched from the courthouse to the prison between a number of threatening police officials, their uniforms and drawn swords emblematic of state violence. The work seems to embody a defiant statement, but as an example

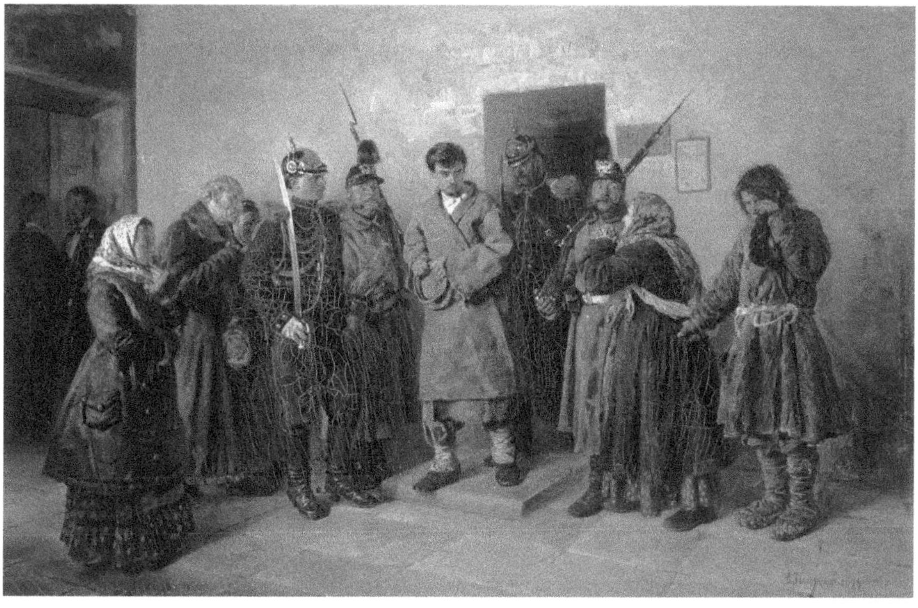

11 Vladimir Makovsky, *Sentenced*, 1879, 76.5 x 113 cm

of psychological drama, whereby viewers were expected to read the reactions of participants placed in moments of tension or crisis, it is equivocal. The grief of the man's family is unrestrained but the convict's reactions are ambiguous. He appears pallid and nervous, perhaps even ashamed to confront his family as he plays nervously with his cap. It is an unconvincing image of populist heroism or suffering, and since all of the characters are of peasant stock it might be conjectured that his offence is not a political one. The willingness to confront these issues, however, should not be underestimated as a facet of progressive endeavour. Makovsky's image remained a rarity at exhibition. It was predictably praised by Stasov, who applauded its accurate and tragic depiction of contemporary life, and the artist was sufficiently exercised by its agenda to return to the theme between 1879 and 1890, producing a variant that portrayed a pair of male and female students, thereby connecting his protagonists with the intelligentsia and activist youth of the day.[7]

Penal imagery provided a degree of ambiguity in that incarceration *per se* was not necessarily tied to political dissent but might connote broadly reformist and humanitarian overtones. That such images would be equated with political activism was merely a by-product of social sensibilities which imbued such works with sentiments not necessarily implicit in their production. Yaroshenko's *The Convict* (1878, GTG) portrays a solitary figure in his spartan cell standing on a table, his back to the viewer as he seeks to catch a glimpse of sunlight at a small, high window. Though the scene is fraught with seditious potential merely by *what* the artist depicts, official and public sensitivity was less likely to be provoked by images of personal reflection, devoid of social interaction. Despite its controversial topic it is, ultimately, a scene of introspective isolation rather than political proselytising; perhaps the result of political activism, but not the act itself.

A rash of images also centred on the *étape*, the halting-place for groups of deported convicts in transit, which enjoyed a fearsome reputation. Vladimir Makovsky produced *At the Etape* (1884, Kiev Museum of Russian Art), depicting an arrested peasant, part of a convoy appearing in the dusty distance, the accent of injustice and oppression somewhat diluted by a masterly landscape. A bold denunciation of the institution came from Sergei Ivanov in 1892 with *Etape. One Did Not Survive* (1892, unlocated) a scene of wretched squalor that will be returned to in chapter 9. Abram Arkhipov's *At the Etape* (1893, unlocated) shows a train of ragged convicts set against a parched, sun-filled landscape, which evokes the suffering of the forced march and the miserable condition of the convicts.[8]

The artist most consistently and controversially associated with the revolutionary genre was Ilya Repin. From his student sketch of Karakozov's execution in 1866, Repin developed a persistent interest in images of political engagement. His earliest canvas, *Under the Guard* (1876, GTG), depicted the miserable conveyance of a convict through a grey, muddy landscape flanked by two soldiers with drawn sabres, the deft use of a series of receding telegraph poles anchoring the events firmly in the present. Beyond an obvious sympathy for the prisoner there is little suggestion where Repin's allegiances lie, though the subject is of an undeniably political hue.

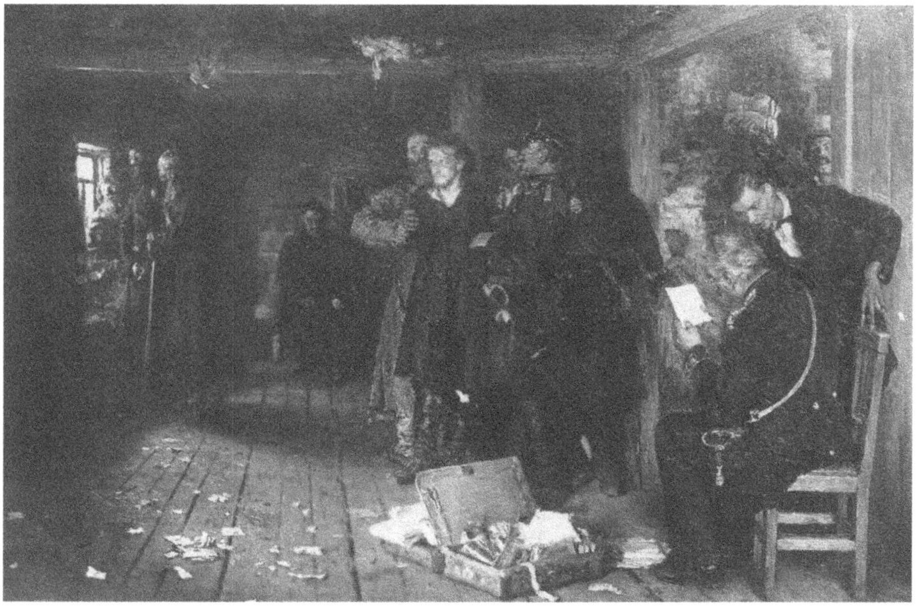

12 Ilya Repin, *Arrest of a Propagandist*, 1880–92, oil on wood, 34.8 x 54.6 cm

Repin's mature works were produced during the period of Populism's greatest activity and subsequent repression, and developed towards evermore subtle and incisive contemporary documentation. *Arrest of a Propagandist* (figure 12) was the artist's first sustained work that attempted to come to grips with the evolving populist drama.[9] Repin addresses his audience via a theatrical space, the story evolving centre-stage, in the wings, and in the rear. The young propagandist is shown as a resolute figure bound to a post in an austere dwelling crowded with *muzhiks*, his suitcase of illegal leaflets scattered about him. A police official scrutinises the contraband literature overlooked by a couple in evening dress, the local landowners who have interrupted their entertainment for more pressing concerns. To the far right a zealous official triumphantly discovers more papers, adding to the abasement of the populist. The revolutionary is divorced from the peasantry, the very people he has come to inform and educate; some shy away as if fearing infection, whilst those near him actively collude with the militia in pinioning their victim. Bound and humiliated, the revolutionary appears trapped in a scene of martyrdom, or possibly the Passion, both of which accord with the modern tragedy. A small group of conspiratorial elders almost lost in the dark background look with a mixture of guilt and complicity at the arrest. Repin confirmed that the malignant figure in the rear, contemplating the arrest with an air of satisfaction, takes the role of Judas: 'In the painting *Arrest* I have repainted a complete figure, in the far background. In place of the sleeping *muzhik* ... there now sits a local tavern keeper or perhaps a factory worker, looking doggedly at the arrested man. Is he not the informer?'[10]

Despite the dramatic and contrived nature of the scene, the authenticity of the work is credible. Repin used a young activist, Nikolai Ventsel, as his model for the protagonist. Ventsel's autobiography paints a typical picture of young populists during the 1870s: he read Dobrolyubov, Pisarev, and seditious journals on his way to becoming a skilled, professional revolutionary. This placed him in an ideal position to advise Repin on the veracity of the incidents depicted. Of the Wanderers' output *Arrest of a Propagandist* most successfully and explicitly reflects contemporary developments. It is, primarily, a 'current affairs' painting. At the time Repin began painting, the notorious mass trials of populists had already begun, including in 1878 the 'trial of the 193' at which almost two hundred defendants, some of whom died in prison before proceedings commenced, received summary justice. His propagandist's educative mission is not without tangible dangers; students were hanged for nothing more than the distribution of leaflets.[11]

Yet the painting is far from a polemic on revolutionary heroism. In highlighting the tragic division between the propagandist and the peasantry, which destroyed the movement as effectively as the mobilisation of police, he uniquely interrogates the decisive role of the peasantry in that failure. In doing so he imputes to them some of the blame for the increasingly desperate actions of the next wave of revolutionary activity. In common with many political themes *Arrest of a Propagandist* was not exhibited publicly until long after completion, but the spirit of the painting seems unmistakable. The ascetic features of the propagandist, his isolation and humiliation, all show a sympathetic attitude for the failed idealism of the *narodniki*; the revolutionary as victim, or social martyr, rather than modern Prometheus. At the same time the work might be said to embody a manifest concern with the futility of kicking against the powerful autocratic system, a question that permeates other canvases in this genre

Terrorism

The assassination of Aleksandr II in 1881 was a political catalyst resulting in judicial reprisals and political repressions, and marking the decline of idealism as the populists turned to violence, confronting the authorities with their own methods. In art these were issues that could barely be hinted at, let alone addressed directly. As such the Wanderers spawned a series of key images whose influence is questionable and whose significance is diluted by censorship. Whilst undoubtedly affecting interventions within artistic circles and so influencing peer development, these challenging images were hardly seen by a wider public, although post-assassination artists do show a greater discernment where political images are concerned in seeking to avoid censorship whilst retaining their integrity.

As the standard bearer within this genre Repin was not always successful. *A Secret Meeting* (1883, GTG) – depicting a heated, clandestine gathering of members *of Narodnaya Volya* – was painted on a large scale, suggesting a serious venture, but never finished. Executed just two years after the Tsar's assassination, the paint-

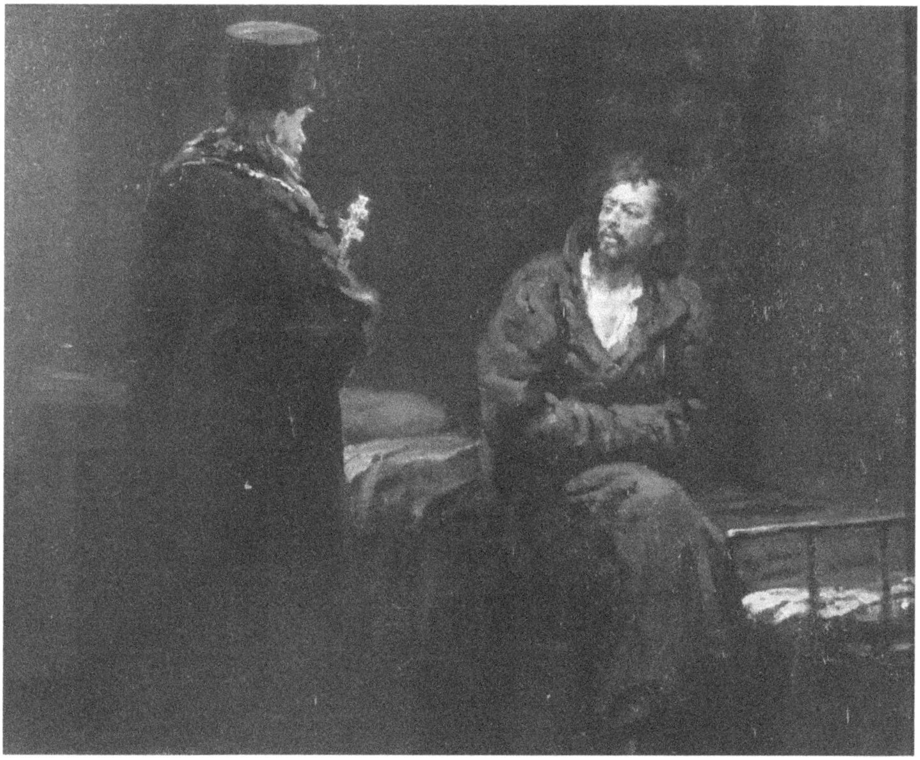

13 Ilya Repin, *Spurning Confession*, 1879–85, 48 x 59 cm

ing's conspiratorial atmosphere and anonymous setting, wherein a central figure berates his comrades in demagogic fashion, suggests an element of the political fanaticism then related to Sergei Nechaev and the followers of Mikhail Bakunin. Such political baggage is an important factor when confronted with images of civic marginalisation. Bakunin, a revolutionary democrat and father of European anarchism, was influential in urging the *narodniki* treks. He believed the *muzhik* to be a born anarchist and held that society required only this spark to incinerate the tsarist regime. Though history might award him zero out of ten for such foresight, his writings were highly influential on subsequent developments, particularly so *The Revolutionary Catechism* written by his follower Sergei Nechaev. Nechaev was a young peasant educated as a teacher whose dispassionate amorality and frightening devotion to political destruction propagated the ideal of the revolutionary as a sociopath, emotionally negated by loyalty to his cause, an outsider to conventions or ethics, knowing only the science of destruction. In a ruthless application of revolutionary ethics that appalled Bakunin, Nechaev developed a creed in which all that served the revolution was good and moral; that which hindered it immoral. As example of this he engineered the murder of a fellow revolutionary who wished to secede, believing this would bind the remaining cell members together in a justified complicity. For these actions, which inspired Dostoevsky's novel *The Devils*, Nechaev was successfully tried for murder in 1873.

Repin's audience would have been painfully aware of these events and the beliefs that sustained contemporary revolutionary activity, but the translation of politics into art was not easy, and frequently impossible. Repin did not manage to exhibit *A Secret Meeting* until 1896, and only then by changing its title to the less provocative *By Lamplight*, potentially reducing its content to nothing more than a fractious debate. However, the 'naming' was important, so much so that when the work was exhibited in Moscow in 1924, after the October Revolution, it was transformed into the pugnacious *Meeting of the Nihilists*.[12]

Repin fared little better with his next offering, *Spurning Confession* (figure 13) sometimes referred to as *Spurning Confession Before Execution*. A small and laconic canvas set in a darkened cell, Repin uses only two figures, a priest and a condemned prisoner, to suggest a muted drama; the priest invites repentance, the populist refuses. The work was prompted by a poem by the revolutionary Nikolai Minsky called 'The Last Confession', which appeared in 1879 in the first edition of *Narod-*

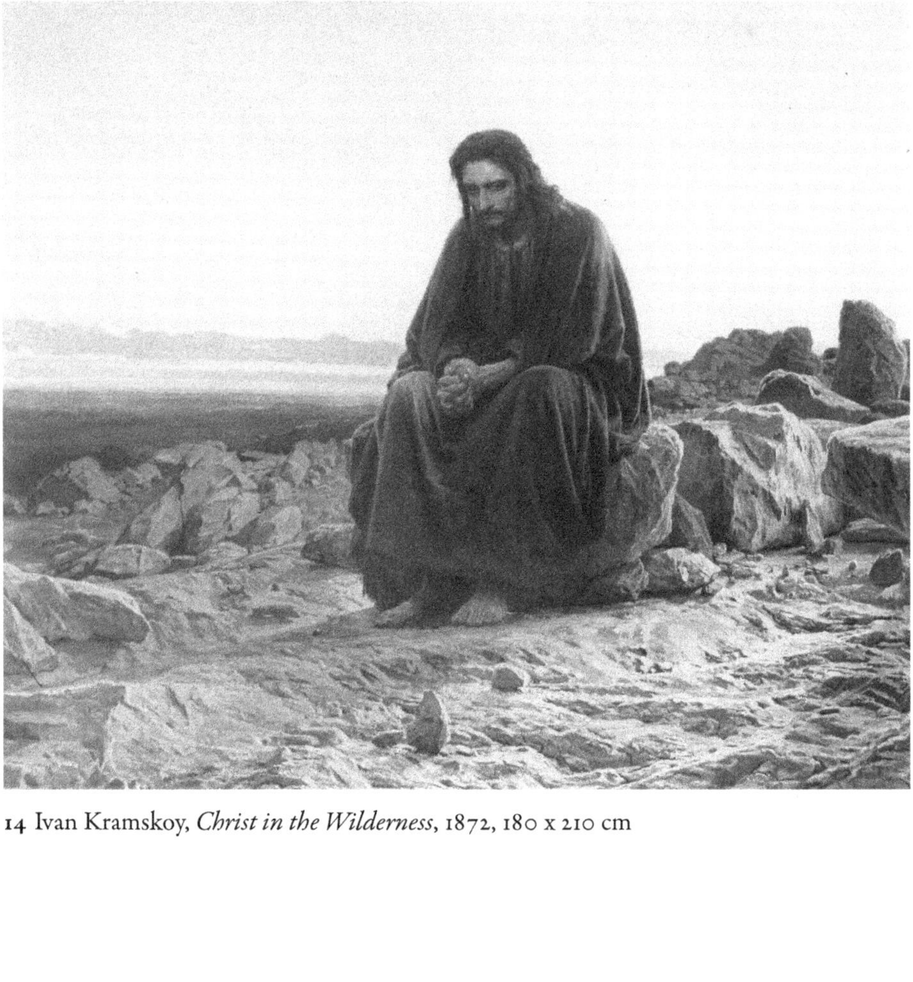

14 Ivan Kramskoy, *Christ in the Wilderness*, 1872, 180 x 210 cm

naya Volya, the illegal newspaper of the organisation. Its genesis and completion took place against the transition from populism to terrorism. Early studies show a robust and agitated revolutionary berating a corpulent priest, but the final version is static and solemn, replete with tragic overtones, stressing the altruistic, sacrificial role of the revolutionary, but also the gulf of misunderstanding between the priest, symbol of the state, and the condemned populist. Whilst the revolutionary is the true subject of the work, whose face alone is seen fully lit, the priest seemingly embodies a condemnation of the role played by the Orthodox Church in upholding the autocracy, since he is represented by only a hint of profile whilst his crucifix, symbol of his office, is highlighted.

The defiance of the prisoner – as well as his isolation at this, his final hour – has elicited comparisons with religious iconography, a correlation between the death of Christ and the revolutionary's sacrifice being apparent from Minsky's poem. As one commentator has remarked: 'He is consecrated by death, but by no means defeated'.[13] Even on the most superficial level there is a coactive relationship between Repin's pensive *narodnik* and Kramskoy's contemplative *Christ in the Wilderness* (figure 14) regarded by many as a quintessential image of the social outsider, a lone warrior against suffering and injustice comparable to the revolutionary's social immolation on behalf of his fellow man. The subject and sentiment of both works is paralleled by Vladimir Makovsky's small canvas *Prisoner* (1882, Kharkov State Museum of Fine Art), depicting a solitary populist brooding in his cell. Like Repin's canvas it is an intimate scene making use of few details other than the prisoner himself, his face similarly lit as the painting's focal point and posed identically to Kramskoy's Saviour, seated with hands clasped on his lap, leaning slightly forward in thought. These analogies will be returned to when considering the use of biblical subjects and their potential to mask contemporary critiques.

Spurning Confession was completed in 1884, intended for the twelfth Wanderers exhibition, to be seen alongside Repin's masterpiece *They Did Not Expect Him* but was banned due to its inflammatory content. Yet whilst aspects of the painting are implicitly but undeniably a rebuke to the autocracy, the work is far from being a blindly partisan sermon. Its stress is on a tragic note of ideological irreconcilability and self-sacrifice that addresses the theme of forgiveness later taken up in Repin's highly controversial *Ivan the Terrible and His Son Ivan* (figure 25). Here though reconciliation is not achieved, and the consequences for modern Russia will be disastrous.

They Did Not Expect Him

Standing outside of this standard fare of tragic suffering, gloomy incarceration and political isolation is Repin's seminal work *They Did Not Expect Him* (colour plate 2) presenting a bright, airy interior and a complex social and family drama which has largely defied adequate interpretation. Of all his major works this caused Repin the greatest anguish in perfecting the desired image and earned him the most critical hostility, marking as it did a more subtle and ambitious attempt to delineate the contemporary political scene.

An earlier version begun in 1883 showed a female revolutionary and is generally translated as *They Did Not Expect Her* (1883; 1898, GTG) though in fact the succinct Russian title *Не ждали* carries no gender expectations, denoting merely an unexpected occurrence in the past tense witnessed by more than one person (such are the subtleties lost in translation to heavy-handed English equivalents that conjure images of Victorian melodrama). This showed a stern, progressively dressed young woman confronting her surprised bourgeois family, which would have been highly topical in light of the general role played by female activists and more specifically in the planning of Aleksandr II's assassination. This will be returned to in relation to Yaroshenko's contentious use of female protagonists and particularly his house arrest in 1881, which may have been a factor in Repin's decision to change the sex of his main character. Repin undoubtedly had in mind the need to avoid censorship, but the restructuring is perhaps less of a retreat than a prudent accommodation. Despite the fact that *Arrest of a Propagandist* and *Spurning Confession*, both small works, had fallen foul of the censor, Repin's statement on political destabilisation is here made on a large scale which could hardly be ignored by officialdom or the public.

Superficially the content seems plain; the domestic reunion of a returning political exile to his surprised family who clearly have not anticipated the event. On closer inspection, however, Repin presents his audience with a series of ambiguous and ambivalent possibilities. The exile's return might be unexpected, but could it also be unwelcome? The maid ushers the hesitant figure in with dispassionate indifference, maybe even disapproval. The young girl at the table stares suspiciously at the dishevelled figure; possibly his sentence has been sufficiently long that she does not remember him. The young boy is the only figure who registers delight and recognition. The older female with her back to the viewer is startled to her feet, whilst the younger woman at the piano has just realised who the intruder is and registers wide-eyed surprise, her hand clutching convulsively at her chair arm, but in neither case are we sure whether joy or shock is their motivation. The whole is a model of psychological tension, on the point of erupting into domestic rapture or perhaps bitter recriminations, but which remains eternally unresolved. Repin never even elucidated the many confusions about the characters' relationships. The elder woman is often referred to as the exile's mother, the younger woman his wife or sister. The children are often assumed to be his own. Stasov, however, identified the children as younger siblings and it is perhaps to Repin's credit that he never insisted on a unitary exposition of the work divining correctly that its central ambiguity is its intellectual appeal.

The detailed iconography, which is uncharacteristic of both Repin and the Wanderers, proves similarly elusive in interpretation. The interior is affluent, respectable and decorously furnished, with servants in attendance – a country dacha of the type familiar in Chekhov's plays, with a hint of bright landscape glimpsed through the French windows to the left. Pictures and prints on the walls confirm the educated standing of the family but are semiotically confusing. On the back wall is a large popular print of *The Golgotha* by Karl Steuben, which hung in St Isaak's Cathedral in St Petersburg. This may denote conservative tastes or another link between the revolutionary and the theme of Christ's sacrifice. In one sense the work clearly represents a scene of resurrection and it has been noted that amongst political activists 'Golgotha' was popular slang for standing in the dock.[14] To the right of Christ is a portrait of the eminent populist poet Nikolai Nekrasov, a colleague of Chernyshevsky's, and to the left an image of Taras Shevchenko, a self-taught peasant artist and political activist who suffered prolonged internal exile for his radical convictions.

On the right-hand wall we see the beginnings of a large map of the Russian empire next to a small photo of the assassinated Aleksandr II lying in state. The latter confirms the modernity of subject – that the participants are living amidst the contemporary terrorism – but a tension is established between these and the representatives of nonconformism, Christ included, on the rear wall. One set of signs speaks of a continuing involvement with the now failing liberal-reformist ideals of the 1860s usurped by terrorism, the climax of which is represented in the dead Tsar's photo. Simultaneously the photo denotes sympathy within this respectable family for the 'Tsar Liberator' and with it the possibility that the exile's political convictions are not shared. (Ironically it is possible that the exile could be amongst those released as part of an amnesty to mark Aleksandr III's coronation in 1881.) If the iconography of images is read as cause and effect, Repin appears to mourn and reassert the validity of the liberal values rejected in favour of violence, with Christ acting as moral guarantor. But the mood is also insular; this is a family crisis, not merely a carrier of wider political symbolism. In large part the canvas is similar to other Wanderers' offerings in terms of addressing personal suffering, the human price the exile pays for his political ideals. Uniquely, however, Repin takes his viewer into the uncharted territory of the home, to remind his audience that belying the stereotype of Nechaev's robotic sociopath, political activists do not live in isolation, but that their acts have severe domestic repercussions.

Problems with deciphering Repin's work are exacerbated by technical difficulties that saw the canvas reworked on four occasions between 1883 and 1888, at one point utilising the writer Garshin as model for the exile, until eventually neither he nor his patron, Tretyakov, was happy with the outcome.[15] The exile suggests a range of emotions that might give the key to the events under scrutiny, but none seems positive: guilt, suffering, shame, confusion, despondency, timidity? Earlier versions and sketches show an evolution from more confident to ever more diffident models, possibly in line with the depressing turn of events as extremism and violence saw the revolutionary become ever more estranged from society.[16]

The controversial nature of Repin's work ensured a large public attendance at exhibition, whilst its politically sensitive subject matter provoked an unprecedented level of abuse from the conservative press:

> Mr Repin undoubtedly executes with genius ... A pathetic genius, swamped in artistic errors, pandering to public curiosity in the most vulgar manner ... If you do not feel tears coming to your eyes at the sight of such shocking family events as Mr Repin depicts, then you can be sure that the reason for this is the cold contrivance of the subject, the prevalence of immature thoughts on top of superficial feeling.[17]

Another writer found the work guilty of 'too much tendentiousness', the environment 'unattractive, untidy and comfortless', the children 'scrofulous and emaciated', and worst of all, the painter's intentions bogus, full of 'pseudo-liberal denunciations and protests'. Prince V.P. Meshchersky, writing in *Grazhdanin*, rejoiced that the artist had defeated his tendentious purpose by making the exile 'offensive and ugly', concluding 'there is evil, discontent, rage and animosity in his appearance ... he looks at his family with hatred'.[18]

Outside of Repin's circle of friends and admirers it is difficult to find a positive review for a painting which clearly hit a raw nerve in conservative circles, and as usual it fell to Stasov to mount a defence, hailing it as Repin's most important creation and 'one of the very greatest works of the new Russian painting'.[19]

Despite the concentration on deconstructing and deciphering the narrative content and the supposedly tendentious motives of its creator, *They Did Not Expect Him* marks a watershed for the Russian realist school in terms of a maturing aesthetic. Repin successfully retained much of the freshness and spontaneity of his Parisian period within this ostensibly political polemic, as evinced by the impressionistic manner of some passages and the softly diffused interior lighting. Aleksandr Benois – one of the Wanderers' principle detractors, who would later spearhead the aesthetic rebellion against the realist-narrative tendency – was nevertheless alive to Repin's painterly genius.

> I left the show quite overcome by the impression made on me by Repin's picture *The Unexpected Guest*. The freedom of the style and the freshness of the painting surprised me. I found it daringly simple and genuine, although utterly unlike everything that had hitherto been considered worthy of attention at home.[20]

They Did Not Expect Him was an ambitious and, by Repin's previous standards, complex attempt at controlled psychological subtlety. The ambiguity or enigma of the painting is perhaps its abiding strength. Repin's concern is chiefly humane, for the exile and his family and whether or not they are pleased at his return, the episode presents a social and domestic tragedy which might have prompted observers of both political persuasions to ask why matters had come to this lamentable pass. Above all the painting is both a moving and eloquent attempt to create a contemporary document of crumbling, thwarted ideals, combined with a universal comment on the individual cost and wider consequences of personal principles. Though both the ethical and painterly problems were not resolved to the artist's satisfaction, the bold attempt to tackle both have long made this the most highly regarded and painstakingly analysed of all Repin's paintings, a fact which speaks for the timeless concerns at the heart of the work.

The 'progressive' woman

> I'm talking about those short-haired females ... They try to get into the Academy, study anatomy. Do you really think that if I fell ill, I'd call in some young female to treat me? Ha, ha![21]

Repin's initial version of *Ne zhdali*, and his decision to drop *They Did Not Expect Her* in favour of a male protagonist, raises a more problematic spectre which artists largely circumvented: the debate over women's rights and role in society. Though rarely configured in the visual arts, the topical and contentious issues surrounding progressive female activity or aspiration, the so-called 'women's question', were vigorously contested in Russia and ensured lively press and public attention. Despite Russia being further advanced than many European countries in terms of women's access to education (women began to attend universities in the late 1850s), the female student was scapegoated in the early 1860s for a wave of university unrest. A student strike at St Petersburg University in October 1861 was followed by closure of the institution for a year in 1862, and was in part attributed to the so-called 'advanced' women agitating for greater access to higher education. In the wake of the unrest women were officially excluded from universities in 1863, and although by the end of the decade extra-mural activities were being arranged for women, and some universities admitted them to lectures unofficially (Moscow's first higher courses for women were opened in 1872), the public profile of the female student became synonymous with disruptive, anti-government tendencies.[22]

In the realm of political activism, trial and police records show that 25 per cent of populists during the 1870s were women and when activity moved into a terrorist phase they followed. Notable amongst many female activists was Vera Zasulich, a revolutionary and publicist; a member of the Nechaev circle who in 1878 shot the Governor of St Petersburg but was acquitted by a jury, leading the state to curtail the jury system and suppress reporting of the trial. Vera Figner was a prominent terrorist leader arrested in 1883, some time after the execution of Aleksandr II's murderers, and sentenced to hang in September 1884, though this was commuted to life in solitary confinement of which she served twenty years. A third of the members of *Narodnaya Volya*, the organisation that planned the Tsar's assassination, were women, as was the director of its executive committee, Sofya Perovskaya, who was hanged for the privilege in 1881.[23]

Imaging this state of affairs was highly problematic and artists tended to soften the blow. In *The Acquitted Woman* (1882, GTG) Vladimir Makovsky portrayed a female activist being released from the law courts to reunite with her family in a warm domestic scene; clearly not a dangerous terrorist. The work is, however, still a daring and rare image of a current social trend and must have prompted the questions: what crime has she been accused of, and what might drive a respectable young woman to the courts, to risk her own welfare and the security of her family? Two years later Repin produced *Revolutionary Woman Awaiting Execution* (c.1884, Private Collection) a single figure engulfed by the darkness of her cell. The work was reputed to have been painted in connection with the trial of the Tsar's assassins and by the 1890s was supposedly known amongst activists as *Vera Figner in Prison.*[24] The date of the trial and the painting correspond, but it is by no means certain that Repin intended Figner as the model. As a secular icon of female revolutionary commitment and suffering the canvas is both potentially explosive and highly emotive, but it was banned from exhibition until 1896, and then appeared more tamely under the title *Anguish*.

Not all images of progressive female activity needed to pertain to political agitation. Works showing women's aspirations to professional status might be similarly contentious in so conservative a society. Makovsky painted a positive image of educated female endeavour in *The Arrival of the Village Teacher* (1896–97, GTG) whilst Repin's *In the Laboratory* (1881, Private Collection) shows a female medical student conducting an autopsy; both rare but serious-minded images of progressive Russian womanhood. Repin had frequent charitable involvement with funding surgical courses for female medical students through sales of his works, and when *Revolutionary Woman Awaiting Execution* was sold in 1896 the proceeds were donated to the Women's Medical Institute.[25]

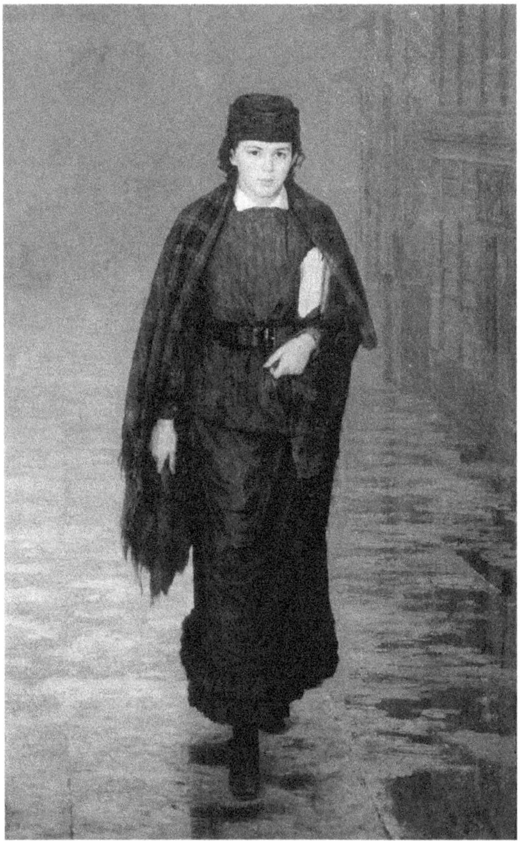

15 Nikolai Yaroshenko, *Kursistka*, 1883, 134 x 83 cm

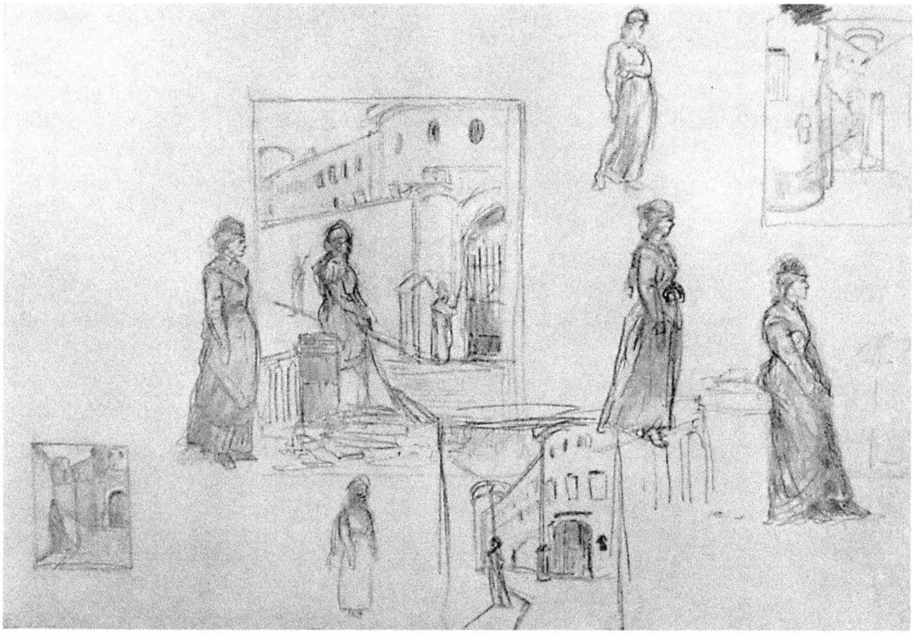

16 Nikolai Yaroshenko, *At the Litovsky Fortress*, sketch, 1881, 21.6 x 30 cm

The most successful image in this category, Nikolai Yaroshenko's female student, *Kursistka* (figure 15), however, was not the most controversial, though its success stemmed from an earlier controversy which undoubtedly shaped its conception. Sometimes referred to as 'the conscience of the Wanderers', Yaroshenko was a hard-line ideologue for the Society yet amazingly followed the two careers of art and military service, retiring in 1892 with the rank of Major General. Notwithstanding this curious professional dichotomy he produced a series of controversial paintings including *The Convict*, *Nevsky Prospect at Night*, *The Stoker* (figure 8) and *Dismissed. At the Station* (figure 9). Yaroshenko is the only artist from among the Wanderers with known revolutionary associates, including Vera Figner who took great consolation from his work *Life is Everywhere* (1888, GTG) depicting the transportation of prisoners, who from their barred carriage watch some birds feeding. In this she saw an affirmation that incarceration could not suppress the love of life, nor of human comradeship.[26] Yaroshenko is perhaps best remembered now for his images of revolutionary youth, such as the hirsute and romantically rebellious *Student* (1881, GTG), an earlier male counterpart to *Kursistka*, but more fundamentally those of female activists. These include such titles as *The Progressivist* (1878, GTG) and *For Reasons Unknown* (1884, Russian Art Museum, Odessa) depicting in a female suicide the death of a failed revolutionary. In 1887 he also sketched his own version of *Arrest of a Propagandist* showing a female agitator.[27]

The catalyst to *Kursistka* was an earlier work of 1881, *At the Litovsky Fortress*, now lost, presumed destroyed, and for which only sketches survive (figure 16). From these it is possible to conjecture the original image of a defiant female student in front of this notorious prison. The combination of a female protagonist and an identifiable symbol of state oppression proved explosive and occasioned the artist's house arrest, a unique event in Russian art.[28] That it appeared at exhibition on the day of Aleksandr II's assassination did not help.

Undeterred, Yaroshenko returned to the theme in 1883. Though at first glance *Kursistka* may not appear to fit the rubric of 'political painting' it provides a telling case study in strategy. Yaroshenko approaches his subject tangentially via the use of 'type' favoured by many left-wing critics, an appeal to the general rather than the particular as a means of encapsulating broader truths – a strategy already encountered in Stasov's advocacy of the need to construct positive prototypes of the Russian *muzhik*. So, whilst the model for Yaroshenko's canvas is one Anna Chertkova, the progressively minded daughter of an army general active amongst the working classes through publishing educational material, the *Kursistka* is not specifically any one woman. She is representative of a type, a trend, a broad social phenomenon, which widened the scope of the canvas causing extensive press discussion on the women's question.

Decoding the image presents us with a more complex set of issues than are immediately apparent. These reside chiefly in the interchangeability of the terms *kursistka* and *nihilistka*, as well as a subversion of conventional dress codes. Though *kursistka* denoted nothing more than a female student, it connoted, as already mentioned, the general insurgent tendencies associated with the 'progressive' woman (the term was applied pejoratively and frequently ironically, being no more a positive designation than modern uses of 'feminist', depending on the user). *Nihilistka* (a female nihilist), however, denoted a set of more dangerous, radical left-wing values; an adherence to a scientific rationality which advocated a complete overthrow of society and its restructuring along egalitarian lines. At a time when many viewed women as merely an extension of their father's estates and marriage as another form of serfdom, nihilism drew in many female adherents through its insistence on personal emancipation and sexual equality in the fields of education, employment and economy. Chernyshevsky's *What Is to Be Done?*, published in 1863, advocated a similar programme of sexual equality, communal living, and the redundancy of marriage, sentiments echoed by Bakunin and later anarchists. So scandalous were these views and so imprecisely and misleadingly was the terminology applied, that by the time of Yaroshenko's canvas the terms *nihilistka* and *kursistka* became synonymous, connoting at least a political activist, at worst a terrorist.[29]

Yaroshenko relied for the impact of his work upon the popular tendency to associate one with the other, since the title *Nihilistka* would undoubtedly have resulted in censorship. To promote the association and blur the distinction, the artist also experimented with the signifiers of dress. The *nihilistka* favoured functionalism, rejecting the ostentatious costumes of the conventional Russian lady as fit only for pampered, helpless creatures. These sentiments were echoed in Tolstoy's scandalous story 'The Kreutzer Sonata', written in 1889 but refused permission for publication by the Minister of the Interior. Here and in his work of 1886, *What Then Must We Do?*, Tolstoy condemned matrimony and equated the rearing of girls for breeding stock for the marriage market as akin to prostitution, an amazingly audacious correlation for the time.

The *nihilistka* and/or *kursistka* rejected conventional dress and hairstyles as marks of sexual attraction which led to domestic serfdom. Her dress speaks of radicalism; a plain dark woollen skirt that falls straight from her waist and a modern, mass-produced knitted sweater. Dark glasses frequently hid the eyes (though Yaroshenko clearly felt this inappropriate in a picture designed for the viewer to make contact with its subject) and her hair was cut short (men grew theirs long) and straight, often covered by a cap or hood. She embraces knowledge (the book) rather than social acceptability or romantic sentimentality. In short, her image is 'defeminised', made boyish, in an age that demanded voluptuousness. The aggregate of these cultural signs that diminish the contemporary social and cultural distinctions between the sexes – intellectual interests, short hair, plain dress – are all evident in Vladimir Makovsky's *Vecherinka* (figure 10).

The strength of social codes within a rigidly structure society should not be underestimated. Several incidents illustrate how seriously the state took breaches of accepted dress. In 1867, following Karakozov's attempt on the Tsar's life, the Moscow Chief of Police ordered the banishment of all women wearing the 'nihilist' costume; the Governor of St Petersburg issued 'nihilist' women with yellow internal passes intended for prostitutes; in Saratov a woman was punched to the ground by two men incensed at her dark glasses; and the Governor of Nizhny Novgorod gave orders to banish from the province any women with short hair, blue glasses and hoods who refused to wear the crinoline.[30] Nihilists of both sexes also subverted or rejected small but influential affectionate manners. Women might appear blunt whilst men would refuse to stand for a woman, affronting chivalric expectations. As one of Dostoevsky's characters notes: 'she understood excellently the question about kissing of hands ... that a man insults a woman by kissing her hands because he shows that he does not consider her to be his equal'.[31]

More vituperative myths that developed from the *nihilistka*'s indifference to sexual and emotional attachments conjectured she was unconcerned with cleanliness and lived in a state of odorous fornication; even that women studied medicine solely to perform abortions on each other. Thus a wide range of debate, informed and hysterical, was aired by Yaroshenko's work as press and public pondered its message. Is she a positive representative of emancipation and enlightenment or the personification of an unwelcome political and social discontent?

Conservative opinion predictably saw a rebellious outcast destined for the ignominious end granted to Sofya Perovskaya, contended that the female brain was too small for academic concerns, or reaffirmed motherhood and domesticity as the preordained roles for women. For Yaroshenko she embodied the idealism and social commitment of her generation, a paradigm for social and intellectual equality.

Gleb Uspensky, a liberal revolutionary who had modelled for *The Convict*, saw her as an intelligent, dedicated activist, prototype of the 'new woman' and representative of those who would affect a positive change in society. In 1885 Garshin was moved to write his short story 'Nadezhda Nikolaevna', which provides a sympathetic portrayal of a female terrorist whose initial appearance is clearly based on Yaroshneko's painting.[32]

The important point concerning Yaroshenko's gambit was that by adopting a less confrontational strategy with more subtle nuances, this painting, which seems superficially less adventurous than *At the Litovsky Fortress*, had a far greater impact. The 'women's question', the issues of female political emancipation and activism, was aired, debated, contested, and the censor, though presumably not happy, found no excuse to ban the painting. Though a brave statement, *At the Litovsky Fortress* had no intellectual impact – it remained unseen and was as such a wasted effort on the artist's part – whereas *Kursistka* became a rallying point for debate and an exemplar of the Wanderers' use of 'type', using the individual to comment on a wider social phenomenon.

Artists and revolutionaries

An integral part of the Wanderers' imaging of political developments is that artists, unlike writers, had scant personal connections. Yaroshenko is the only painter known to have had revolutionary associates, and whilst Repin followed current political events avidly and met activists through various contacts, using one as model for *Arrest of a Propagandist*, most of his images are based on research rather than experience. The controversy that surrounded these images suggests, however, that they were considered accurate by press and public, and presumably by the state that sought to curtail them. Benois recalls how, as a young man, there would be 'uproar' at the dining table when a 'progressive' uncle expressed approval of a new work by Repin, Surikov, Makovsky or Savitsky, and how his own family, believing that art outside of the Academy was a destructive influence, labelled these painters 'nihilists'.[33] Amongst similarly affluent, conservative households, the Wanderers doubtlessly enjoyed a comparable standing.

We know also that many revolutionaries identified with such images, as Vera Figner's comments attest. Nikolai Minsky's memoirs describe Repin as an artist who portrayed the late populist period of struggle with great veracity, noting that he eschewed depictions of heroic feats: 'The hero, depicted by Repin, lives in the world of liberatory ideas ... these are educators and transformers ... fighters.' The revolutionary socialist Vladimir Bonch-Bruyevich suggested that the youth of the day drew great strength from such paintings and that they swore oaths in front of many at the Tretyakov Gallery including Yakobi's *The Prisoners' Halt* (figure 2) and 'the painting in which the proud revolutionary, resolute in his belief, refuses the priest's blessing before execution'.[34]

Despite these notable examples, few painters made use of political symbols, particularly of convicts or revolutionaries. And whilst no artist openly supported terrorism, in their images pertaining to political affairs Repin, Yaroshenko and Vladimir Makovsky exhibited a keen interest in social phenomena and a concern for the fates of the individuals caught up in contemporary events. A personal commitment, then, must be regarded as a prerequisite for addressing these themes; a willingness to tackle difficult and sensitive issues. But the genre was relatively short-lived, confined to the years of populism's greatest activity, after which artists appear to lose appetite for the subject. A sense of disillusionment, rather than defeatism, perhaps permeates the final version of *They Did Not Expect Him*. With the exception of Yaroshenko's remarkable *Kursistka*, the consistent factor in these disparate images is a concern for the revolutionary as a social victim, pariah or martyr, seldom as a positive hero and never as a bomb-wielding insurgent. The tone is sympathetic but politically astute, which in turn successfully charted or foreshadowed the increasingly tragic turn of events.

5

Meritocracy: portraiture

The outstanding body of portraits produced by the Wanderers is rightly considered one of their finest achievements, fixing for posterity definitive images of Russia's intellectual and cultural élite. The decision by Pavel Tretyakov to establish a collection of contemporary notables, a pantheon of Slavic culture, was undoubtedly the most important influence on portrait painting in the second half of the nineteenth century. Always a popular art form with wealthy patrons, Russian portraiture up to the 1860s displayed, by and large, a steady stream of imposing or decorative royals and aristocrats, the peasant portraits of Venetsianov and his school being far from representative. The genre of professional 'types', surrounded by the accessories of their trades, epitomised in the works of Tropinin, was also prevalent, but images of writers and thinkers were noticeably absent, Kiprensky's romantic portrayal of Pushkin (1827, GTG) observing the ethnic traces of his negro ancestry remaining an exception.

The reforming 1860s saw no shortage of intellectual heroes, but whilst artists were industriously indulging in social exposé, and the peasant portrait was striving for artistic autonomy, few depictions were produced of the thinkers who inspired their efforts. Ge painted Aleksandr Herzen (1867, GTG) with whom he made contact whilst in Italy, but this remained an aberration until Tretyakov's conscious decision to amass a body of Russian portraits precipitated an explosion of earnest, serious-minded depictions of celebrated national figures.

Prior to 1869 Tretyakov had been a keen collector of portraits by Russian masters such as Borovikovsky, Bryullov, Levitsky and Kiprensky, acquired chiefly on the grounds of the artist rather than the sitter, but from 1869 to 1870 he began seriously collecting and commissioning works on the basis of whom they depicted.[1] At the first Wanderers exhibition of 1871 Ge exhibited his portrait of Turgenev (Armenian State Art Gallery, Yerevan) and Perov showed a portrait of the playwright Aleksandr Ostrovsky (GTG). The following year saw portraits by Ge of the writers Mikhail Saltykov-Shchedrin (1872, GRM) and Nikolai Nekrasov (1872, State Hermitage, St Petersburg) and by Perov of Turgenev (1872, GRM), the poet

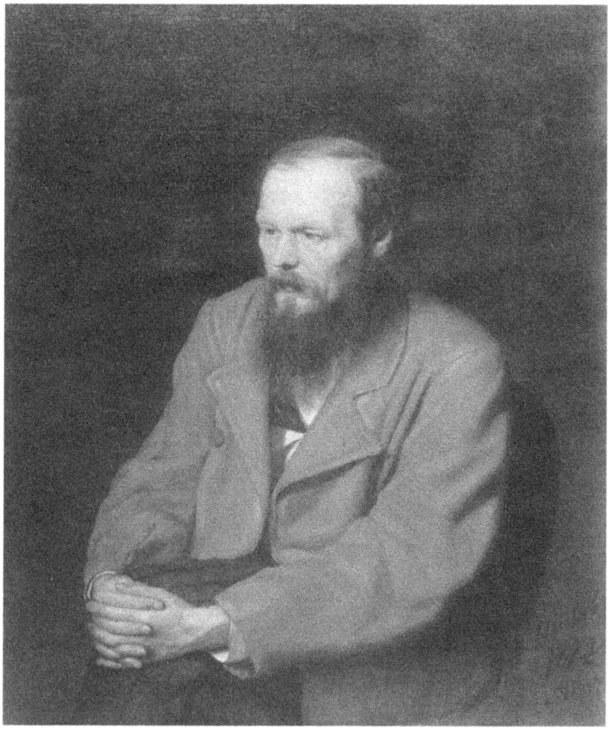

17 Vasily Perov, *Portrait of Fedor Dostoevsky*, 1872, 99 x 80.5 cm

Vasily Maikov (1872, GTG) and, still regarded as one of the greatest achievements of Russian portraiture, his psychologically incisive image of the gaunt and pensive Dostoevsky (figure 17). The trend, bolstered by Tretyakov's acquisitions, was quickly established and succeeding exhibitions saw fresh, often powerfully laconic images of Russian celebrities.

A common conception at the time was to regard Tretyakov's collection as a form of meritocracy in action, since in the broadest sense the sitters appeared to be of a reformist-liberal character. Thus, Ostrovsky's plays are concerned critically with the despotism of contemporary Russian mercantile life, Saltykov-Shchedrin and Nekrasov, co-editors of *The Contemporary*, were of the radical intelligentsia. Even the more conservative figures of Turgenev and Dostoevsky were keen and sharply analytical contributors to national cultural debate, both with a fierce sense of moral probity and an independent if mercurial turn of mind. In this sense, whilst never constituting a programmatic gallery of politically active radicals (such would have been anathema to the loyalist Tretyakov) the specific and personal nature of the genre, which superficially spoke of introspective individuality, was pressed into the more general service of engaging with societal generalities and national discourses.

The Wanderers' output in portraiture is certainly characterised by a paucity of aristocratic, noble or establishment sitters, replaced instead by an assortment of exemplars of national and creative aspiration. The list of cultural figures is prodigious and too long even to hint at in terms of its comprehensive and inclusive nature, but its scope was immensely varied ranging between writers, critics, musicians, actors and actresses, scientists, physicists, doctors, scholars, lawyers, artistic patrons and public figures. Particularly telling in this respect is the Wanderers' impetus to paint themselves into the cultural life of the nation as fully fledged members of the progressive intelligentsia. Almost all of the major painters of this period portrayed one another in intimate and public modes and together with a large output of psychologically insightful self-portraits this reciprocity of cultural legitimisation embedded artists into national life with a forcefulness and self-confidence previously unknown.

Given the disparate nature of the genre which stemmed largely from commissions, the output of the school cannot be regarded as a planned or systematic collection, but Tretyakov's often variable acquisitions at least represent a project with an ostensible cultural teleology, which given the chauvinistic nature of the collector is remarkably free of conservative or reactionary figures. Kramskoy's portrait of Aleksei Suvorin (1881, GRM) a noted journalist for the right-wing *New Times*, is something of an exception to the rule, but commemorates an inconsistent reactionary who also published cheap, popular editions of literary classics and later praised Repin's supposedly seditious *Ivan the Terrible* (figure 25).

There were, however, boundaries of tolerance, even if they remained undefined. When Tretyakov proposed to Repin a commission to paint the journalist Mikhail Katkov, the artist's rejection was unequivocally couched as ideological rather than aesthetic objections, even drawing parallels between the proposed sitter and the terrorists who had assassinated Aleksandr II on 1 March, little more than a month before:

> Your intention to commission a portrait of Katkov and place it in your gallery disturbs me, and I cannot refrain from writing that by it you will cast an unpleasant shadow over your fine and enlightened collecting activity ... The portraits which you have amongst your paintings at present, are of a chance character, they do not constitute a systematic collection of Russian figures, but with few exceptions they represent the faces of those dear to the nation, its best sons, who through their selfless activity bring positive benefit, well being and advantage to their homeland, believing in a better future and fighting for this idea ... What sense is there to accommodate here a portrait of a retrograde, who so long, with such rigorous consistency and insolent candour attacks every enlightened thought, and holds every free word up to shame ... With their Turkish ideals, of sheer slavery, merciless punishment and arbitrary power, these people provoke horrible opposition and such shocking events as, for example, March 1st ... Should such people be placed alongside Tolstoy, Nekrasov, Dostoevsky, Shevchenko, Turgenev and others?! No, for God's sake refrain!![2]

Repin's inclusion of Dostoevsky amongst this list of Russian worthies is also curious since, less than two months before, writing to Stasov on the death of the writer, he had decried Dostoevsky's reactionary beliefs, even linking him with Katkov:

> I hate his convictions! ... He frightens and confines, and without this our depressing lives are already narrow and full of prejudices ... And why such mud-slinging at the intelligentsia? And his crude hatred of the Poles, the obsolete, home-spun notion of the supposed perniciousness of the West, and his popish glorification of orthodoxy ... and much more in this vein, is as obnoxious to me as Katkov himself.[3]

The significance of these comments shows not merely that artists were beginning to find their critical independence, but that those commissioning the works were served noticed that the artists' services were not simply 'for hire'.

Type and typicality

As with the Wanderers' output in general, the theoretical conceptualisation of 'type' was utilised in assessing portraiture and here perhaps with the greatest consistency. But whilst the specific symbols of genre painting might be abstracted, or 'read out' from their contemporary narratives to assume a universal significance, portraiture presents us with an unremitting series of specific and particular individuals. This carries an essential paradox of how to draw out meaning from likeness. Many see the best works of the Wanderers as providing a commentary on the general via the use of the particular. But if the employment of 'type' is to be successful, then presumably the portrait has to transcend the individuality and likeness of the sitter, so that these aspects must, logically, be sacrificed to the typicality and topicality of wider trends in social development. As a likeness the portrait has a transitory life. Whether or not Perov's much admired image of Dostoevsky (figure 17) is 'good' in the sense of an accurate, faithful rendition of external physical features is of little interest to posterity. We have no definitive method of judging. In this sense a 'good' portrait will of necessity need to say something more of the individual by giving us insight into his or her inner being, whether one construes that as spirituality or psychology. If this is successful, then future generations may find Perov's portrait fascinating not as a likeness, but as a potential window into Dostoevsky's mind and character.

The additional burden placed upon the Wanderers, however, was the pressure somehow to allow these individuals to incarnate general social trends and truths, to become emblematic of deeper and more significant developments within modern Russia. Perov's portrait provides a good instance of this; not merely the image of a famous writer but the embodiment of the troubled, introspective intellectual, sign and symbol of a tormented generation of thinkers seeking answers to life's most fundamental questions of freedom and responsibility. Certainly this was how the image was initially received and how it continues to be assessed. Reviewing the work in 1872 the critic P.M. Kovalevsky pointed to the portrait's transcendental nature, that it surpassed likeness to encapsulate an intellect grappling with life's 'accursed problems'.[4]

In one sense this may appear fanciful, or at best the result of privileged knowledge about the sitter, but Perov wields a decisive influence in structuring this reading, giving us little alternative but to confront the writer's psychology. He concentrates primarily on the face, providing no interior detail, and setting the gaunt, ascetic, distracted figure against a neutral background. Only the finely drawn and expressive hands clasped around the writer's knees, producing a vulnerable or maybe troubled body language, are similarly susceptible to an emotional or psychological analysis. No 'clues', no accessories are allowed to detract from the man, or the symbol. It can hardly have been coincidental that the following year Kramskoy depicted a similarly troubled Saviour (figure 14) in near identical pose, contemplating a similar set of spiritual, moral and ethical questions. In this respect the images complement one another, configuring Christ as a thinker and the intelligentsia as enjoying the highest moral sanction.

A more explicit exemplar of the individual as sign for the collective is provided by Repin's *The Archdeacon* (figure 18), produced at a time when the use of type was becoming common currency. The person depicted is a known individual, as much as is Yaroshenko's *Kursistka*. Ivan Ulanov was Archdeacon of the cathedral in the artist's native Chuguyev; by all accounts a great drinker, a man of good humour and boundless energy who enjoyed the contentment of his rural diocese. Repin asserted that the solid, imposing figure was a transference to canvas of living actuality, but he claimed it intellectually as both a 'type' and an 'extract' of the genus archdeacon, typifying a breed 'who have not one iota of spirituality – all flesh and blood ... our deacons are the last echo of the pagan priesthood, still Slavonic, and this is how I have always regarded my dear deacon – as the most typical, the most fearful of all deacons'.[5]

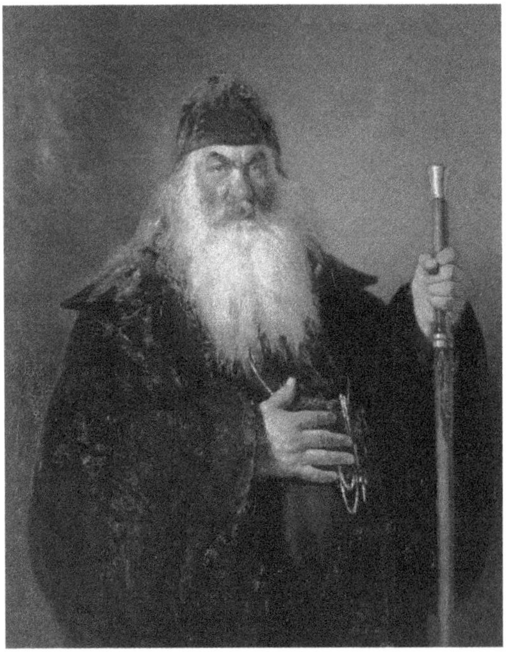

18 Ilya Repin, *The Archdeacon*, 1877, 124 x 96 cm

Unequivocally this is intended to depict something beyond the individual, to capture and summarise an archetype, a species. In this respect the *Archdeacon* speaks of much more than the sitter. With its insistence on physical size and presence, on corporeality where one should expect spirituality, it stands for the rapacious and venal nature of the rural clergy as a body. Indeed it constituted so unflattering a portrait of a servant of the Church that it was withdrawn from the Russian pavilion at the 1878 Paris Universal Exposition on the intervention of Grand Duke Vladimir, the Academy's President.

Reinforcing the universal or abstracted nature of the work, Repin combines an anonymous title with a vacant background and neutral colours to focus attention solely on the sitter who appears in a connotative and representative role, rather than a purely denotative or personal one. It is, perhaps, small wonder that *Religious Procession in the Province of Kursk* was considered seditious when this single study for the work contained by association so much underlying criticism of the existing order.

Similar motives underpin other examples of Wanderers portraiture, confirming that the genre was in some measure being adapted to accommodate contemporary progressive aspirations. Kramskoy's *Nekrasov at the Time of His Last Poems* (1877–78, GTG), showing the pensive poet on his deathbed, has been read as a prime example of the breadth of intellectual concerns contemporary realist portraiture sought to convey.[6] Early sketches for the work, combined with correspondence between the artist and Tretyakov, indicate that Kramskoy planned to depict his subject in a passive manner, weak from illness, powerless and confined to his bed. The motif of spent force and prostrate creative impotence was initially contrasted with souvenirs of the poet's enthusiasm for hunting, including a gun case and hunting hound. On the writer's death, however, Kramskoy radically rethought the composition to stress a life dedicated to intellectual activity. Nekrasov was raised to a sitting position with pencil and paper in hand, his mien and expression indicative of an engaged intellect to the last. An ancillary iconography now assisted a reading of the canvas. The hunting accoutrements were replaced with symbols of cultural activism: a bust of Belinsky, images of Dobrolyubov and, recalling Katkov's reactionary anti-Polish sentiments (and Repin's disdain for them), a picture of the patriotic romantic Polish poet Adam Mickiewicz provided a commentary on, and sanction of, Nekrasov's liberalism. Nekrasov was thus transformed from a pitiable individual to an empowered paradigm, a 'type' of the dedicated progressive intelligentsia

In practice, however, and as theory turned to convention, not all images of cultural significance fit this pattern. Repin's *Portrait of Modest Musorgsky* (figure 19) provides an instance of fixing temporal particularity seemingly without social agenda. Repin saw Musorgsky during the last days of his life when, as a former army cadet, he was lodged at the Nikolaevsky Military Hospital. After an earlier period of illness, when he rallied and optimistically planned new works, Musorgsky succumbed to the alcohol abuse with which he had sought to keep emotional prob-

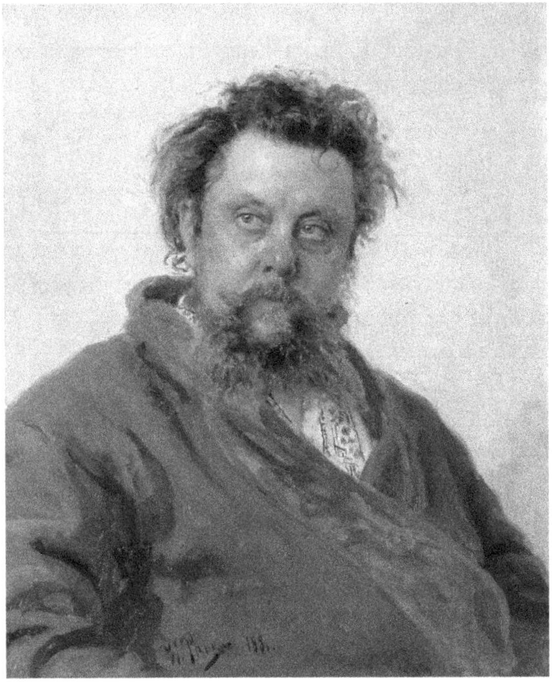

19 Ilya Repin, *Portrait of Modest Musorgsky*, 1881, 69 x 57 cm

lems at bay. Repin had always been on intimate terms with the composer whose candour and child-like naivety he admired. Sensing that the musician was unlikely to survive he set about painting a candid tribute to a friend and man of national significance. The work was completed in Musorgsky's sick room in only four sittings and shows the composer in a military dressing gown, the decoration on his embroidered nightshirt just visible. Although Musorgsky entered a more extreme phase of his illness, dying less than two weeks later, a combination of fortuitous timing and personal devotion to his subject allowed Repin to capture an image of the composer balanced between normality and physical degeneration, clearly suffering the effects of a dissolute lifestyle, yet retaining a spark of animation in his tousled state of undress.

Stasov regarded Musorgsky's death as a great loss to Russian culture, viewing his work as profoundly national and progressive, the antithesis of conservatism in the arts. For him the portrait was a revelation and proof of his faith in the realist national school which provided the visual complement to Musorgsky's work. On his recommendation Tretyakov bought the work unseen and in a long review of the Wanderers exhibition that year Stasov's praise was unstinting:

> I have witnessed the admiration and joy of friends, colleagues and many of our best artists – all are worshippers of Repin ... One of the greatest amongst them, Kramskoy, simply sighed in amazement. After the first seconds he grabbed a stool and sat in front of the portrait, in line with the face, and did not leave it for ages. 'What Repin

has done here', he said, 'is simply inconceivable ... how it is drawn, with what skill, what plasticity, how everything is brought out; look at the eyes, how lifelike they are, they see, they are alive with thought, all the emotion of the moment is reflected in them; how few portraits will you see with such expression!'[7]

The personal nature of this portrait sets it apart from the Wanderers' standard output (Repin refused a fee, asking that the money be put to establishing a memorial for the composer). Disarmingly but forcefully direct, the sitter is placed against a neutral background without the use of superfluous accessories, relying solely on the confrontation between spectator and subject. Lacking a high finish and exposing its spontaneity, the impromptu nature of Musorgsky's portrait reveals the essential characteristics of the sitter at an intimate state of physical and mental decline, his eyes rheumy, his nose red and inflamed with peeling skin, possibly from one of the composer's many falls to the gutter, from where Repin frequently retrieved him. It could, of course, be construed as a 'type' of tortured and self-destructive genius, and despite contemporary controversies surrounding the propriety of depicting a cultural dignitary in a state of distress it has undoubtedly a wider, national significance simply in terms of the sitter. But predominantly it speaks less of the timeless and universal, of the general and typical, than of the individual and momentary, of transience, of personal dissolution and temporary but terminal affliction.

Tolstoy on art

By far the most consistently depicted Russian was the writer Leo Tolstoy. Throughout his long and productive career Tolstoy was keenly engaged with cultural developments, maintaining close associations with some of the leading artists of the Wanderers, particularly Kramskoy, Ge and Repin. Like Stasov he was a domineering and at times over-bearing influence, but one whose colossal pre-eminence in the arts – in terms of fame, celebrity, notoriety – made him impossible to ignore. Indeed his dramatic flight and death at the small railway station of Astapovo in 1910 is arguably the first event attended by an international 'paparazzi'.

Artists were genuinely flattered to make Tolstoy's acquaintance and responded to his challenging, volatile nature. Many imbibed his influence at firsthand, through portrait sittings, and it is worth digressing here on the nature of Tolstoy's musings on the traditional arts since artists were undoubtedly attracted to his democratic central tenet, that the arts were predominantly artificial, elitist and a frivolous waste of a powerful medium which could better benefit the human condition by a positive promotion of moral goodness. Tolstoy's meditations occupied him for fifteen years and were published in 1898 as *What is Art?* The more outlandish examples of his rectitude have tended to overshadow the serious substance in the treatise. These include his dismissal of Goethe and Shakespeare, as well as a hilariously apposite parody of Wagner's Ring Cycle, aimed at exposing opera's over-elaboration and incomprehensibility to ordinary people. *What is Art?* is primarily an attack both on the German idealist philosophy which long guided critical theory under the notion that Art and Beauty are synonymous absolutes. Additionally, Tolstoy is unstinting in his disdain for the proscriptive and elaborately concocted theories which sought to legitimise the aesthetic of a wealthy ruling élite. The idealist concept of art – whether as a reflection of a Platonic eternal and absolute Beauty, or merely as an altruistic, pleasurable experience – he considered useless. In their place he substituted his own broad but concise definition:

> To evoke in oneself a feeling one has once experienced and having evoked it in oneself then by means of movements, lines, colours, sounds, or forms expressed in words, so to transmit that feeling that others experience the same feeling – this is the activity of art. Art is a human activity consisting of this, that one man consciously by means of certain external signs, hands on to others feelings he has lived through, and that others are infected by these feelings and also experience them.[8]

This attempt to define art as an activity confined to the fixing and transmission of unmediated ideas could comfortably accommodate any school of thought, whether it be a disciple of Chernyshevsky communicating, through the transmission of experience, the inequality of Russian society, or Malevich recreating in the spectator his utopian project to order society's collective nervous system. In terms of the direct propagation of 'worthy' ideas Tolstoy acknowledged that there were many similarities between *What is Art?* and Chernyshevsky's *Aesthetic Relationship of Art to Reality*, though he considered Chernyshevsky's work much cruder.

Tolstoy, however, progresses via a relentless logic, expanding his argument thus: is the thing communicated something we desire to impart, in other words is it worthy of transmission, and if not, should we not better use our creative powers in communicating something of worth? Put simply, who but a fool would communicate trivialities rather than truths? This rationale, driven by his own religious, moral and aesthetic philosophies, led the writer inexorably towards the promotion of a pre-Renaissance artistic simplicity and Christian religious sincerity. The best art is that which enhances life and contributes towards human well-being, expressed by clear, unalloyed, intelligible means, that will reach the largest numbers, rather than by an erudite and artificial tongue directed through complex symbols and imagery towards an initiated few. The supreme task of the artist then is to convey high-minded messages in a universally intelligible form: great, good art, is clear, original and sincere.

There is no doubting the earnestness of *What is Art?* and the work is still a powerfully compelling read, but if one departs from Tolstoy's logical chain of thought at any given link, the thesis becomes implausible. The unswerving rationality of his argument is itself the chief contradiction of the irrationality, emotionality, and the empathy of sentiment to which Tolstoy himself was susceptible. He is reputed to have been seriously disturbed by music for the very reason that it played unchecked on his emotions and that he could not logically account for it nor resist it. At times he would become agitated when listening to music 'in a way that seemed to express fear'.[9]

Many artists felt that the insistence on rational, ethical elucidation in art, though something they were at times sympathetic towards, was not a philosophy to which they could fully surrender. The artistic nature wilfully indulges, even within canvases which fit these criteria, in the aesthetic delights of line, form and colour, and the inexplicable process of creation remained for artist and audience one of art's abiding fascinations, which could not be explained or confined by any theory. But few intellects could survive the writer's matchless cross-examination. Levitan found the work 'brilliant and absurd at the same time', whilst away from Tolstoy's assertive influence Repin told a friend: 'I simply cannot agree with Tolstoy's work – *beauty does exist*. But he himself is terribly interesting! He wants to achieve something completely original in art ... What a lively and powerful genius this man is. But he has a passion for paradoxes.'[10]

If we look beyond the superficial dogma and seeming creative restrictions of Tolstoy's work, *What Is Art?* presents itself as a text much due for reassessment. Tolstoy sought to contextualise art fully within society, rather than view it as the outpourings of inspired genius. Money, the market, critical reception, education, and countless other factors, he argues, are always present. Whilst reaching very different conclusions on the nature of art, Tolstoy shares many post-modernist concerns: his iconoclasm, a refusal to accept art as a canon of famous and untested names, his acceptance of art as a social construct acting as an inclusive and excluding agent in seeking to promote, establish and defend itself or its masters, and most importantly the recognition that art is a sophisticated, manipulative and never disinterested system of symbolic and semiotic signifiers – even though such terminology was not available to him.

The central paradox of all this is that whilst arguing for an objective set of principles on which to structure 'good' art, Tolstoy's refusal to countenance received wisdom, such that Shakespeare is a 'great' writer (on what grounds? who says? how can this be proved?), renders his own thesis unstable. If there are no objective, scientific grounds from which to argue for genius all must be subjective, including Tolstoy's findings. He himself maintained that art is always a pejorative term regardless of who uses it and why. This should not, however, distract from the many fascinating and theoretically challenging questions Tolstoy poses about the canon of art, issues of race and nationality, or his assertion that art never touches the lives of the masses who should be its true audience. In this sense it is possible to view his religio-moral stance as merely an expression of a then current 'political correctness'. Tolstoy argues for Christian ethics, not spiritual instruction, nor does he confuse morality with prudery. Even at his most proscriptive, agreeing with Plato that no art is better than bad art, a central strain of altruistic philanthropy is always evident towards what is now termed the 'other'.

Portraits of the writer seem imbued with his own ideas; similarly dedicated in their desire to present an image of intellectual probity whilst illustrating a variety of agenda in imaging the individual as national hero. Notwithstanding Tolstoy's view that portraits were a manifestation of worldly vanity, a huge number of finished

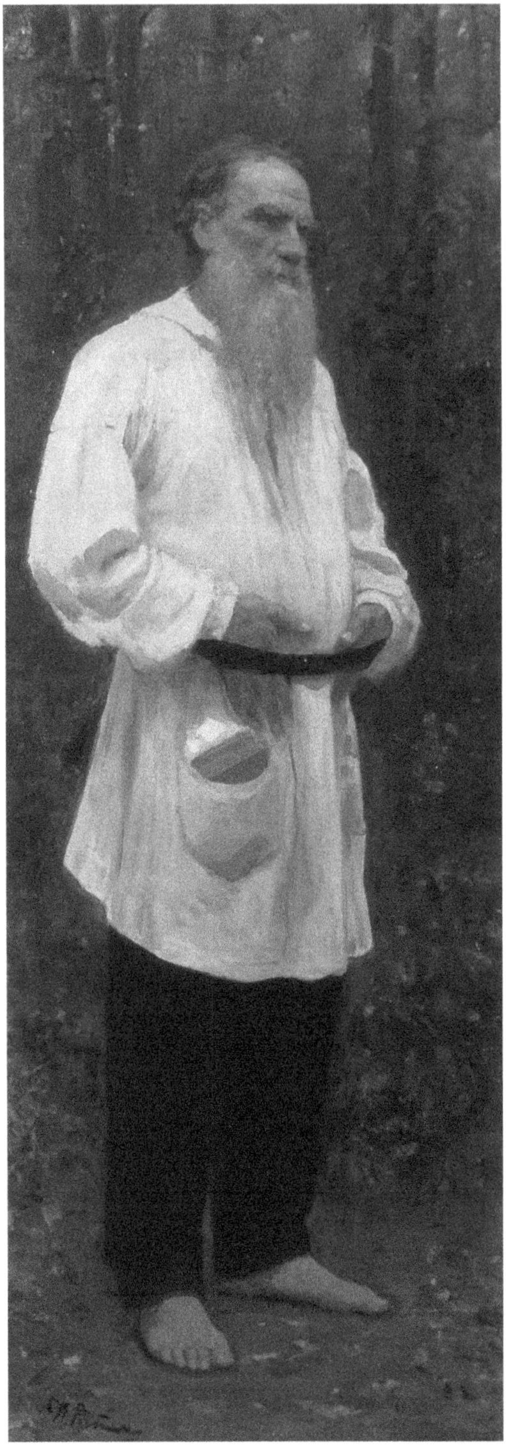

20 Ilya Repin, *Leo Tolstoy Barefoot*, 1901, 207 x 73 cm

works and studies exist, some even produced posthumously, incarnating the writer in serious, studied, unaffected images, seated and looking intently at the viewer as in Kramskoy's *Portrait of Leo Tolstoy* (1872, GTG) or writing at his desk as in Ge's similarly titled portrait (1884, GTG); a more intimate but creatively active scene. A close friend and disciple of Tolstoy, Ge presents a prosaic view of the writer's profession, though what appears to be a private image of the man has, of course, very public associations with Tolstoy the national figure. A similar structuring was deployed by Repin in his *Portrait of Leo Tolstoy Seated* (1887, GTG), which fuses Kramskoy's meditative figure with Ge's assertion of profession by showing the seated writer lost in contemplation but with two fingers lodged at separate places in his open book, as if interrupted by sudden thought (a similar strategy would later be utilised for images of Lenin and Stalin). In line with other Wanderers portraits these standardised images of intellectual proclivity adopt neutral backgrounds with few clues as to the sitter's profession – though this would hardly be required in Tolstoy's case.

These images are straightforward, unfussy, faithful likenesses, well executed and perhaps fitting Tolstoy's own dictum of an art accessible to all. All are conventionally posed and structured around the obvious themes of reading, writing and thinking. More meaningful if idiosyncratic images are provided by Repin's frequent visits to Tolstoy's country estate of Yasnaya Polyana and his Moscow home. In *Leo Tolstoy Ploughing* (1887, GTG) he depicted the writer engaged in a simple but, for him, meaningful activity, the composition and subject matter somewhat reminiscent of Repin's *Burlaki* (figure 3). The work caused a rift after Tolstoy temporarily withdrew permission for it to be reproduced. His family, particularly his wife, believed this to be a personal and sacred occupation, too easily open to ridicule and misunderstanding, though Repin likened Tolstoy to the hauler Kanin and later to the heroic ploughman of Russian legend, Mikula Selyaninov.

A similarly audacious image is *Leo Tolstoy Barefoot* (figure 20). In compositional terms this unusually tall, narrow work hints at conventional images of Orthodox saints, whilst its realistic *plein airism* and sharply observed characteristics anchor it firmly in the present. The painting is sometimes referred to as *Tolstoy at Prayer* as he is seen at his unconventional outdoor devotions. With the writer standing like a pagan deity or an Old Testament prophet, his bare feet firmly in contact with the Russian soil, the portrait offers a compelling image of intellectual and personal nonconformity. Tolstoy was reputedly very unhappy with the work, particularly his bare feet, but his disapprobation was not shared by the general public. When the writer was formally excommunicated Repin's canvas became the focus of a number of student demonstrations at the Wanderers' exhibition, being bedecked with flowers amidst speeches of support. As a consequence it was withdrawn from the St Petersburg exhibition, and permission to display it in Moscow and the provinces was denied.[11]

The portrait sheds light on a crucial development of Tolstoyan thought at this time as the writer increasingly espoused the simplicity and integrity of peasant life. His advocacy of the harsh environment from which Repin had extricated himself, and his condemnation of the artificial and superficial 'civilised' life, to which Repin considered himself elevated, was something the artist found irritating and laughable by turns, but which informs this image of the peasant theologian. A memoir of a visit to Yasnaya Polyana gives an amusing description of the 63- year-old writer, dressed in peasant garb, striding barefoot to the ice-cold river, oblivious to his thorny route, to undress and plunge straight in. Behind him the dapperly dressed Repin struggled to keep pace, arriving late to carefully undress and gingerly enter the water. On a separate occasion Repin noted with irony the quizzical look of a peasant family watching open-mouthed as Tolstoy ploughed under a scorching sun. Whilst painting his portrait of Tolstoy ploughing, Repin observed the powerful, muscular action of the writer at work, but when he tried to plough himself the horses ignored his orders and chaos ensued.[12] The irony of their respective attempts, each to pursue a way of life from which the other was escaping, is encapsulated in this vision of the aristocratic ploughman and the urbane peasant. Images arising from these personal clashes of philosophy, more successfully than the plethora of static, studio-based, respectful portraits of the revered writer, give genuine insight into Tolstoy's unorthodox lifestyle and intriguing character.

The peasant made visible

Integral to the peasant theme, and in crucial respects a genre in its own right, was the peasant portrait. Though precedent existed in the works of Venetsianov and his school, their idealised images of rural contentment are distant evolutionary relatives to the Wanderers' more forceful and consistent treatment of the *muzhik* portrait as a legitimate subject outside a narrative context. This genre became the preserve of the Society and was regarded as characteristic of its ostensibly liberal and reformist ethos, rendering the faceless masses faceless no more. This is not to suggest that the Wanderers merely painted peasants, which in itself might be regarded as progressively eccentric, but that they focused on the *muzhik* with the same rigour, candour and psychological intensity as they accorded the nation's élite. Consistently peasant portraits hinted at the sitter's integrity and sagacity, but chiefly their singularity as thinking individuals. Turgenev's *Sketches from a Hunter's Album* published in 1852 proved an earlier agent in awaking the educated public to the revelation that the peasant, far from being a bestial inchoate entity, was a thinking being with opinions of his own, should anybody see fit to ask for them.

Lagging somewhat behind literary developments Perov's *Fomushka sych* (1868, GTG) – literally 'Owl-faced Tommy' – an individualistic, worldly wise portrayal of a hirsute, sagacious old peasant, proved the forerunner of many memorable images of rural worthies, important for their sympathetic and serious treatment of seemingly insignificant subjects. Many *muzhik* portraits shared characteristic elements of compositional simplicity, presenting frequently anonymous but highly individualised sitters against vacant backgrounds, focusing attention solely on the legitimacy of the subject. Kramskoy's *Miller* (1873, GRM) and *Mina Moiseyev* (1882, GRM) both showing elderly, bearded peasants in bust format, allowing the maximum encounter with physiognomic peculiarities, grant their sitters all the dignity of royal portraiture. Frequently *muzhik* portraits would abstract the sitter from specific identity into generic types. Two of Repin's works, *Peasant with an Evil Eye* (1877, GTG) and *A Cautious One* (1877, Nizhny Novgorod Art Museum) present sympathetic and serious treatments of subject, but whilst clearly modelled on individuals their anonymity denotes the preoccupation again to define Russian 'types'. The titles give clues merely to traits thought to be prototypical of the *muzhik* – in these instances slyness and timidity, or perhaps hinting at the rural superstitions that coexisted with Orthodoxy.

Often the use of type was eclipsed, investing the peasant with the status of an ethnographic analysis of almost forensic objectivity. Kramskoy produced many peasant portraits titled simply as 'studies from nature' or with unelucidated commentary that placed the images seemingly in the realm of human taxonomy.

The Peasant Ignaty Pirogov. Model at the Academy of Arts (1874, Kiev Museum of Russian Art) offers the viewer an image of a human specimen propped against a wall as if exhibited for scientific inspection, whilst the laconically titled *Portrait of a Peasant* (1868, Morava Gallery, Brno, Czechoslovakia) appears little more than the product of a passport photo booth or an impersonal 'mug shot' from a police archive. In each instance the fidelity to life, the delineation of each single hair, the rendition of the minutiae of physical peculiarity, is tantalisingly off-set by the anonymity of the sitter, wholly seen but never known.

Occasionally this pattern was broken and more was invested in the peasant intellect, as in Kramskoy's *The Contemplator* (1876, Kiev Museum of Russian Art) depicting a *muzhik* in a winter landscape, lost in meditation, immune to his inhospitable surroundings. Dostoevsky's reading of the canvas provides a case study of how the intelligentsia might configure the peasant in nationalistic romantic terms not merely as devout, but as possessing unsuspected spiritual depths.

> He seems ... to be standing there thinking, but he is not really thinking but only 'contemplating' something. If you were to nudge him he would give a start and look at you as though he had only just woken up, but without understanding. He would, it is true, have come to life at once, but if you asked him what he was thinking of while standing there, he would most certainly never forget the sensation he had experienced during the time of his contemplation, but would always keep it hidden away inside him.[13]

Kramskoy produced some of the most progressive and positive images of peasant psychology. His *Woodsman* (1874, GTG) is exceptional in this genre as a portrait which aimed not merely to humanise the peasant, but attempted to depict a politically and socially informed individual, a social loner who harbours a great deal of ill-will against his oppressors and the injustices inflicted on his class. Kramskoy likened him to the participants of the great peasant uprisings of previous centuries as one who stands in readiness to respond again.[14] The knowledge of the woodsman's profession gives us a reference point frequently absent from peasant portraits, affording the viewer at least some relief from uncertainty. Naming the individual also lessens the impersonal nature of these works, but seldom develops the image. As likenesses we have no means of assessing their success, and even the named sitters remain essentially anonymous.

In his portraits of the peasant Mina Moiseyev (colour plate 3), however, Kramskoy produced warmer, more humane images of his subject, lacking in forensic disinterest but instead expressing the vitality and vivacity of the aged Mina, seen here with the accoutrements of a skilled and profitable profession. Composed with a seemingly nonchalant ease and executed in a technique of breathtaking dexterity, the photographically 'real' subject presents a fully formed psychology and, we feel, an insight into the specifics of his ebullient personality. Here and in the close-up bust portrait of 1882 Kramskoy presents his audience with images that are unusual in depicting a peasant who appears to be happy, maybe even contented with his societal position. The risk of ideological misrepresentation, that viewers might read such images as redolent of *muzhik* satisfaction with the status quo, accounts for their rarity, although here Kramskoy's intention to show individual character seems unambiguous. The sitter might be said to be of a cheerful disposition, but is not seen in relation to his wider material existence, his inferior living conditions or low social standing (as were Kasatkin's miners).

The peasant is sometimes a named individual such as Mina Moiseyev or Ignaty Pirogov, or occasionally – as with *The Miller*, *The Woodsman*, or Kramskoy's superlative study of an aged *Bee Keeper* (1872, GTG) – identified by his trade. More frequently he is labelled merely as 'peasant' or a human 'study', preserving his ethnological typicality. In a broad sense the specific, personal incarnations of Wanderers portraiture, the 'famous names', were the complementary obverse of the generic peasant portraits, symbolising twin aspects of the Russian character: the moral, cultural and intellectual exemplars of Russian achievement and the embodiment of national traits and values. Where intellectuals might embody strands of cultural dedication, peasant portraits more frequently became incarnations of perceived national characteristics; such was Stasov's review of the individuals delineated in Myasoedov's *Reading the Emancipation Manifesto*. And where Turgenev's writings allowed the peasant a psychology and a voice, Wanderers' portraits, whilst progressive and unorthodox, more frequently label them in terms of facets of character or profession. In Kramskoy's photo-realist images this is broadened by the sheer detail and intimacy of physiognomy which demands to be 'read', as if the ambition of the image is to say something about the condition of work, age and social class.

The innovation and important consistency in these images is that they are fully developed works in oils exhibited cheek-by-jowl with portraits of the Russian intelligentsia, not relegated to inferior media as were, for instance, the rare observations of *muzhik* depravity. The Wanderers' inclusion of ordinary, often nameless peasants, into the pantheon of national achievement is surely a statement of intent, a recognition that these unassuming representatives of the people were also invaluable contributors to the life of the nation.

Domestic informality

The last category in which the Wanderers were active was that of the domestic portrait. Most of the Society's members left images of friends (frequently their artistic brethren) and family. From these one gains a view of a bourgeois tranquillity as painters sought to advertise their social aspirations and successes, as well as the distance their profession had brought them from often humble beginnings. Poses, fabrics and costumes are indistinguishable from those of Russia's affluent middle-class, though the Wanderers' trademark candidness and lack of idealisation is a constant.

Some of the best examples are provided by Repin who, despite a turbulent personal life, produced a huge variety of serenely unruffled portraits of his wife

Vera and their family. *Vera Repin Resting* (1882, GTG), painted at a time when the couple's relationship was under considerable strain, shows the sleeping Vera reclined gracefully in an armchair, a model of peaceful intimacy, gentle repose and classical beauty. Painted without a public in mind, and away from the pressure to conform to Stasov's shaping of the critical realist credo, Repin produced some of his best works in this genre. These include a portrait of his five-year-old son Yury (1882, GTG) swaddled amongst the rich tones of a large Turkish carpet, juxtaposing the pale, wide-eyed, delicate child against an ornate decorative background; a fine example of aesthetic considerations being pursued in tandem with an accurate rendition of the sitter, neither facet unbalancing the other, but acting as complementary agents.

The integrity of Wanderers' work in this genre is exemplified by Kramskoy's *Portrait of Sofya Kramskoya* (figure 21), where the artist images his daughter in the fashionable silks of a young woman of polite society. The trappings of her existence as well as her importance as the sole substantial subject of the canvas suggest prosperity, whilst her pale and thoughtful countenance intimate an introspective intelligence and emotional intensity. But whilst these facets might privilege the sitter as a well-to-do, educated member of society, the young Sofya is rendered

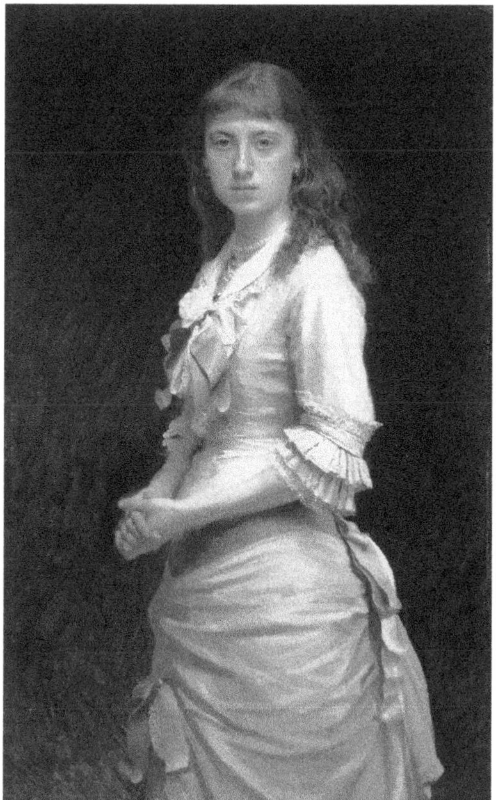

21 Ivan Kramskoy, *Portrait of Sofya Kramskoya, the artist's daughter*, 1882, 118 x 70 cm

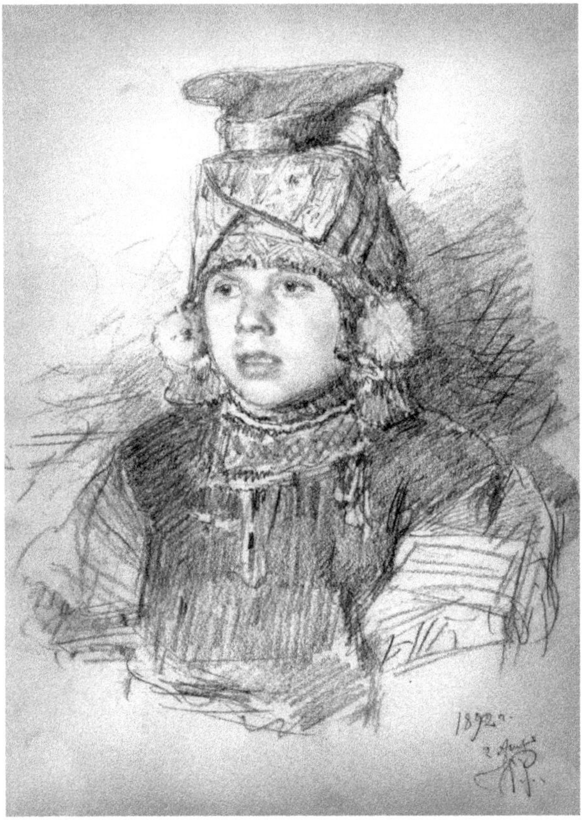

22 Ilya Repin, *Portrait of Aleksandra Tolstoy*, 1892, 40 x 27 cm

without flattery, her strong features and physical specificity, her appealing ordinariness, delineated with a severe but loving honesty.

Similarly Repin's *Portrait of Aleksandra Tolstoy* (figure 22) the writer's youngest daughter, offers a delightfully ingenuous image worked in a hurried but assured manner redolent of the artist's then infatuation with experimentation and the status of the sketch as a legitimate means of artistic expression. The explicit nature of this appealing work encompasses the precise documentary data of its execution at Tolstoy's Moscow home on 2 April 1892 whilst the artist was in the city to attend the closure of his solo exhibition.[15] Perhaps in keeping with Tolstoy's promulgation of the integrity of the peasant existence he chose to draw the eight-year-old Aleksandra in the costume of a peasant from Tula province in a decorative tunic and elaborate headdress with characteristic cotton earrings. The young sitter is depicted in a gauche but engagingly childish pose with her mouth distractedly open and a dreamy countenance. Giving vent to a type of expressive panache less evident in his oil works Repin presents a pleasing aesthetic contrast between the finely worked face and the roughly sketched remainder. One of his finest and most intimate portrait sketches from his mature period, the work fulfils the function of being an important documentation of the individual, offspring of Russia's greatest cultural figure, but at the same time remains a disarmingly frank portrayal of a child, a 'family' portrait sketched from the privileged viewpoint of an insider to the Tolstoy household. Additionally it reflects a period of late Wanderers output when pluralism in the arts and the forces of aesthetic innovation occasioned both artistic doubts and greater technical freedom in the work of the society's pre-eminent master.

In all a sense of gentle, intimate, harmonious family life pervades these portraits as if they bespeak a depth of genuine, unforced emotional warmth which, clearly, the artists felt more able to express through the reflective process of their least public output. They also utilised the informal nature of family portraits to explore and experiment with technical and formal considerations. A preoccupation with *plein air* tonality and colourful, painterly execution can be seen in many works of this period, for instance Repin's unidealised portrait of his daughter Vera, *Autumn Bouquet* (1892, GTG), or that of his daughter Nadya, *In the Sunlight* (1900, GTG), where aesthetic concerns of pure and reflected light are spectacularly to the fore.

Occasionally these images of bourgeois leisure shade into a seemingly more ambiguous mode that combines anonymity with wealth and status. Kramskoy's *Portrait of an Unknown Woman* (1883, GTG) shows a haughty aristocratic beauty in an unspecified architectural space looking through the viewer with nonchalant disdain, whilst the recumbent *Woman with an Umbrella* (1883, Nizhny Novgorod Art Museum), dressed all in white, presents a self-assured image of a class elite. Repin's elegantly nonchalant study of Russian chic, the magnificent *Portrait of Varvara Ikskul von Hildenbandt* (1889, GTG) appears to venerate an aloof society beauty, but is also a celebration of a woman of progressive ideas, a collector and founder of numerous philanthropic societies and hostess to celebrated literary, artistic and musical salons.

These forays into formal or establishment portraiture would appear to contradict the critical realist as well as nationalistic ethos of the Wanderers, and their production and exhibition raises problematic issues. However, they remained relatively rare, the province mainly of Repin from the mid-1890s and of Valentin Serov, a sometime exhibitor and late member of the Wanderers whose overt aestheticism and predilection for upperclass sitters sites him between the realist school and its later opponents (figure 36).

Facing the nation

> It was the objective of the Peredvizhniki to convey the general, the typical, to go beyond the individual by emphasising those qualities that would carry a positive message and give the picture a deeper significance.[16]

Whether or not generality and typicality as a means of influencing public opinion or massaging the national consciousness was a recurrent feature in Wanderers art is debatable. There are instances, certainly, of images that seem hardly to go beyond the individual, but to make a positive virtue of momentary physical specificity. Ideologically, however, there is sufficient evidence of intellectual aspiration towards the use of type to observe it in practice. Its use raises interesting issues that impacted on late nineteenth-century Russian culture and beyond to the Soviet era. From a Marxist-Leninist standpoint the typical was not a statistical mean, but that which most persuasively expressed the current direction of the social impetus and as such it was always considered a political aspiration. Maksim Gorky asserted:

> A fact is not the whole truth; it is merely the raw material from which the real truth of art must be smelted and extracted ... the accidental and inessential is mixed with the essential and typical. We must learn to pluck the fact of its inessential plumage; we must be able to extract meaning from the fact.[17]

In seeking to separate the typical and meaningful from the inessential, the Wanderers certainly utilised portraiture like any other genre, whether intentionally or otherwise, to reinforce allegiances to liberal and progressive social exemplars. In this respect many works became socially shaping agents, but this does not classify such usage as an objective, defined and undeviating tenet of Russian realism. The consistency of the Society's output is that of treatment. Their portraits are frank, unflattering, unidealised, sincere but sympathetic images of an unswervingly concrete nature. As the poet Afanasy Fet told Tolstoy: 'If a portrait is a good one, then it will have a mouth; and if you open the mouth you would find a tongue; and under the tongue, there would be bone, and so on.' The artist Leonid Pasternak, who reported this remark, and who was himself an assured but unconventional portraitist, did not regard this insistence on tangibility as an obstacle to artistic creativeness, commenting: 'Fet's incisive graphic expression is relevant to the very essence of each work of art: everything evolves naturally, one thing flows from another with the inevitability of life itself.'[18]

This is not to suggest that the Wanderers adhered to a prosaic realism that delineated external features with unerring constancy. The social and intellectual objectives of these concrete productions approached a variety of agendas, of both a general and specific nature with concomitant public and personal outcomes. Ultimately, however, this is not to deny the progressive aegis of the Russian realist portrait in reconfiguring the public face from one of hereditary status to that of justified and legitimate merit, whether of the intelligentsia or the peasantry. As Solzhenitsyn noted in *The First Circle*: 'if I look at the person whose portrait I am painting and discern potential qualities of mind or character ... why shouldn't I depict them? What's wrong about helping a man to find his higher self? – That's pure Socialist Realism!'[19]

6

History painting: sedition and tradition

History painting in Russia was, from the inception of the Academy in 1764, staple fare. As elsewhere in Europe it confined itself chiefly to images drawn from the Bible, ancient history and classical mythology, and was regarded as a morally improving vehicle which, through its selection and elucidation of worthy exemplars and antique grandeur, would instil virtue in the viewer. Its mixture of Neoclassicism, melodrama and theatricality found early expression in the work of Anton Losenko and later its greatest exponents Karl Bryullov and Fedor Bruni, although for a long time scenes from Russian history were notably absent, considered inappropriate for this pre-eminent of genres. When in the second half of the eighteenth century native subjects began to appear, the indigenous element was confined to the titles alone. Losenko's *Vladimir and Rogneda* (1770, GRM) and Grigory Ugryumov's *Yan Usmar's Feat of Strength* (1796–97, GRM) cloak Russian history in a swathe of classical drapery and grandiloquent gesturing with little concession towards archaeological accuracy nor any attempt at personalisation, the figures merely acting as moral or dramatic ciphers.

The cultural trends which shaped the first generation of liberally minded realists during the 1860s eventually came to bear on this most venerated of artistic hierarchies, though with slower results. The contribution that art could make to the solution of existing and evolving social problems was less evident in the case of history painting than with the inferior genre class, which had a tradition of social commentary and conscience-pricking. During this period, however, history painting fused with genre to produce greater archaeological accuracy and consistency of period dress, furniture and coiffure, depicting historical personages as individuals, often in anecdotal settings. The best proponent of this documentary brand of history was Vyacheslav Shvarts, whose descriptive works include *Scenes from the Domestic Lives of the Russian Tsars: Playing Chess* (1865, GRM) and *The Vernal Train of the Tsarina on a Pilgrimage at the Time of Tsar Alexei Mikhailovich* (1868, GTG). Shvarts combined historical authenticity with a modern, natural treatment, his characters moving in real worlds rather than concocted grandeur. His works accurately reconstruct the mien and manners of the period but with little attempt to capture the psychology of his participants.

Other exponents included Pavel Chistyakov, a gifted and progressively minded academic tutor, and Konstantin Flavitsky, who produced the luridly arousing *Princess Tarakanova in the Petropavlosk Fortress at the Time of the Flood* (1864, GTG).[1] This painting, one of the most popular of its day, exposed the tensions and ambivalences inherent in the academic roots of Russian history painting. The narrative, concerning the incarceration of a pretender to the throne of Catherine II who drowns in her cell during a flood, had become part of popular legend despite lacking historical foundation. Flavitsky depicted the Princess standing on her unsanitary bed as the water fills the infested cell and rats encroach. Against such stark realism the treatment of the Princess is melodramatic and incongruously sensuous, her mouth languidly open, her eyes closed as if in sensual ecstasy and her upper garments unaccountably peeling off of their own accord. Yet Flavitsky was a politically astute painter who, in the first stirrings of what became a preferred strategy – using historical subjects to draw an analogy with the present – planned his image as a denunciation of despotism. The hegemony of his academic education, and particularly his tutor Bruni, proved inimical to the artist's progressive ambitions and the result is simply pathos mixed with titillation, an historical 'bodice-ripper' of conventional style and artificial structure.

Hidden histories?

History painting then proved slow to don the interrogative mantle or was, perhaps, incapable of doing so. Two early works by Ge nevertheless gave cause for critical concern in their innovative reworking of the genre. *The Last Supper* (1863, GTG) painted seven years before the Wanderers' inception, but the same turbulent year of the secession from the Academy and the formation of the artists' *Artel*, seems superficially a conventional working of a commonplace theme. In reviewing the work, however, the liberal-reformist writer Saltykov-Shchedrin interpreted it more broadly as a commentary on the conflict between spiritual and materialist ideologies: those like Christ embrace ideals, whilst those like Judas are preoccupied with self-interests. He praised Ge for prompting society towards higher, more altruistic ends, such as social and political reform, and for demonstrating that personal convictions should be followed through by action. According to contemporary reports this moment depicting Christ's revelation that one of His disciples would betray Him was intended also to symbolise the collapse of the circle around the leading liberal revolutionary Aleksandr Herzen. Christ's face was reportedly modelled on Herzen, whom Ge had met some years previously and whom he later painted in 1867. It is surely not coincidental that when in 1865 Herzen had his photographic portrait taken in the studio of Sergei Levitsky he adopted the same pose as Ge's Christ.[2]

Whether or not Ge intended his work to be read so specifically in terms of

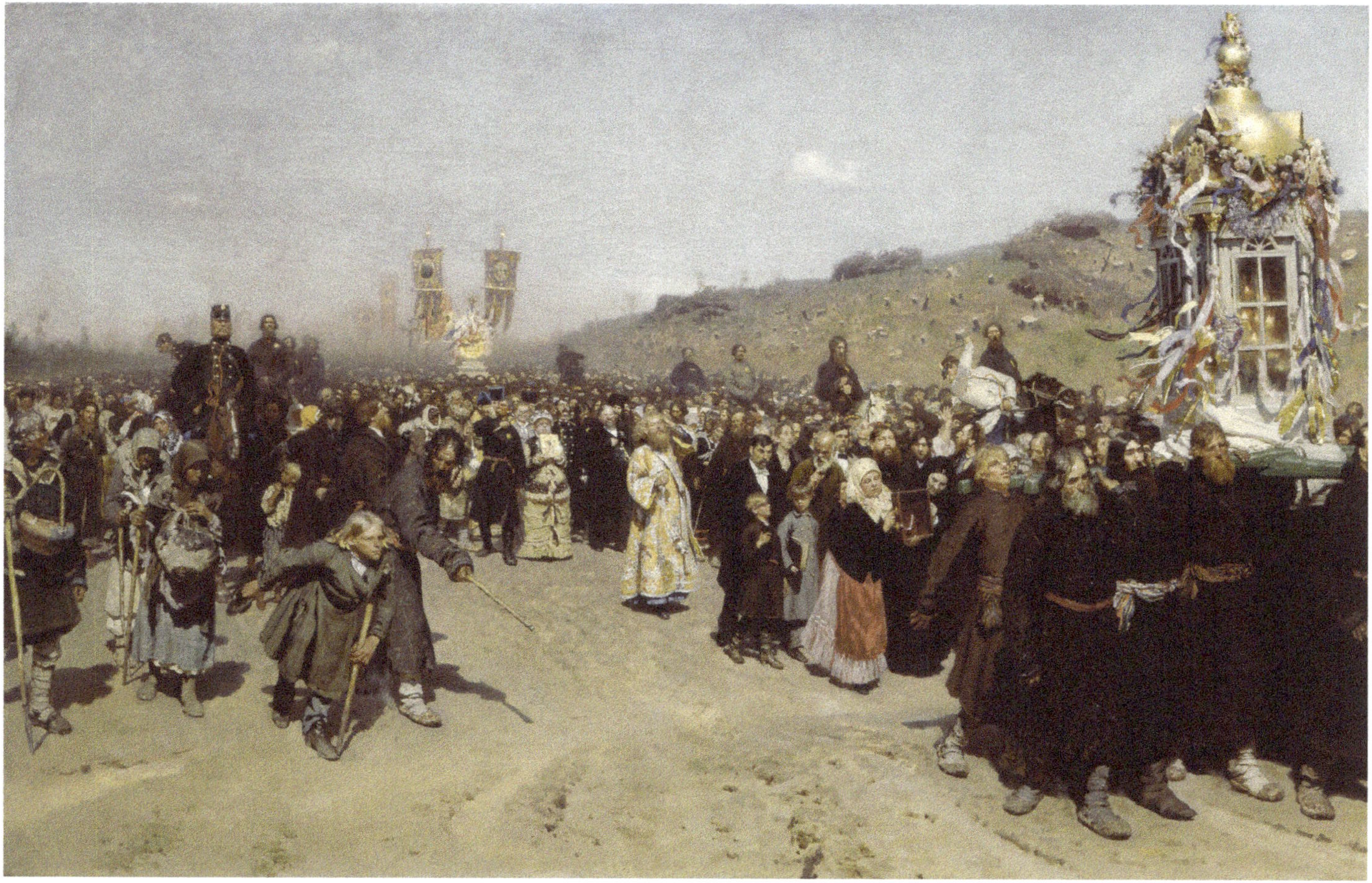

1 Ilya Repin, *Religious Procession in the Province of Kursk*, 1880–83, 175 x 280 cm

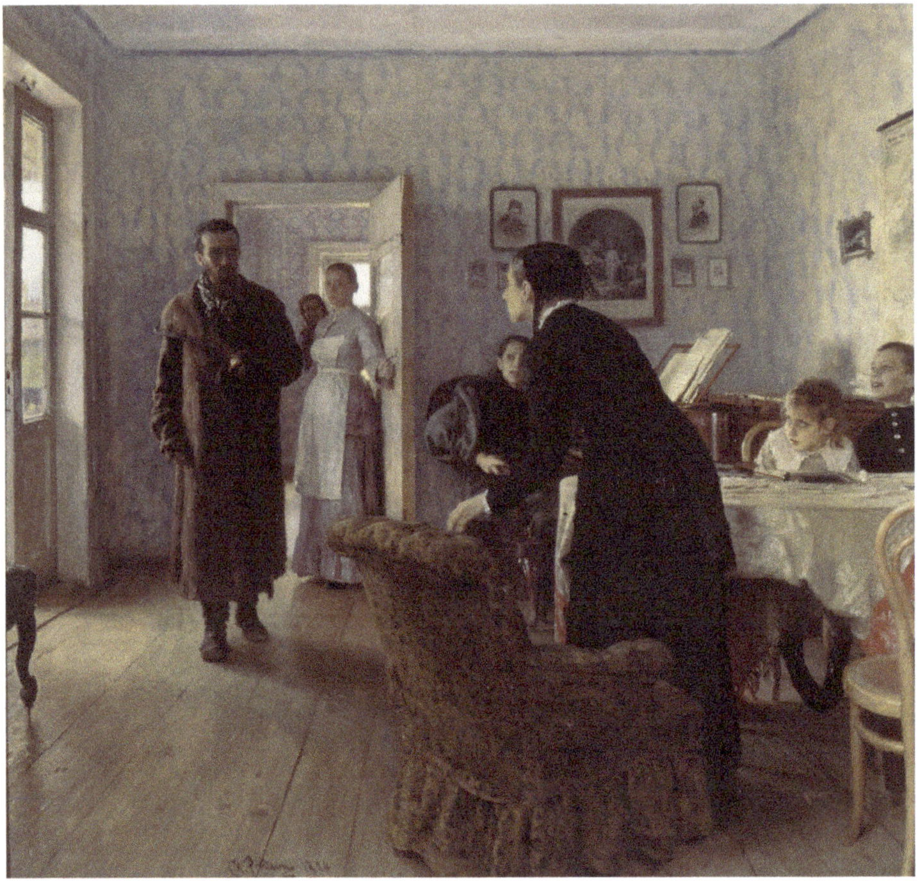

2 Ilya Repin, *They Did Not Expect Him* (*Ne zhdali*), 1884; 1888, 160.5 x 167.5 cm

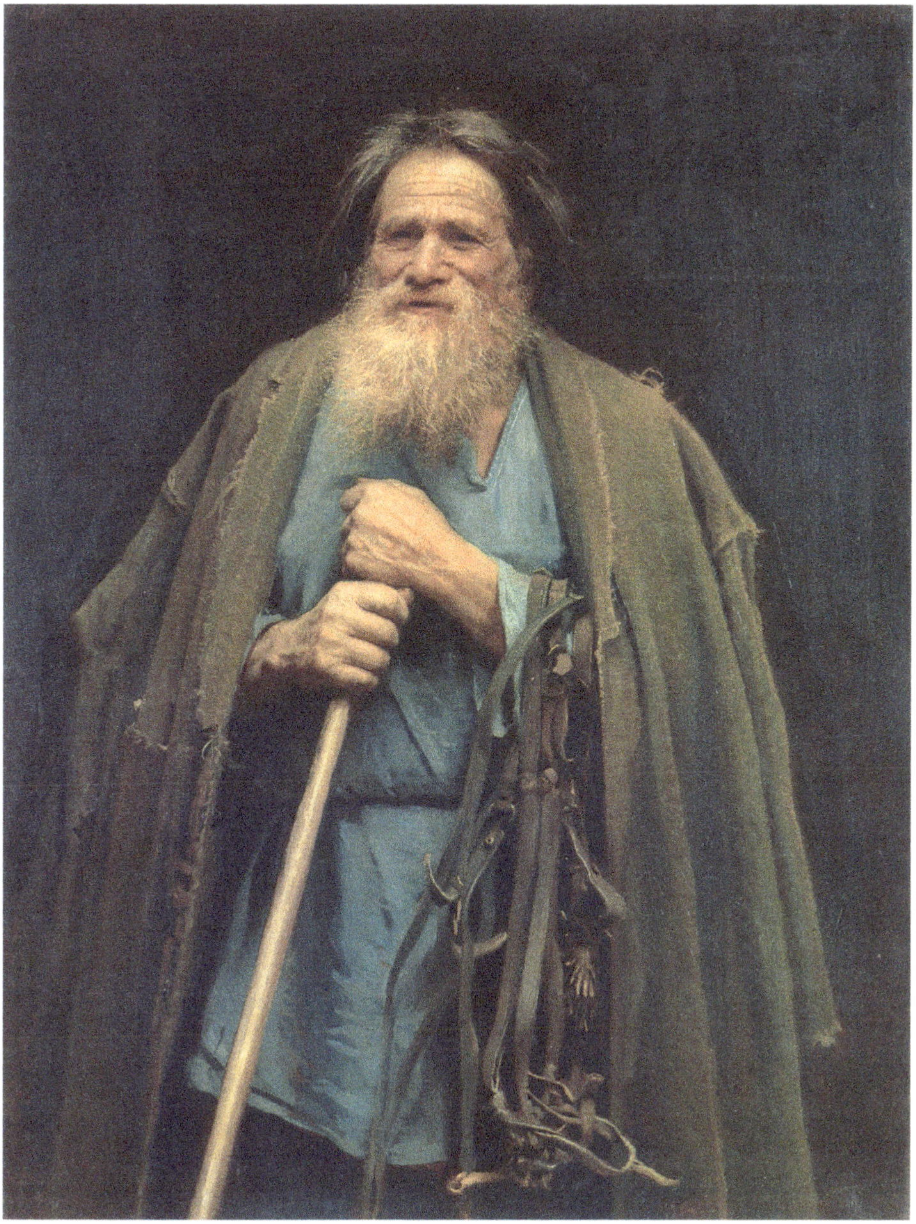

3 Ivan Kramskoy, *Peasant Holding a Bridle (Mina Moiseyev)*, 1883, 125 x 93 cm

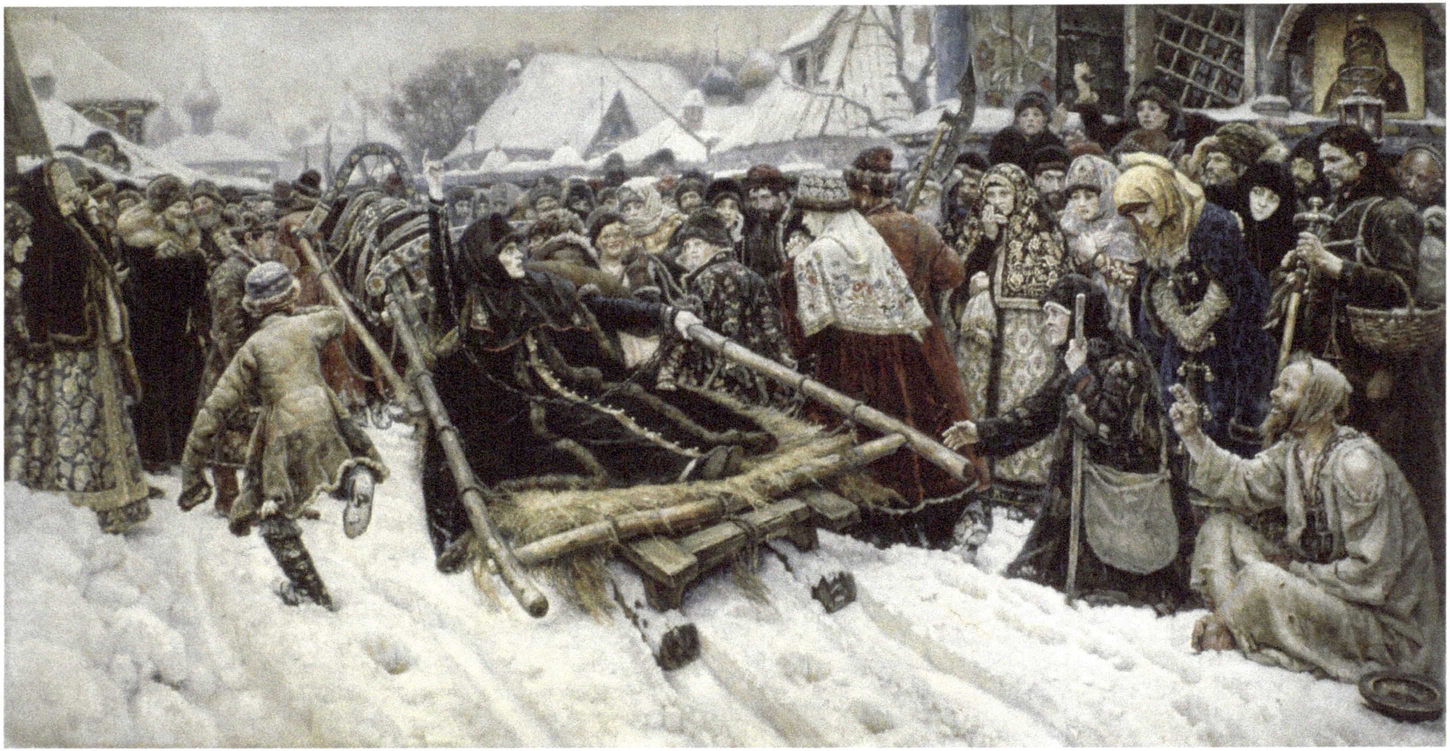

4 Vasily Surikov, *The Boyarina Morozova*, 1887, 304 x 587.5 cm

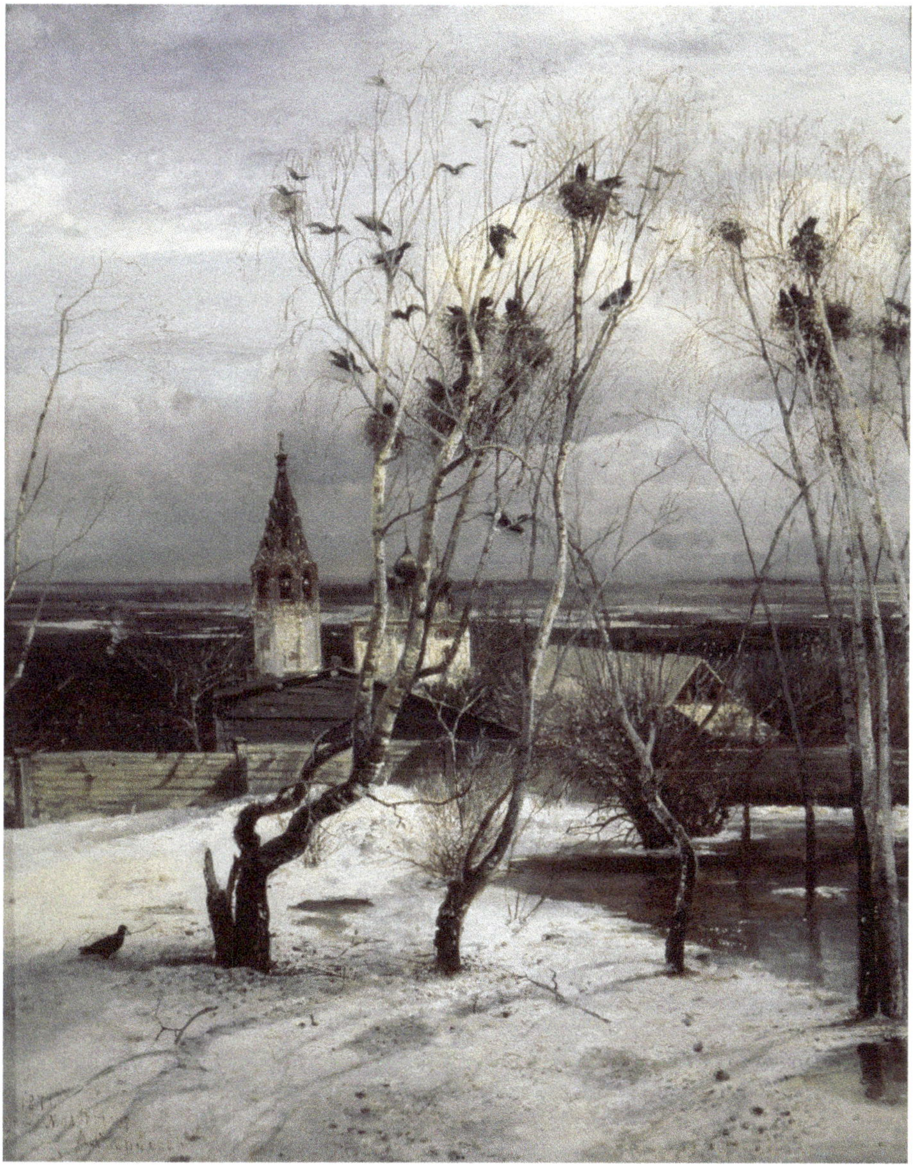

5 Aleksei Savrasov, *The Rooks Have Returned*, 1871, 62 x 48.5 cm

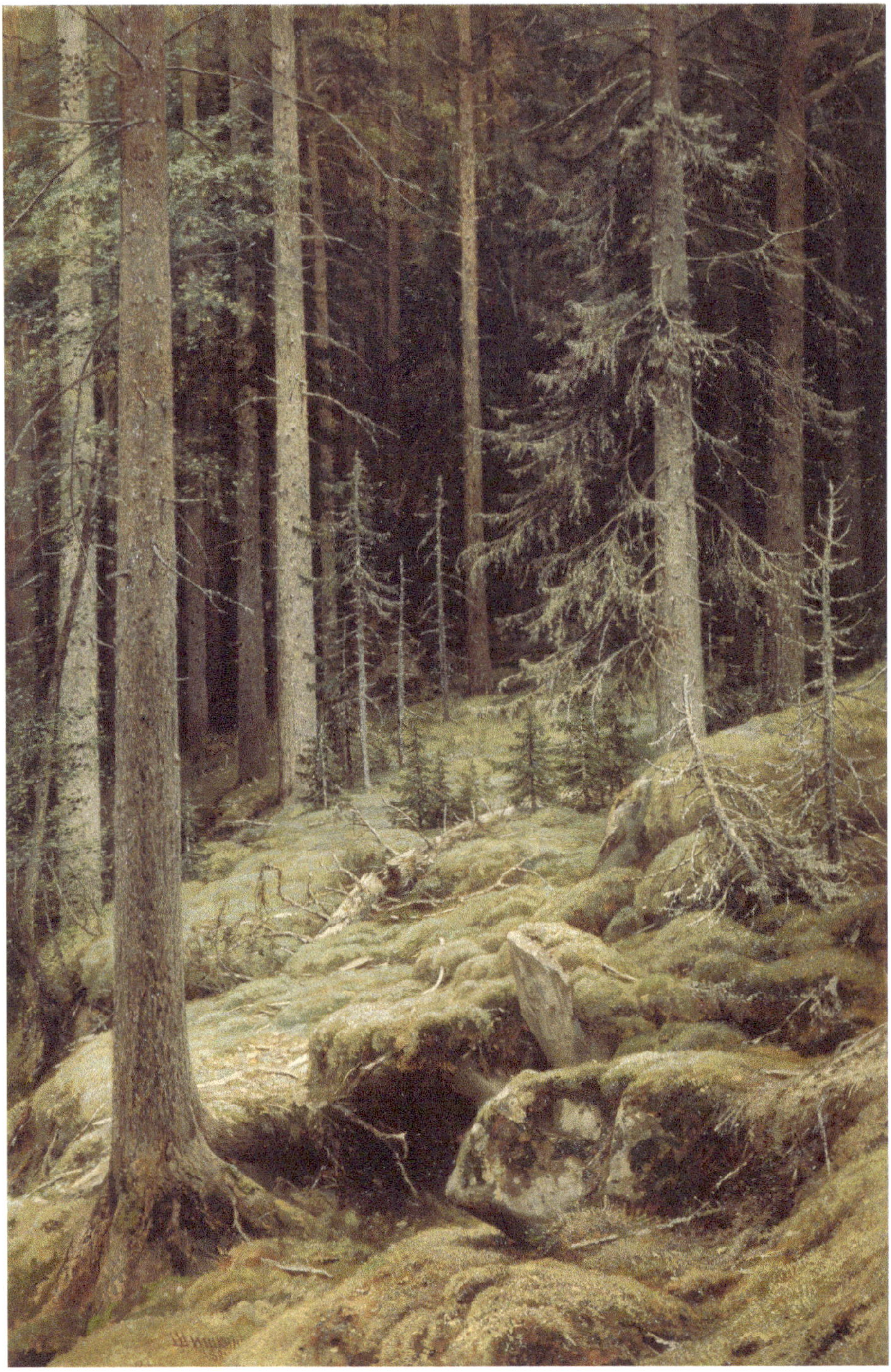

6 Ivan Shishkin, *The Thicket*, 1881, 142 x 93 cm

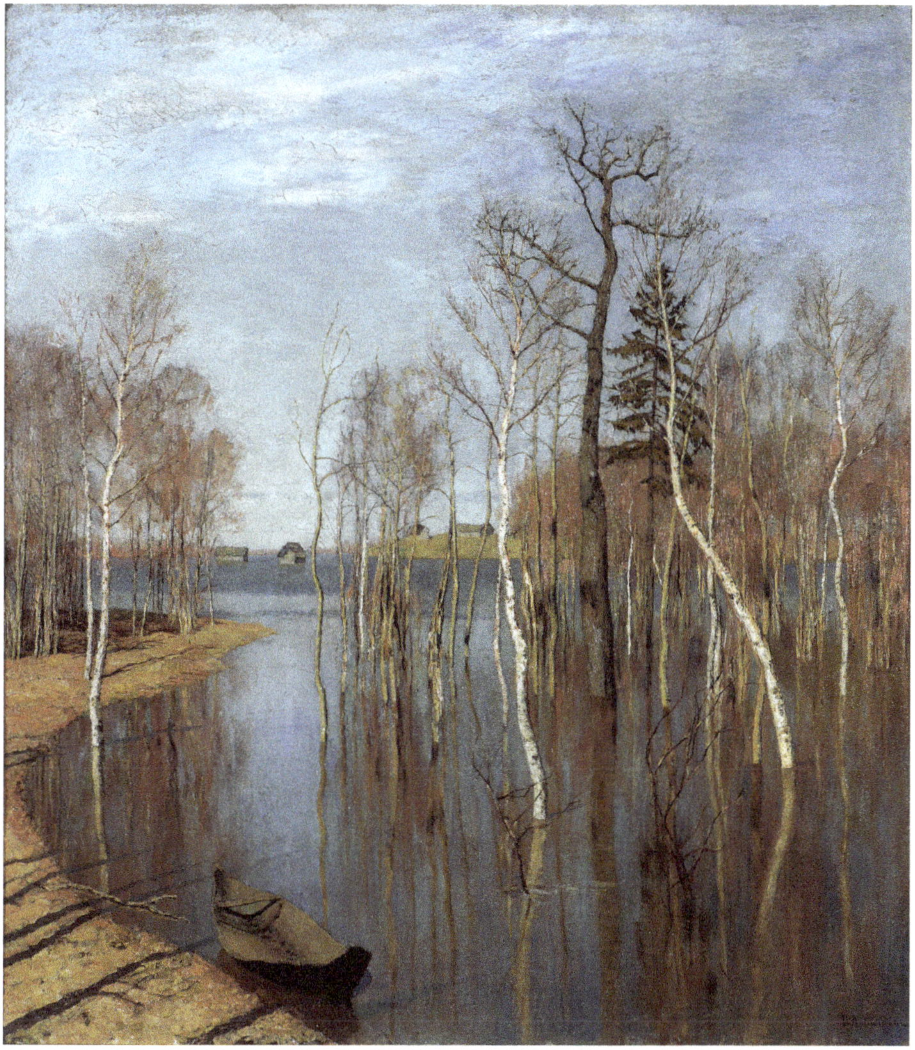

7 Isaak Levitan, *Spring Flood*, 1897, 64.2 x 57.5 cm

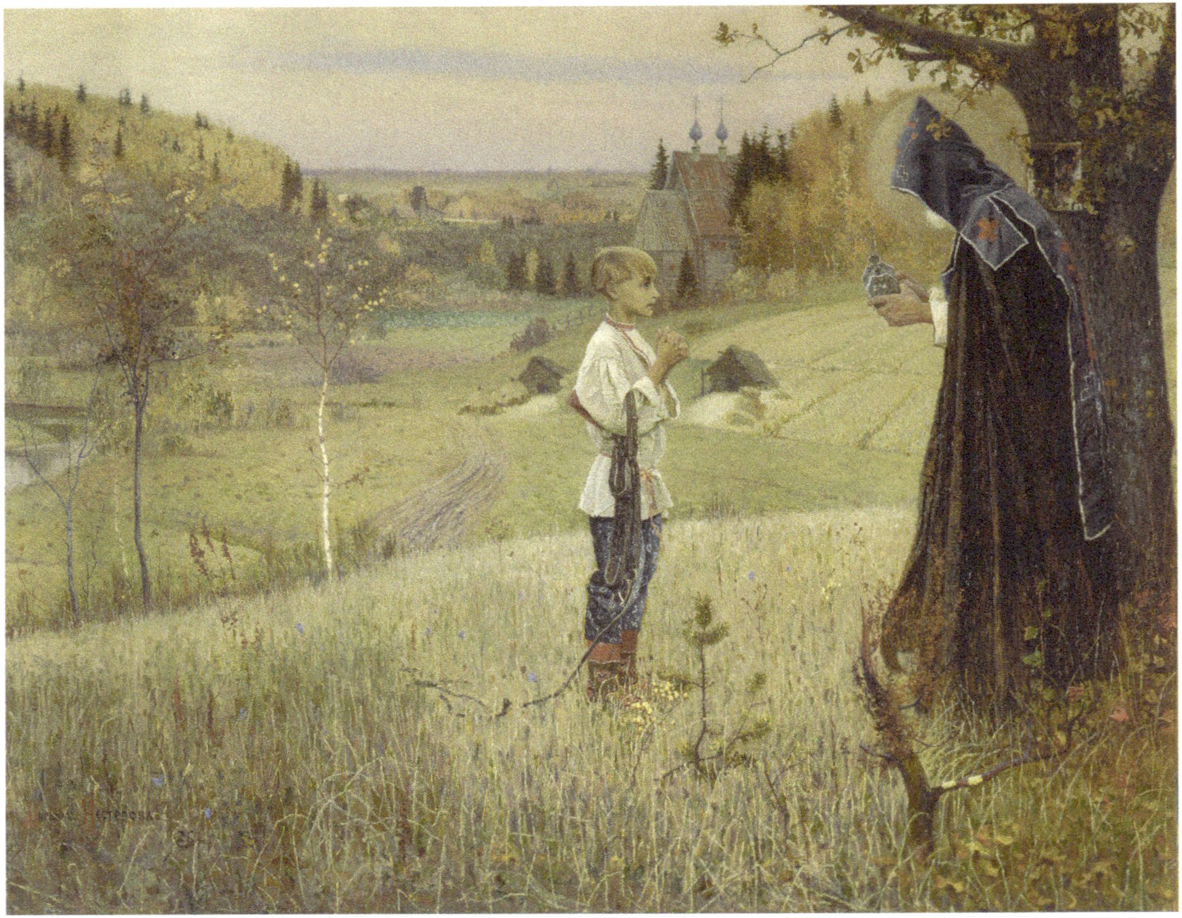

8 Mikhail Nesterov, *The Vision of the Boy Bartholomew*, 1889–90, 160 x 211 cm

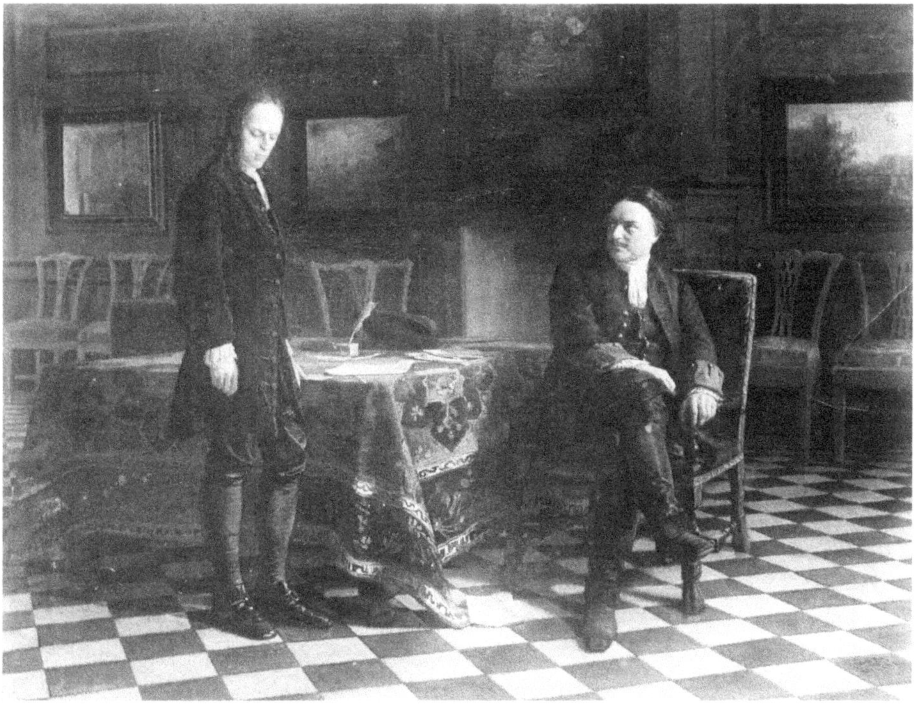

23 Nikolai Ge, *Peter the Great Interrogating Tsarevich Aleksei at Peterhof*, 1871, 135.7 x 173

contemporary issues is unclear, but *The Last Supper* proved to be a precursor of a tendency in Russian criticism to seek subtext (подтекст or 'podtekst'); secondary readings or concealed meanings. In 1871 the inaugural Wanderers' exhibition saw the revelation of Ge's *Peter the Great Interrogating Tsarevich Aleksei at Peterhof* (figure 23). As with Shvarts, Ge put great store by historical accuracy to convince the viewer of the 'realism' of his works: setting, costumes, portrait likenesses, were thoroughly researched. The shift affected, however, was to subordinate that accumulation of detail to a more subtle exposition of history presented through the psychologies of its prime movers and the clash of ideologies, rather than the depiction of momentous events. Ge's masterful study of Peter, the human dynamo brooking no obstacles to his reformation of Russia, was imaged as history in introspection.

Saltykov-Shchedrin again read the semiotics of Ge's work, concluding that it formed an adverse commentary on the unfinished political and social reforms of the 1860s which, like the confrontation between Peter and Aleksei, were being jeopardised by obstructive, uncomprehending traditionalism. Peter thus becomes symbolic of the modern Westernisers, dynamic and progressive, and his diffident son emblematic of retrogressive Slavophilia; at best well-intentioned, but undoubtedly misguided. Garshin too identified Aleksei as representative of reactionary forces.[3] Though often the underlying critical sentiments of historical paintings could be more in the eye of the beholder, Saltykov-Shchedrin's remarks verify that even as the Wanderers were forming it was established practice (and the source of much tenuous criticism) to look for latent messages in historical canvases.

Notwithstanding the genre's potential as a means to circumvent Russia's draconian censorship laws and to make veiled references to contemporary problems, history painting was not universally welcomed. Examples appeared regularly at the Wanderers' annual exhibitions, but Stasov was not alone in his consistent opposition to what he regarded as a dilution of the original ethos of the school, believing the observable present, rather than some imagined past, took precedence, and that critical comments were best made directly rather than analogously. An admirer of Proudhon and Courbet, the standard-bearers of French democratic realist painting, Stasov denied the validity of history painting and concurred that art could consist only of contemporarily observed and tangible phenomena. Kramskoy shared some of these reservations but felt that relevance of subject matter was key, insisting such paintings might stimulate intellectual debate through their analogy with the present, by mirroring contemporary issues.

Though the historical genre continued to flourish at the Academy, epitomised by its greatest adherent Heinrich Semiradsky, for realist artists the treatment of such themes carried possibilities beyond antique grandeur. As the Academy cloaked nudity and sensuality in the guise of classicism, so history painting offered the Wanderers a chance to voice delicate or unacceptable criticisms by association with past events. But a preoccupation with history to the detriment of contemporary concerns could compromise an artist's credibility and standing within reformist intellectual circles. Repin for instance, whom Stasov had taken considerable trouble to shape after his own image (to the point of misrepresentation), was kept under close scrutiny to ensure his creative powers were not enervated by encounters with irrelevant, unobserved phenomena.

An example of the ideological pressures maintained on artists to keep within confines set by the intelligentsia is provided by Repin's first major historical canvas after joining the Wanderers, the pithily titled *Tsarevna Sofya in the New Maiden Convent at the Time of the Execution of the Streltsy and the Torture of All Her Servants in 1698* (1879, GTG). Depicting Sofya Alekseevna Romanova (1657–1704) – half-sister to Peter the Great, who, when he came of age and ascended the throne, was forced into the Novodevichy convent – Repin painted her incarcerated on the anniversary of her unsuccessful attempt to incite a rebellion, at which time the gruesome events so graphically described by the title are taking place. The work was painted in the face of robust opposition from Stasov even though Repin planned and executed it with a scrupulously realist methodology: sketching in Novodevichy, studying period documentation, costumes and accessories, visiting historical locations, immersing himself in period literature, and scouring relevant museums. Out of this objective rationalism, however, came a melodramatic and psychologically unsubtle piece of Grand Guignol, the canvas dominated entirely by Sofya's bulky figure, consumed by suppressed fury and seething hatred.

The work was poorly received by the critics, and Stasov's confidence that Repin had embarked on a disastrously misguided course found outlet in a series of articles condemning the work as well as the artist's approach.[4] Stasov held that Repin was squandering his proven talent for the elucidation of phenomena observed at firsthand, from modern life. In this way the artist was manoeuvred back towards contemporary critical realism with the bonus that both the work and its adverse reception might serve as a deterrent to others considering encounters with Russia's past.

Censoring the past: subtexts in historical and religious works

Whilst the full rigour of Russian censorship has already been encountered in relation to images of contemporary hardship and political activism, it is perhaps paradoxically fitting that the full weight of official opprobrium was eventually to fall upon the historical genre. As Stalin was later to prove with ruthless efficiency, the strategic subversion of history was an awesomely powerful tool of propaganda: who controls the past controls the present. The nature of censorship under Tsarist control was, however, more haphazard – draconian but frequently incompetent and prone to inconsistencies and bungling such as that which let Chernyshevsky's *What Is to Be Done?* through the net of official scrutiny. One legend has it that the manuscript was passed around so many government departments, accruing imposing wax seals and ribbons on its journey, that it eventually took on the appearance of an august official document and so proceeded to publication. Whatever the reality it illustrates the characteristics of censorship under the autocracy: harsh, arbitrary, inequitable and frequently farcical. Driving this state of affairs was the fact that once approval was granted the individual censor rather than the writer or artist became responsible for any repercussions. This is not to say the protagonists of dissenting or undesirable creativity went unpunished, but since censors were primarily accountable, they were as a group cautious in the extreme; one even suppressed a cookery book which mentioned the suspiciously revolutionary concept of 'free air' circulating in an oven.[5]

Therefore, the tactic of evading censorship by effectively outwitting the office and making one's criticisms tangentially or by association would seem an attractive one, particularly where overtly contentious topics were simply unapproachable. It has frequently been conjectured that this tactic was singularly fitted to the Russian psyche which, as a result of centuries of training via the highly complex but legible iconic tradition, was exceptionally skilled in comprehending and interpreting visual data. Artists made the assumption that their works would be scrutinised patiently and at length, and that additional 'podtekst' would be unearthed. This may be a contributory factor to the Russian penchant for close reading of visual material, but the notion that artists could thus hoodwink the censor seems hardly tenable. It presumes that artists were capable of expressing in encrypted form seditious commentary which would remain invisible to the censor but simultaneously comprehensible to the public. It has to be assumed therefore that where subtext was intentional its import was visible to all, but that unless the censor was willing to impose a total ban he would be restrained by not wishing to draw attention to it. Once 'outed' in this way the author could simply deny the accusation, thereby suggesting over-sensitivity on the part of the state which in turn implied that perhaps it had something to hide. Adverse criticism, then as now, might be the quickest means of ensuring nationwide interest by which the censor would assist in the dissemination of radical thought. Where protest was concerned, the Russian bureaucracy understood that there is no such thing as bad publicity.

The process by which art was censored was also curiously inconsistent. Initially works were freely exhibited but might be removed after the show had opened to general scrutiny. This meant that for a while at least the most problematic and potentially insurgent images might be seen in public, although in general artists strategised carefully, favouring the permanent exposure of tempered criticism to brief sensation followed by an enforced withdrawal. In 1881 Yaroshenko's *At the Litovsky Fortress* fell foul of the latter, being hung at the Wanderers' exhibition but swiftly removed. Four years later Repin's *Ivan the Terrible* (figure 25) provoked a new and comprehensive censorship law enacted in 1886 whereby exhibitions became liable to examination by representatives of the government and Church prior to their opening. Eventually Kramskoy skilfully brooked this by inviting the Tsar to a personal preview reasoning, rightly, that if he did not object to what he saw his minions could hardly do so.[6]

Artists therefore worked under stressful, ill-defined and problematic rules of engagement. For some, history painting offered a respite from the demands of contemporary realism, while for the more astute it promised additional ammunition and diversionary tactics for critical engagement. Religio-historical works provided fertile ground for the latter, being neither 'realism' as contemporary theorists recognised it, nor 'religious' in terms of aspiring to devotional status. Building on the precedents of Aleksandr Ivanov's *Christ Appearing to the People* and Ge's *Last Supper*, imaging a demythologised Christ configured largely in historical terms, popular, secularised narratives of biblical events were frequently interpreted as conveying modern messages, the spiritual preoccupations of contemporary society. The exemplar in this respect is Kramskoy's *Christ in the Wilderness* (figure 14), already discussed as a hero-martyr image of revolutionary endeavour, a pensive icon of selfless sacrifice. Its affiliations with Perov's *Portrait of Dostoevsky* (figure 17) also placed it in the category of intellectual introspection; Christ as thinker and activist. Picking up on these aspects a contemporary critic remarked of Kramskoy's Saviour: 'Christ is here shown as the ideal human being ... all perfection expressed in the purest human features ... representing a lofty moral ideal ... as a man who, aware of the suffering and tears of mankind, has found the inner strength to embark on a *podvig*.'[7] The term *podvig* [подвиг] means broadly a heroic deed or valiant exploit and is commonly used in tales of epic adventure, but it was also used specifically of those involved in the Populist movement to the people, invoked here in a none too subtle nuance that the public would understand. In this respect Christ is fashioned as a crusader against injustice who, at great personal cost, takes his revolutionary message 'to the people', an image which sits comfortably with His Gospel mission as well as its modern political analogy.

Though there was some debate as to whether it was an image of resolution or disillusionment, the consensus interpretation was that of a moral insurrectionist. Garshin averred that this purposely 'humanised' Saviour was not a contemplator but a man of action, not a Hamlet but a Don Quixote. When asked to clarify the controversy Kramskoy was elusive but obliquely in tune with Garshin's reading, saying: 'I see clearly that there are moments in every man's life ... when he must ponder on whether he is to go left or right, whether to accept the silver coins and betray his God or whether to refuse to yield an inch to evil.'[8] The moral dilemma encapsulated here – of whether to act on one's convictions or become a bystander, or worse still to collude by turning away from an ethical imperative – was a highly topical question which much exercised contemporary Russia. In this respect Kramskoy is interested in a general and philosophical ideal of Christ the man, symbol like Dostoevsky of somebody wrestling with society's moral and ethical 'accursed problems', but also, spiritually, offering a solution not encrypted by more concrete documentations of political militancy.

Similar concerns resonate in Kramskoy's canvas of Christ's flagellation, *Mocking. 'Hail King of the Jews!'* (1877–82, GRM), which bears a strong compositional resemblance to Repin's *Arrest of a Propagandist* (figure 12). Both show centrally bound figures surrounded by their captors and are depictions of state power breaking and humiliating the noble-minded. Kramskoy's work was painted during the height of populist activity and completed shortly after Aleksandr II's murder, which heralded the end of revolutionary altruism. Conservative critics were certainly not blind to the ideological bifurcation offered, one commenting that but for the costumes what in essence was depicted was the arrest of an agitator in the Russian provinces.[9]

This process of reading the present from the past might work both ways. Repin's *They Did Not Expect Him* (colour plate 2) images a political resurrection whilst Makovsky's *Sentenced* (figure 11) might be read as a variation on the traditional theme of Christ meeting His mother at one of the Stations of the Cross. More overtly, Sergei Korovin's *Before Punishment in the Volost Administration* (figure 24) seems a naked transition of biblical events to a contemporary agrarian setting. This depiction of a peasant about to be flogged at the offices of the local jurisdiction has clear affinities with the Flagellation of Christ and is permeated by a fittingly solemn and reverential air, the drama muted but ominous. The spectator is witness to a physical outrage about to be committed by the powerful on the meek as the state exercises its formidable corrective muscle. Though no clue is given to the peasant's crime his dignified demeanour and calm surrender elicit sympathy and make of him a model of Christian sacrificial resignation. Such images set up a chicken and egg scenario: which came first, revolutionary paintings patterned after religious iconography, imbuing contemporary causes with moral sanction, or religious works covertly commenting on contemporary events as they sought to avoid censorship? A definitive answer remains elusive. The genres in Russia were deeply interrelated and frequently interchangeable.

Vasily Polenov's *Christ and the Woman Taken in Adultery* (1887, GRM) provided a case study of this Russian propensity for encoding or 'podtekst'. In an accomplished piece of archaeological naturalism evolving from the artist's travels around the Holy Land with the professed desire to depict the historical reality of Christ's life, Polenov produced a skilful ethnographic recreation of biblical events with documentary-like fidelity. The contemporary analogies read from this unremarkable canvas, however, saw the forces of modern arrogant officialdom cast in the role of the Pharisees.

> The man hauling the woman away to be stoned drags her off with the conscientiousness of one of our policemen to wherever, he assumes, it is for some reason necessary to drag people ... Don't we see such sinners on our streets every day, newcomers to the path of vice? ... Look at Polenov's adulteress: isn't it the same face that constantly passes before our eyes, the naive face of a child unaware of its degradation?[10]

The subtitle of the painting, 'He that is without sin amongst you ... ', is scripturally correct, but was perhaps too strong an invitation to cast the first stone in the direction of the state. Associating Polenov's work with contemporary police brutality and child prostitution is within the literary convention of the 'fallen woman', employed as a tool with which to expose the hypocrisy and moral bankruptcy of a social system that creates, uses, and then abuses her. In the visual arts, however, the correlation is audacious and invokes a violent disruption with the superficially illustrative nature of this narrative from biblical history.

At times, however, the alignment of history and contemporaneity seems more plausible. A current analogy seems manifest in Semiradsky's *Torches of Christianity* (1876, National Museum, Cracow) depicting the burning of pitch-covered Christian martyrs before the Roman Emperor Nero. The work swiftly became infamous for its dramatic excesses but also drew on aspects of current political relevance: arrest and execution, autocratic injustice, altruistic victims, courageous martyrs, and an impotent or indifferent public contrasted with the vanity and arrogance of the Imperial Court. Whether or not Semiradsky intended the public to read a precise set of analogies, the work's exhibition in 1877 when the Populist cause was suffering its most severe repression makes it likely that contemporary events were influential in the choice and treatment of so violent a subject.

In a similarly macabre piece of near-expressionist intensity, Fedor Bronnikov's *The Field of the Damned. Place of Execution in Ancient Rome. Crucified Slaves* (1878, GTG) surely alludes to a repression characteristic of the bloody present. Biblical subjects were rare at Wanderers' exhibitions but this type of anguished treatment even rarer. Why, one wonders, should such a work appear at this time, when the clash between the state and the *narodniki* was at its fiercest? And why

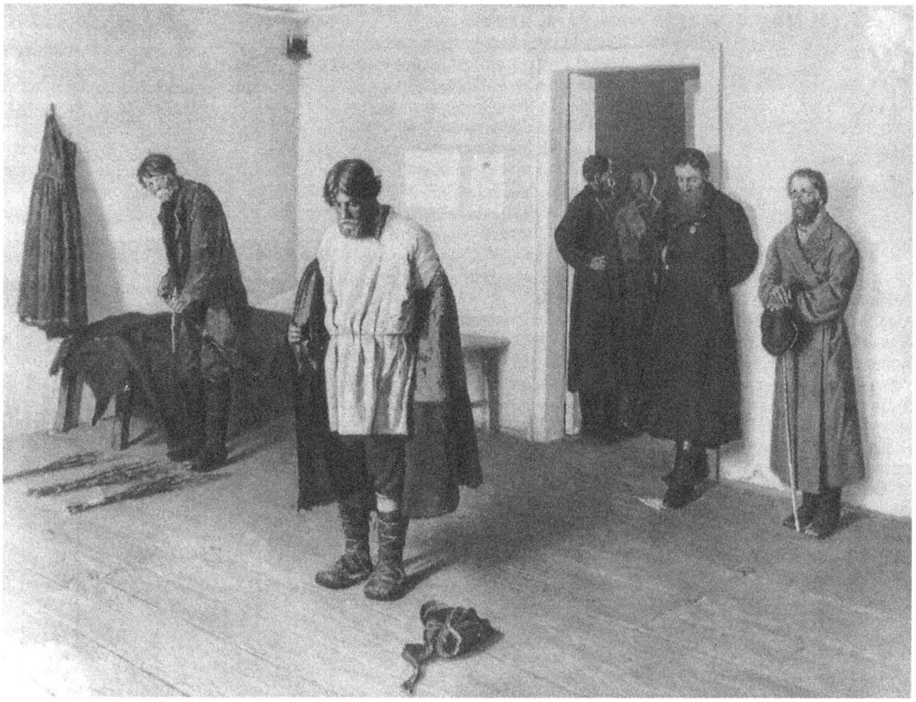

24 Sergei Korovin, *Before Punishment in the Volost Administration*, 1884

does Bronnikov choose to depict not the Crucifixion, but a mass of common crucifixions, identified by title and treatment as a brutal death inflicted by the state on the rank and file? Such painterly histrionics can hardly be coincidental and, like Semiradsky, Bronnikov seems to be exorcising the horrors of contemporary life, even if subconsciously.

The exorcist: Repin's *Ivan Groznie*

A conscious exorcism and exegesis of contemporary events as seen through the mirror of history was given candidly by Repin's *Ivan the Terrible and His Son Ivan. 16 November 1581* (figure 25). Repin explicitly confirmed its ties to the revolutionary theme, evolving from the assassination of Aleksandr II and the subsequent executions of his murderers, which he witnessed, commenting: 'My emotions were overwhelmed by the horrors of contemporary life. This mood was then a common one. Terrible scenes were in everybody's mind, but no one dared paint them ... It was natural to look for a way out of this painful and tragic situation through history.'[11] Repin subsequently confirmed the link between the canvas and the executions of the People's Will organisation, making this work unique in that a current political analogy is professed rather than surmised. He recalled being possessed by the image, working in frenzied bouts of activity accompanied by insomnia and ghastly visions. This immersion in the psychology of his protagonists, as sort of 'method painting', was crucial to an unconventional imaging that avoids confrontation and violence, relying instead on the mutely discarded steel-tipped staff to suggest the preceding action. Instead of the violence of anger, when Ivan, in a fit of rage, struck the Tsarevich a fatal blow, Repin depicts the equally terrifying violence of remorse, as the delirious Tsar cradles his dying son. Garshin, who purportedly posed for the figure of the Tsarevich noted: 'Ivan the Terrible deserted by the Tsar in him ... the tyrant, the sovereign – there's none of that; before you there is an animal ... which struck by a terrible blow, has for a moment become human.'[12]

Repin dropped the original and more provocative title of *Filicide* (*Сыноубийца*), doubtless in an attempt to avoid censorship, but its appearance at the Wanderers' exhibition in 1885 was a cultural bombshell evoking such mass curiosity that police had to intervene to keep public order. The painting provoked severe reactions ranging from vitriolic denunciation to ecstatic praise. Andrei Prakhov, former editor of the conservative journal *The Bee* (*Пчела*) now turned convert to democratic realism, gave the work a favourable review, whilst Aleksei Suvorin likened Repin to Rembrandt and praised his psychological insight. Tolstoy adopted a

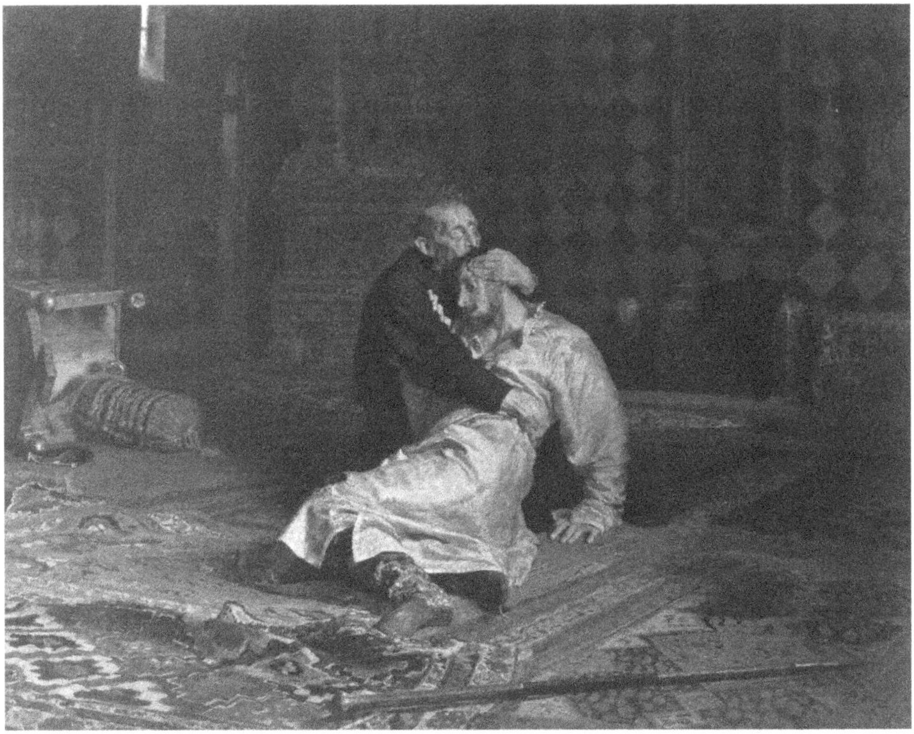

25 Ilya Repin, *Ivan the Terrible and His Son Ivan. 16 November, 1581*, 1885, 199.5 x 254 cm

pacifist philosophical view and praised what he regarded as Repin's exposé of how violence harms the perpetrator as much as the victim, a view Tolstoy proffered when appealing unsuccessfully to Aleksandr III to spare the lives of his father's assassins.[13]

Suvorin's article was prompted by a long description of the painting sent to him by Kramskoy, in a letter which provides fascinating insight into the intensity with which works were then regarded, a facet of critical reception which scorns detached, objective analyses, but which is characteristic of the times. In an intense and ecstatic outpouring Kramskoy urged his reader to surrender to the work's powerful emotional catharsis:

> What is conveyed and brought most sharply to the fore is the unexpectedness of the murder! This most phenomenal, and extremely difficult aspect, is achieved by means of only two figures. The father has struck his own son on the temple with his staff, and the son has collapsed, pouring out his life's blood! A moment, and then the father cries out in horror, rushes to his son and seizes him. Dropping to the floor he lifts him on to his lap, and firmly, firmly, presses with one hand the wound at the temple (but the blood gushes out between the slits of his fingers), and with his other hand round his waist, clasps him to his breast and firmly, firmly, kisses the head of his poor (and unusually attractive) son, and he roars (positively roars) from horror, in his helpless condition. Throwing himself upon his son, tearing at his hair, the father has stained the upper half of his face with blood; a touch of Shakespearean tragicomedy. This animal of a father, shouting with horror, and this sweet, precious son, resigned to his death ... But how it is painted, God how it is painted! ... You simply must see it!!![14]

Kramskoy's view was not, however, shared by an officialdom outraged at this depiction of the Tsar as murderer. When the exhibition moved to Moscow, the scene of Ivan's crime, the painting was ordered to be removed and Tretyakov was forbidden to exhibit it or to disseminate its likeness. The comprehensive censorship law introduced the following year was intended to ensure that such potentially offensive works could henceforth be weeded out before being seen in public. Advising Aleksandr III in his illiberal reign was Konstantin Pobedonostsev, Chief-Procurator of the Holy Synod and a man of legendary conservatism. He wrote to the Tsar:

> I saw *that* painting today and was unable to view it without disgust ... the art of today is remarkable: without the slightest ideals, only the sense of naked realism, critical tendentiousness and denunciations. Previous paintings by Repin were distinguished by this inclination and were also offensive. It is hard to understand what thought induced the artist to describe in such total realism these particular moments. And why Ivan the Terrible? Besides a determined tendentiousness you will not find another motive.[15]

This official disapproval of course only further endeared Repin to the radicals, leaving the state to mount a reactionary campaign to discredit the painting and its author. In an unprecedented but concentrated attack on an artist Repin was subjected to abuse, smears and innuendo in the best traditions of yellow journalism.

These ranged from the charge that he had appropriated the idea from one of his students (quickly retracted when the artist threatened litigation) to a long and erudite article in the Academy's journal seeking to prove the painting's serious anatomical and medical inaccuracies.[16]

Since the Academy's President, Grand Duke Vladimir, was the Tsar's brother, and Repin's work was effectively arraigned on a charge of *lèse majesté*, and since the controversy arose so soon after Aleksandr II's assassination and the ensuing political executions, countering these views was potentially hazardous. When Stasov wrote a rejoinder dismissing the Academy's fatuous observations the Grand Duke wrote to the Minister of the Interior requesting that a penalty be imposed on *Novosti*, the journal that had printed Stasov's article. He singled out Stasov and Repin as perpetrators of 'a tendency in art ... full of expressions of impermissible protest against all forms of establishment'. *Novosti* received a strict warning, but the over-zealous Minister instigated a comprehensive ban forbidding any favourable reaction to the painting, threatening 'a fitting punishment' for any breaches, and warning editors to abstain from criticisms of the Academy or its 'most august leader'.[17] The authorities showed themselves to be extremely sensitive towards any criticism, implied or explicit, and willing to invoke their considerable powers to suppress all views contrary to their own.

Notwithstanding Repin's questionable reputation as the doyen of radical circles, it is not difficult to see how shocking the painting must have been to an audience in the 1880s, whether through political analogy or sheer emotional impact. One might accept Pobedonostsev's view that Repin need never have tackled the subject, but having done so he takes it to a logical if not obvious conclusion. Could one depict the terrible consequences of Ivan's violence and the reality of the brutal slaying of his own son with restraint? Though the notoriety of the work resulted in accusations of artistic excess this seems an obvious strategy to castigate its political content. There are examples of suspect taste which outstrip this but which did not engender the same controversy. Perov's *The Torture of the Boyarina Morozova* (1881, GTG) – depicting a fetishised image of a trussed-up, upturned, bare-breasted beauty being strung up in readiness for a beating – is particularly distasteful in its lascivious sadomasochism. In European art possibly only Henri Regnault's fascinatingly repellent *Execution without Trial Under the Moorish Kings of Granada* (1870, Musée d'Orsay, Paris) can compare for shock value, though here the subject seems arbitrary, the violence unnecessary, and the painting entirely lacking in pathos: a case of bare sensationalism.

Outside of its public life, for Repin the painting was clearly an emotional release, a means to placate the horrors of contemporary life, and the public and a few discerning critics, weary of the round of political violence, responded in like mind. Suvorin praised its theme of conflict resolved by Christian forgiveness and considered that it carried a timely message, though as a loyalist he did not consider that it apportioned blame.[18] In this respect the ideological content managed to be both universally humane and immediately topical, but whilst the much-vaunted contem-

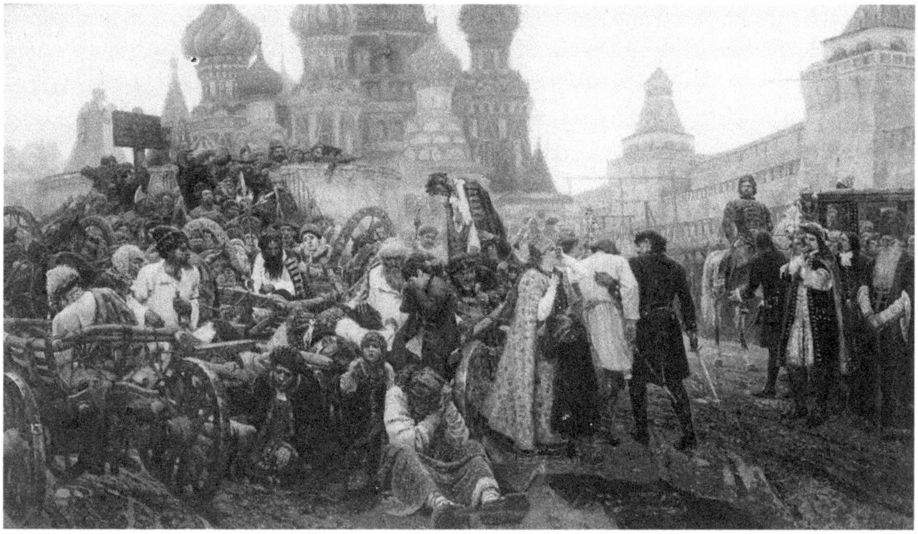

26 Vasily Surikov, *The Morning of the Execution of the Streltsy*, 1881, 218 x 379 cm

porary analogy upset the Tsar (or more correctly Pobedonostsev) and affronted the dignity of the Academy's President, this was not, ultimately, the work's enduring facet. The intense emotional content, raised to a shrill pitch, superseded all other considerations, and it was on these terms that the painting was judged. Nowhere, for instance, was a voice raised to protest that the historical Tsarevich was a worthy protégé of his father who participated in much of the Tsar's brutal debauchery. In this respect most commentators were willing to suspend their historical knowledge and accept the painting on a broad, moral level, participating in Repin's manifestly humanitarian portrayal of Ivan as victim of his own violence, at once terrifying and pathetic.

Ethnographic history: Surikov and after

Repin's painting appears to crown the summit of historical critical analogy, its comparisons with the bloody present overt enough to upset the state, sincere enough to unite the public and critics to regard its Christian ethic. History painting after the assassination tended more towards a non-partisan view of the past, even at times to heroic and patriotic mythologising. As liberal critics feared, historical works too frequently detracted from an observation of contemporary ills, but the intelligentsia's involvement with Populism, its shift towards lauding, preserving and studying the national culture, rather than seeking to supplant it with Western models, assisted an association of the Wanderers with a nationalist agenda, thereby depleting its reformist image. In part this was due to market forces as merchant patronage shunned the tastes and subjects of the aristocratic Academy in preference for contemporary naturalism, simultaneously sponsoring Slavic subject matter rather than insurgent opinions.

These factors are most clearly embodied in the career of Vasily Surikov, arguably Russia's only 'pure' history painter in that he devoted himself to vast, densely populated reconstructions of the political and social upheavals of the nation's past, particularly the cultural schism of the Petrine period. Born in Siberia where serfdom had not taken hold, of an old Cossack family steeped in the independence of that race, Surikov's background was at odds with the subordinate status and European-Russian origins of many of the Wanderers. Coupled with this ethnic difference was a conditioning from a culture which lagged picturesquely behind European Russia. The customs and mores of the sixteenth and seventeenth centuries lived on in a patriarchal life-style, traditional modes of dress and a strong oral tradition of story-telling.

Like Repin, Surikov needed the auspices of a wealthy patron, the gold-mine owner P.I. Kuznetsov, to fund his academic tutelage in St Petersburg, but it was Moscow that made its impact on him, particularly the remnants of the Old Russia which Peter the Great had tried so assiduously to destroy. From 1877 he made his home here, incorporating historical sites and period architecture into his large and ambitious panoramas chronicling the movements of a nation. Working from meticulous historical studies, Surikov nevertheless avoided a lifeless archaeological correctness, making the viewer a participant in his teeming dramas where the power-brokers are pushed to the sidelines and the Russian people are imaged as the history-makers. Though his models are individualised and drawn from life, Surikov is seldom concerned with psychological portrayals of individuals, nor are his participants abstracted to 'type'. The masses are given a face, are personalised, but are not pressed into the mould of political and social signifiers.

The absence of partisan moralising in Surikov's work seem quite remarkable given that his major canvases depict times of upheaval and loss of life when the character of the Old Russia beloved of the Slavophiles was mercilessly pushed aside. Similarities with contemporary Russia as it struggled with its cultural destiny and agonised over its past, polarising society and creating political divisions, might seem inviting, and certainly some were tempted to see contemporary analogies in these strife-ridden images. But Surikov was vehemently against grafting modern mores onto previous epochs and professed no overt or conscious correspondence between his works and modern Russia. His first major work, *The Morning of the Execution of the Streltsy* (figure 26), illustrates these tensions. A realistic imaging of a cold, bleak winter's dawn, it depicts the last moments of members of this military corps instituted by Ivan the Terrible, which enjoyed great privileges, becoming a law unto themselves. Attempts to curb the power of this unrestrained and retrogressive body triggered a revolt in 1698 which was quelled, precipitating several days of tortures and executions in which, reputedly, the Tsar took a hand. Surikov pictured the defeated traditionalists as victims of Peter's westernisation, clutching the candles that symbolise their repentance as they await their deaths.

In this sense the work might easily be read as a disquisition on Tsar versus people, prophetic too of the modern terror and executions. But Peter might just as easily be regarded by the liberal, westernising camp as a positive influence on a backward Russia seeking to rid itself of these self-serving thugs. The individualised, sympathetic portrayal of the Streltsy as real, suffering individuals, their weeping wives and children in attendance as they are torn from their loved ones and crushed by Peter's reforming zeal, may have appealed to conservative Slavophilia; the price Old Russia paid for its westernisation. But Surikov's Peter is strangely impassive, neither flattered by the artist nor denounced. The Streltsy's protectionism and Peter's mission to modernise Russia are on a tragic collision course. Peter and his new-style regimental army that oversees the executions are the new order, and the old is on its way out. But this is matter of fact; Surikov, it seems, is impartial.

In part the lack of critical appraisal of this huge and important canvas was due to the unfortunate timing of its exhibition at the ninth Wanderers' show, which opened the day of Aleksandr II's assassination. This and the removal of Yaroshenko's *At the Litovsky Fortress* doubtlessly stifled critical debate, and although some felt the work in poor taste most were perhaps disinclined to dwell on Surikov's depressing theme during a time of national shock. Nevertheless, Surikov does appear to refrain from moralising in a manner which might easily have polarised contemporary debate. Perhaps the most telling aspect in this respect is that he avoided the blood and gore of the executions which would surely have proved emotively sympathetic to the condemned. Instead he focused on the gravity of the participants, the Streltsy and their friends and relations, the Tsar, his Court and army. The canvas therefore evokes mass suffering without actually portraying Peter's fiendish tortures, a conscious strategy on Surikov's part confirmed by a recollection of a visit to his studio in 1880 by Repin who, amazed at the lack of bloodshed, advised him to include some hanged figures in the rear. Against his better judgment Surikov acquiesced, incurring the displeasure of Tretyakov, but more so of his own grandmother who on entering his studio promptly collapsed. Before painting out the lurid figures Surikov laconically remarked of his grandmother's faint that it confirmed his opinion that 'art need not work this way'.[19]

Similar issues of disinterested historicity came to the fore in Surikov's next major canvas *The Boyarina Morozova* (colour plate 4). Taking its subject from the reign of Tsar Aleksei Mikhailovich, the father of Peter the Great, it deals with opposition to religious reforms correcting basic scriptural errors and outward forms of worship. The noblewoman Morozova, along with the self-styled 'Old Believers', rejected these innovations, for which she and her sister, the Princess Urusova, were confined and tortured in 1672. Eventually the unrepentant schismatic or devout martyr (take your pick) was incarcerated in a squalid pit in the small town of Borovsk, where she died in November 1675.

Surikov pictures the Boyarina driven in chains through the streets of Moscow in a peasant sledge to be mocked by the crowds, an obvious parallel with Christ's martyrdom. The sledge cuts the huge canvas obliquely in two, dividing the scene between her supporters and sympathisers on the right, and her enemies or detractors on the left, each carefully individualised. The supporters comprise a cross-section of spiritual and secular society evincing various reactions to the Boyarina's fate. To her right Princess Urusova is led on foot by a *Strelets* to share her sister's fate, whilst elsewhere Morozova's mockers include the sledge-driver, laughing heartily at her fate, and a grinning and derisive priesthood to the far left. But it is Morozova who dominates. Dressed all in black she contrasts dramatically with the ostentatious surfaces – gold and silver, precious stones, multi-coloured fabrics, silk embroideries – as she cuts a dark swath through the canvas. Chained and unbowed she makes the sign of the cross with two fingers (the reforms prescribed three) presenting a compellingly powerful figure of courageous and single-minded dedication.

Whether or not this is a positive image is debatable. Along with her courage Morozova's blind zealotry is also displayed. Stasov believed her a narrow-minded religious fanatic, certainly not a role model of heroic endeavour. As ever he counselled that present-day issues were more important than revisiting the past. Garshin concurred in regarding her image as potentially celebrating a retrogressive schismatic. Whilst he admired the strength of her convictions he found her reactionary fanaticism repellent; the fact that small points of external ritual mattered more to her than life. Had she and her followers prevailed, he predicted, 'there would have been pyres, gallows, executioners' blocks, and rivers of blood'.[20]

An important signifier in this respect is the ragged figure of the 'holy fool' (юродивый) at the bottom right of the canvas, with his begging bowl and heavy penitential chains who, like her, voluntarily endures physical pain and suffering for his beliefs. He returns Morozova's two-fingered sign of the cross and mirrors her ecstatic state. This might seem an overt comment on the unbalanced state of mind of both, but is ambiguous. In Russian religious culture the fool does not necessarily carry connotations of stupidity or ignorance, rather of an 'otherworldliness', like children and other innocents a potentially purer conduit to the divine, unhampered by rationality. Such is the child-like portrait of the peasant Grisha in Tolstoy's autobiographical sketch *Childhood*, who sleeps in chains but whose piety and faith give him a closeness to God which his educated masters cannot hope to attain.

The Boyarina Morozova is therefore again difficult to ascribe political motivation to. Contemporary analogies might be sought in the theme of democratic protest against autocratic abuse, or the unwarranted persecution of schismatics such as the modern-day Dukhobors: an oppressed pacifist, quasi-socialist Christian sect whose victimisation was vigorously renewed in 1895, prompting Tolstoy to publish his highly controversial novel *Resurrection* in support of the Dukhobor Fund. Similarly, the canvas might be thought to hold some latent critique on the efforts to retain national customs and the religious practices of Old Russia against the reformist tendencies of an increasingly dominant state centralism. Varied readings might place Surikov as liberal, conservative or politically indifferent, though it is perhaps telling that the imprisoned revolutionary Vera Figner took comfort also from this work, relating its content to the dedication of Sofya Perovskaya and the women of the Populist movement whose self-sacrificing convictions had brought them to a similarly resolute death.[21]

The vitiating effect that Surikov's work possibly produced on the Wanderers' critical ethos, however, may relate also to aesthetic issues, always a point of controversy when an artist was perceived as abandoning the former for the latter. In his large, painterly canvases, Surikov proved himself more concerned with light and colour than most of his contemporaries, a fact which endeared him to later, more aesthetically minded artists. He frequently travelled abroad and was a great admirer of sixteenth-century Venetian art – Veronese, Titian, Tintoretto – adopting scintillating surfaces of colour. He also expressed a diverse interest in modern foreign practitioners as well as Russian influences, citing admiration for Bastien-Lepage, Manet, Degas and Pissarro, as well as his particular veneration for Aleksandr Ivanov's experimentations with *plein-air* coloration.[22]

Crediting Surikov's aestheticism with breaking the socially minded ethos of the Wanderers, Aleksandr Benois noted: 'It was as though the door was flung open, and fresh air rushed in', whilst of his ability with colour the otherwise radical Repin called him 'an aesthetic aristocrat'.[23] Indeed, as Surikov recorded, the conception of the painting came from an aesthetic impetus, that of having seen a crow land on snow, its black form and carrion associations contrasting with the purity of the scintillating polychromatic surface leading him to note: 'most painters paint silhouettes on the snow. But snow is permeated with light, it is all violet and pink reflexes.'[24] This approach is true of all of Surikov's mature works where the detail of apparently monotonous areas are touched with pure colour, the decorative, impasted surface taking on the aspect of tapestry.

For a burgeoning aesthete of apolitical leanings, however, his works are frequently anchored in socio-political territory, making his subject matter the site of critical ambiguity. That Stasov was decidedly cool towards Surikov, regarding his paintings as expressions of a conservative temperament, is perhaps sufficient evidence that his work was seen by the left as detrimental to progressive propagandising. Allied to the favour Surikov found with a younger generation of aesthetically minded painters, his apparent lack of critical discourse perhaps confirms liberal fears that Surikov's painterly works embody an ideological impartiality. As his biographer noted in a passage approved by the artist: 'in history you can side with either party, depending on your sympathies and antipathies, but you know that in the final analysis nobody is right in history and nobody wrong, there is only the horror of collisions such as this, that are never resolved but with the shedding of a sea of blood'.[25]

To a significant degree that outlook also characterises Repin's last major historical canvas, *The Zaporozhye Cossacks Writing a Mocking Letter to the Turkish Sultan* (figure 27). With broad humour Repin illustrates events from 1676 when the Zaporozhye were threatened with annihilation by the superior forces of Sultan

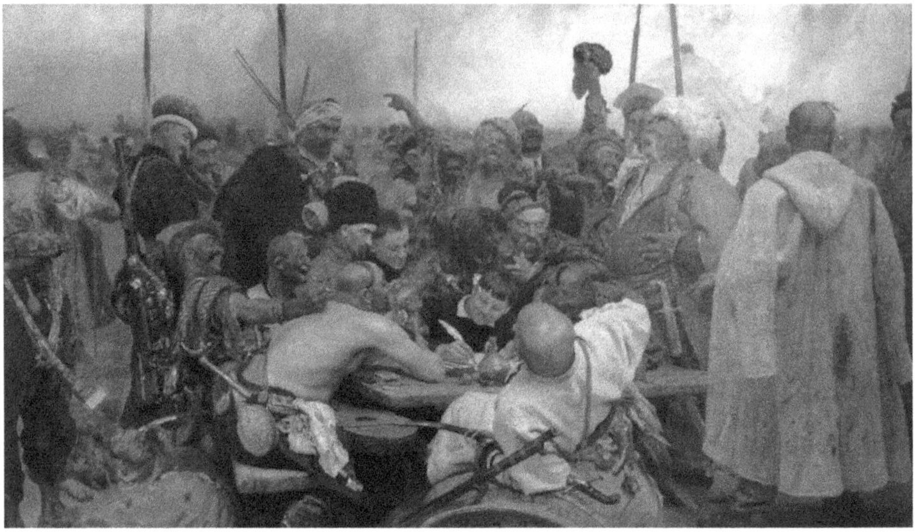

27 Ilya Repin, *The Zaparozhye Cossacks Writing a Mocking Letter to the Turkish Sultan*, 1880–91, 203 x 358 cm

Mohammed IV. Refusing to submit the Cossacks compose a crude and abusive reply, each one vying to outdo his comrades in their choice of scathing obscenities. The result is a huge ethnographic-historical tableau celebrating the traditional values of the artist's Ukrainian Cossack forbears, their rumbustious love of freedom coupled with a fierce sense of independence and national pride, grounded in an autonomous, equitable political culture. Repin worked on the canvas in a manner and scale that mirrors Surikov's practices. He made excursions to the Ukraine to sketch descendants of the Zaporozhye in search of racial likenesses, taking historical and archaeological advice and collecting documentary materials and artefacts of the period and place. Like Surikov he also derived inspiration from the labours of Aleksandr Ivanov in terms of a project spanning more than a decade and generating a profusion of sketches and variants.

It was finally exhibited in 1891, by which time Surikov's interventions had subverted the genre to a more passive mode. It gave Repin his greatest success, critically and commercially, but was in marked contrast to his controversial canvases of the 1880s, produced during the period of *The Zaporozhye Cossacks*' gestation. The intervening years had seen great social and political changes, but significantly the growth of a cultural plurality. As will be discussed in chapter 9, the Wanderers by now had embarked on a self-destructive bureaucratic ossification which Aleksandr III was swift to capitalise on, reforming the Imperial Academy through the agency of a Government Commission to which Repin and other artists were elected in 1890. Meanwhile, a burgeoning diversity in the arts was also threatening the realist style and narrative content. The seed of Diaghilev's *Mir iskusstva*, which was to assume international significance, was sown in 1890 with the formation of a circle of artists around Aleksandr Benois, and the establishment of the St Petersburg Society of Artists the same year further eroded the artistic monopoly enjoyed by the realists.

Indeed, at the time of the work's exhibition Repin had resigned from the Wanderers in March of that year, and so *The Zaporozhye Cossacks* was displayed at a massive independent one-man show amongst 298 works, including 30 studies for the finished canvas, which became the central attraction. During this period of cultural flux Repin's combination of nationalist subject matter and a vigorous, painterly execution found ready admirers, and where formerly opinion had diverged predictably along progressive and conservative lines, this rip-roaring slice of Cossack revelry, lacking tendentiousness or even the most general of critical analogies, was appreciated much in the vein that its creator had intended. Most telling in respect of the painting's political inoffensiveness was that less than a decade after the controversy surrounding *Ivan the Terrible* Aleksandr III purchased *The Zaporozhye Cossacks* for 35,000 roubles, the highest price ever paid for a Russian canvas. Repin used the proceeds to purchase a large country estate in Vitebsk province, thus completing a transformation from indigent peasant to landed gentry.

A lack of the tendentiousness which critics and public firmly associated with Repin not only pleased commentators of various viewpoints but invited closer association with technical and painterly aspects of the work. The composition, which looks natural and obvious, disguises a complex placement of over seventeen figures in the central group alone. As one reviewer pointed out, it is artfully conceived to draw one into the action, the edges of the painting employing cut-off figures to decrease the notion of finite space, suggesting a continuation of events beyond the canvas.[26] Several figures turn their backs to us, increasing the sense of our being unobserved witnesses to events, whilst various Cossack accoutrements and the figure of the bald Cossack reclining on his barrel seem to jut out from the canvas in aspects of compositional daring that enhance the illusion of our being participants rather than bystanders.

Though *The Zaporozhye Cossacks* was a popular and critical triumph for Repin its expansion of a historical anecdote into a major painting was a weakness commented upon by critics who compared it to an over-extended short story. A disappointed Tolstoy, who saw such promise in *Ivan the Terrible*, called it a 'study' (этюд) and lamented its lack of a serious, meaningful idea. Repin's work shows the stage history painting had reached at the time the Wanderers began to lose their status as the sole alternative to the Academy. The employment of critical analogy, at best a short-lived phenomenon, had yielded to nationalist and ethnographic concerns. The celebration of heritage and pride in indigenous characteristics underpins the forced revelry of this thigh-slapping pendant to Gogol's *Taras Bulba*, a roistering piece of virile Russian history, the antithesis of Kramskoy's dictum that history painting might force society to examine its deficiencies by holding a mirror to the present.

With the upsurge of aesthetic tendencies and Surikov's example of elaborate surface decoration, in the hands of artists such as Sergei Ivanov and Apollinary Vasnetsov, history painting during the 1890s reverted to the anecdotal nature of Shvarts, whilst in the works of Andrei Ryabushkin a greater attention to ornamentation becomes an almost terminal obsession. Ryabushkin devoted himself to nostalgic recreations of Old Russia, utilising flat compositions with stiff and stylised figures. In works such as *Tsar Mikhail Fedorovich Holding Council with the Boyars in His Royal Chamber* (1893, GTG), imaging the court of Peter I's grandfather as a group of seated elders surrounding the Tsar, all of whom appear to be asleep, surface detail and colourful costumery dominate an uneventful scene of static ennui. No hint of drama or tension, nor vigorous nationalism threatens to intrude on the decorative beauty of Ryabushkin's images, which were seen by many as self-indulgent, holding no 'purpose' beyond pleasure for the eye – which naturally endeared him to the modernists. He exhibited with Diaghilev's *Mir iskusstva*, his light-hearted, aesthetically based images having much in common with their penchant for recreating similarly colourful fantasies of an imagined Versailles.

Past imperfect

Finding common ground or certainties in Russian 'realist' historical works presents a problematic series of ambiguities complicated not least by the varied interpretations placed upon the term 'history', the meaning of which was debated throughout Europe in the nineteenth century. Academic History Painting (the capital letters are important), though frequently resembling mere historical tableaux, was ostensibly for the embodiment of eternal values, a morally improving force for which the Bible, classical myth or antiquity were deemed compulsory. The transition to historical genre, accurate reconstructions of anecdotal, everyday scenes such as those by Shvarts, broadened the notion of history by accepting that grandeur and elevated moral thought were no longer prerequisites. The development of Ge's histories interpreted through psychology, or Surikov's 'democratisation' of past events, further expanded the limits of what could be regarded as history. These are not particularly Russian traits, however; similar developments can be mapped throughout Europe.

More fundamental was the intervention of Realism in the arts which simply denied history painting in its then current forms, the views of Proudhon and Taine in the 1860s, echoed by Baudelaire in his *Salon* reviews calling repeatedly for contemporaneity (Proudhon's *Du principe de l'art et de sa destination sociale* of 1865 appeared in Russian translation the same year). History became the here and now, the objective elucidation of the epoch in which the artist lived, the only one which he had a right, indeed a duty, to depict. In effect history was turned about from something inherited to something bequeathed.

This viewpoint, the essence of a realist philosophy, was however confused and diluted in art by those who adopted only the realist style (sometimes supplanted by the term naturalism) or realist subject matter, usually associated with low-life scenes or a general lack of idealisation. In such a manner Kramskoy's *Christ in the Wilderness* is corporeal, but not based on observation. The painted solidity and veracity of Surikov's crowd scenes, his concern with specifics rather than generalisations, individuals rather than stereotypes, labels the artist as a realist,[27] though this is not an epithet which the French thinkers would have applied to one who engaged in imaginary fabrications of Petrine Russia, nor was it one Stasov recognised. The Wanderers' contemporary subjects were, in Stasov's view, history paintings, or as he frequently labelled them 'modern history'. In this he accorded with Courbet:

> The history of an age finishes with the age itself and with those of its representatives who have expressed it. It is not given to new ages to add something to the expression of past ages, to aggrandise or to embellish the past. That which has been has been. It is the duty of the human spirit to always start anew, always in the present[28]

But progressive Russian artistic criticism never embraced the supposedly disinterested objectivity of French realism, which might properly be applied only to contemporaneity. A subjective, critical component allied to national subject matter was also a prerequisite for Stasov and liberal critics. Complaining of the lack of 'modern history' paintings throughout Europe, or of past artists who failed to address critically their own epochs, Stasov thundered:

> History as it is generally understood (with such rapture and enthusiasm!) is rubbish, worthless. At the last Universal Exhibition and the huge annual Paris Exhibition last year, where more than 3000 pictures were shown, where was the history? Where were the history paintings? And I do not mean museums with old pictures on past times and people, by past artists to whom everything beyond expression and sentiment was *terra incognita*.[29]

But in this uncertainty concerning past and present, reality and realism, of how the past fathered the present, the utility and legitimacy of historical subjects (as distinct from History Painting) within a realist school became confused and diluted. Repin's *Ivan the Terrible* fits easily into no category, being distressingly 'real', psychologically 'true' and horrifically convincing, yet ultimately an artistic fantasy. That it was interpreted as a discourse on the evils of violence, which would be in keeping with the morally improving nature of traditional academic History Painting, further problematises the image since the squalid, brutal realisation of Ivan's predicament is the very antithesis of the enshrinement of noble virtues. Perhaps in this respect at least realist history painting might have offered a subversive development of a genre traditionally used in the maintenance of the status quo?

Ultimately, however, the imaging of historical scenes, whether in terms of anecdote, drama, psychology or communal endeavour, was a genre seemingly designed to compromise the critical-contemporary ethos of the Wanderers. Its potential contribution to the liberal-reformist cause was highly dubious; at best it might make veiled and coded comments without guarantee that they would be perceived. At worse it might offer abundant possibility for pro-nationalist sentiments, a facet later exploited by Tsar Aleksandr III's campaign of cultural 'Russification'. Reservations or fears expressed by liberals, especially Stasov, about the vitiating effects of history painting within a realist school were largely vindicated. The enormous public success of Surikov eroded the gritty realism which had been Society's hallmark whilst, as we shall see, artists such as Viktor Vasnetsov and Mikhail Nesterov used historical nationalist subject matter as a springboard for straying further into realms of escapist fantasy and poetic spirituality.

7

Landscape painting: styles and ideologies

If history painting was greeted with critical disquiet by liberal commentators, imaging the nation's landscape proved even more problematic as a site for potential capitulation to convention. Notwithstanding the questionable ideological proclivities of the Wanderers, the very basis of the society's output – a literary-derived form of visual narrative – would seem redundant in a genre of limited intellectual possibilities.[1] The fear of form usurping content, of decorative nationalistic impulses celebrating Mother Russia displacing critical interrogation, unsettled the intelligentsia, and with good cause.

In the broadest sense the significance that Russian culture attached to the land can hardly be exaggerated. The concept of a 'Motherland', embodied in the inauspicious feminine noun 'rodina' (родина) defies adequate translation but was universally acknowledged as a heritage common to all, whether the aristocracy that owned most of it, the merchants that traded on it, the literary intelligentsia that sought tendentiously to define and mould it, or the peasantry that worked it. Its ethos, however, surpassed the physical, the land itself, to encapsulate an indefinable and inexpressible sense of belonging that was entangled in a heady mix of fierce national pride and lachrymose nostalgia. Traditionally this was the place of home, the receptacle of the Russian soul, a birthright surpassing social divisions and binding all. The very etymology of the word traces a lineage, its root filtering into those used for nationhood, the people, birth, parents, mother and father.

Geographically too, Russia encompassed a vast, overwhelmingly rural country of diverse topography and climates; a country of avid 'sportsmen' – hunting, shooting and fishing – the legacy of which permeated the nation's literature, music, thought, myth and legend. Nature, the land, 'rodina', were concepts therefore of paramount importance to Russian culture and not easily susceptible to ideological containment. Where, for instance, Turgenev's *Sketches from a Hunter's Album* might be said to have invented the concept of the peasant as a thinking individual, thereby forcing a progressive cultural intervention that the intelligentsia built upon in their insistence that 'the people' be accorded their social due, the land they inhabited remained a site of emotional romanticism. Observing the ragged and drunken participants of a peasant singing contest in one of the sketches, Turgenev' recorded:

> He drew in a deep breath and began to sing ... and each one of us felt a wave of sweetness and shivery anticipation creeping over us ... The honest fiery soul of Russia resounded and breathed through it and quite simply seized us by the heart, plucked directly at our Russian heart-strings ... He sang, quite oblivious of his rival and all of us, yet evidently uplifted, as a spirited swimmer is borne up by the waves, by our silent, devotional aspiration. He sang, and in every sound his voice made there breathed something familiar as our birthright and so vast no eye could encompass it, just as if the Russian steppe were being unrolled before us, stretching away into an endless distance. I felt emotion throb in my heart and tears rose to my eyes.[2]

These concerns are vital to an understanding of Russian landscape painting, the context of which is that of emotive, subjective and highly personal readings, and particularly of the ongoing search for national identity, which in this instance polarised but unwittingly reconciled the social and political divides. In Russian art the cultural baggage encompassed by this ostensibly placid genre ensured it would not remain a supine province of decorative developments, but rather an arena in which were fought some of the most influential artistic debates. Its initial strength, however, was prosaic. It was, even before the Wanderers, a popular genre which found public approval and ready patrons, and in which Russian artists excelled. Early Russian landscape favoured Mediterranean scenery in keeping with the aristocratic belief of the superiority of all things Western, and if tackled at all artists tended to imbue Russia with an Italianate light and treatment. As one commentator noted: 'In these travesties of the truth ... the Steppes are indistinguishable from the Campagna, a street in Moscow suggests Rome, or a sunset on the Neva looks like evening on the Venetian Lagoons.'[3]

The prevailing dominance of the academic tradition, its emphasis on idealisation and the picturesque, of artificially arranging natural phenomena into pleasing constructions, was posited on the dictates of convention and precept. At competition academic students were instructed to include precise detail such as specific flora and fauna or picturesque buildings, and frequently their knowledge of nature was based on studying the Old Masters. Repin recalled how he was sincerely advised by Bruni, the great academic pedagogue, to erase from one of his biblical themes elements of landscape studied from life, and instead to go to the Hermitage to copy Poussin in order to paint truly 'historic' landscape. Like many of his generation Repin found this an unacceptable method of working and was unimpressed by the 'artificial, darkened, unnatural' works of the French master.[4]

During the first half of the nineteenth century, however, moves towards greater naturalism in landscape painting had been made. Venetsianov and his pupils paved the way for a more relaxed and informal approach to native topography comprised of simple motifs. Their landscapes remained the backdrop for human activity but bucked academic trends, becoming occasionally documentary in tone

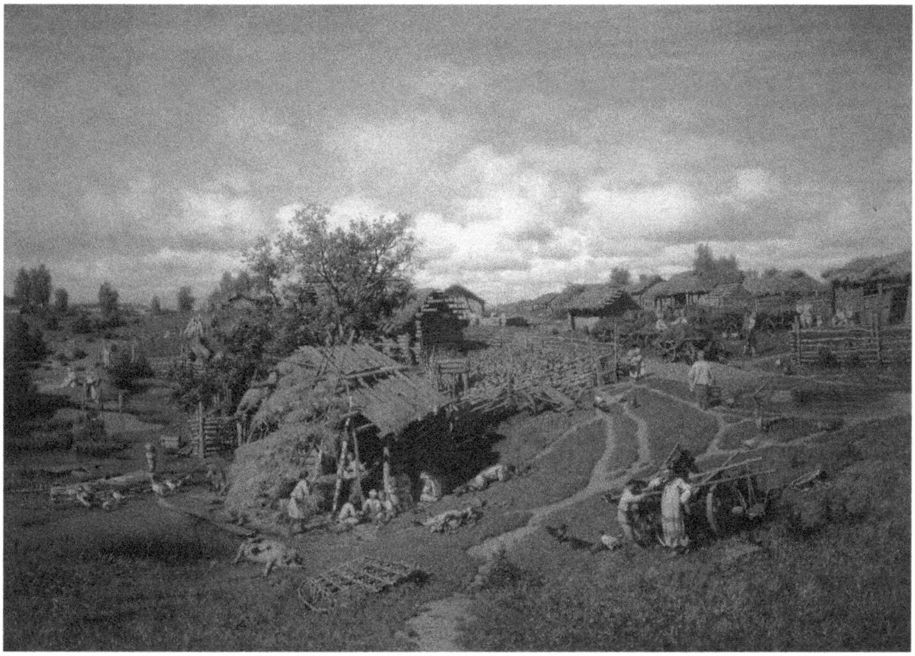

28 Petr Sukhodolsky, *Midday in the Countryside*, 1861, 101.5 x 142 cm

and presented with an unconventional naturalism. For a long time these remained exceptions to the academic norm, the dominance of which continued into the second half of the nineteenth century when distinctly 'native' landscapes began to appear with more consistency. Not until the 1850s were such scenes valued by Russian patrons, audiences and critics, a burgeoning acceptance that accompanied the literary intelligentsia's most consistent agitation for national subject matter as a means to asserting cultural independence.

Even then, and into the 1860s when art found a more overtly critical edge, scenes of human endeavour predominated. Perov's bleak, powerful and radically hard-hitting images of rural and urban hardships frequently made emotive use of landscape as complement to the human condition, paralleling the psychological state of his subjects; a vital component in convincing the spectator of the authenticity of his cheerless scenes. Occasionally, however, examples from the 1860s hinted at the promise to be realised by the Wanderers. *Midday in the Countryside* (figure 28) by Petr Sukhodolsky is a fascinatingly unorthodox work, a rambling, unidealised view of a scruffy, dilapidated Russian village with its haphazardly arranged buildings and seemingly random dirt tracks. The centre foreground, where academic tradition led the eye to something worthy of contemplation, inversely focuses on a rusting harrow, a piece of agricultural refuse littering the countryside, and a large unedifying sleeping sow having the fleas pecked from its rear by a magpie, a common carrion bird. The plethora of figures arranged in pleasing groups and poses still identify this as genre, but the peasants are too small to read physiognomy or emotions. The landscape predominates and the work successfully evokes the soporific heat and lazy air of a hot summer's noon. The whole is quaint and otherworldly for a modern viewer, but for its time represents a transgression of the ennobling, uplifting role of 'Art' via the environment of the tattered indigenous lower orders. In terms of subject and treatment this would have looked disconcertingly modern amongst the standard fare of the period.

Landscape and the Wanderers

The works of Perov and Sukhodolsky characterise in different ways the progressive 1860s when art was tentatively exploring new subjects and new possibilities of treatment. The advent of the Wanderers, however, placed landscape painting in something of an impasse. Where previously it had been sufficient to assert the legitimacy of native scenery over Italianate pastiches, it now faced the task of securing a role within an ostensibly critical-realist school under a more charged atmosphere of official scrutiny. Yet whilst this problem was being debated and its ends pursued, the Wanderers initiated a boom in native landscape painting. The genre was popular with artists, patrons and public alike, and it carried a 'feel good factor', evoking nationalist pride in the previously denigrated native scenery. Though less capable of expressing democratic ideals it was acceptable to all at least in its inoffensiveness and it allowed those artists who were never at ease with incorporating political or sociological overtones into their work to concentrate on purely artistic concerns. This was the place where one might seek relief from the sometimes oppressive content of genre, though the vogue for Russian landscapes was also heavily driven by the market. Merchant patrons paid well for them and can be credited with affecting a shift in purchasing trends that privileged native scenes.

A preoccupation with native imagery was in keeping with the Wanderers' objective of building a realistic, popular, national school of art and at their first exhibition over half the exhibits were landscapes. Their works were more authentic in their evocation of rural Russia, diminishing the picturesque use of models and allowing the land, rendered in natural tones and realistic detail, to become its own subject matter. But as with history painting, landscape was not popular with those who saw art's role as subsidiary to progressive causes. At the very first Wanderers' exhibition Aleksei Savrasov's *The Rooks Have Returned* (colour plate 5) was criticised for having made background its sole subject matter. The liberal paper *The Cause* (*Дело*) noted: 'In general, we do not very much like artists who have chosen landscape for their exclusive and only speciality ... such one-sidedness is strange to us ... Landscape is necessary to the artists as a background, as a decoration ... But by itself landscape is pointless.'[5]

On one occasion Repin admonished Stasov over the narrowness of his tastes, accusing the powerful critic of having no interest in landscape painting,[6] whilst for Garshin landscape was synonymous with superficiality, lack of commitment and leanings towards bourgeois respectability. In Garshin's short story 'Artists', the character of Dedov provides a wicked parody of the gentleman-painter who pursues an artistic animus for trite decorative landscapes.

A more sympathetic but similarly ineffectual image of the landscape painter is provided by Chekhov's short story 'The House with an Attic', subtitled 'An Artist's Story'. It tells of a would-be romance between a landscape artist and the young daughter of a wealthy land-owner which is broken up by the elder daughter. She, a teacher at the local council school who dispenses medical advice to the peasants and agitates for their political rights and welfare, disapproves of the lack of social commitment in his work, leading him to observe: 'She did not like me. She did not like me because, being a landscape painter, I did not depict the hard life of the common people on my canvases, and because she thought I was indifferent to what she believed in so firmly.'[7]

Even as late as 1903 Repin was dragged into speculative controversy in Russia and the United States when his innocent motif of a young couple walking on a tempestuous seashore, *Wide World* (1903, GRM) was subjected to critical scrutiny for subtext. Some, it seems, refused to believe that the one time *enfant terrible* of Russian art could indulge ingenuously in a genre synonymous with lack of commitment. An American writer speculated: 'Is it a warning, or is it a call to self-sacrifice?' An exasperated Repin complained that the public ascribed ulterior motives to his work and sought non-existent allegories: 'And on account of this allegory I am in turn abused, blamed and despised.'[8]

The difficulties evoked by landscape painting proved problematic for many artists, with the result that those most successfully associated with the genre tended to be specialists. The major practitioners discussed here – Savrasov, Shishkin, Vasilev, Levitan, Kuindzhi – are not noted for work in any other fields. They appear undesirous, perhaps even incapable, of working outside the genre. Even the best landscape painters sought assistance for figurative aspects: Konstantin Savitsky painted the bears for Shishkin's *Morning in a Pine Forest* (1889, GTG) whilst the female figure in Levitan's *Autumn Day. Sokolniki* (1879, GTG) was supplied by Nikolai Chekhov, brother of the famous author.[9] Others, like Repin, although highly competent in their use of landscape, tended to restrict it to that of a 'mood enhancer' for human drama. Within a hugely prolific career he produced almost no independent landscapes unconnected with preliminary studies for his major genre works.

The strength of landscape painting, however, was to prove itself over a longer period of time, and in other areas, to those that concerned Russian art criticism at the Wanderers' inception. Freed of constraints to encapsulate or illustrate progressive civic-minded ideas, the aesthetic aspects of art were more readily and consistently observable in landscape painting, and its practitioners surprisingly diverse. Savrasov proved the catalyst in this respect. A founder member of the Wanderers and a product of the more liberal Moscow School of Arts, he travelled widely through Russia, especially the Ukraine, and is almost single-handedly credited with ushering in a new, fresh, lyrical landscape with his work *The Rooks Have Returned* (colour plate 5). Using a restricted palette of browns, greys and blues Savrasov evokes a poetic yet realistic view of an unremarkable village at the end of winter: trees budding, snow melting, the earth beginning to reappear, the rooks returning to nest. Beyond the busy foreground the vast Russian countryside is already brown and snowless. The composition seems artless but is unconventional, the viewer's entry to the canvas and view of its main architectural features not facilitated, but blocked by the dirty bare trees and the scruffy array of birds and nests. But from such prosaic material Savrasov fashioned an image of arresting beauty and meaning. The spring thaw, the end of the excessively harsh, long dark winters, and the awakening of nature and of human activity were eagerly anticipated and celebrated in folk culture. Using such a modest motif the artist alludes to universal themes: nature's cycle and man's place within it, the coexistence and interdependency of nature and society.

A very different vision was provided by Ivan Shishkin another founder member and mainstay of the Wanderers who instead of the shift and variation of nature makes concrete and permanent its transient states in exacting detail. This is true particularly of his major canvases, where he earned himself a reputation for studious precision in a series of iconic images depicting the might and fecundity of the great Russian forests. Shishkin encapsulated for many a pride born of national identity, the quintessence of rural Russia; indeed his subjects – trees in one form or another – rarely varied. For many Shishkin's high-definition finish was the apogee of realist landscape, whilst for others he exposed its limitations. Kramskoy thought the prevalence of detail would distract from the overall harmony of Shishkin's works, and there is something in this. The temptation still, for a modern audience, is to get close to the canvas and marvel at the faultless technique. And yet there is much in Shishkin's work that is unconventional and experimental. In works such as *The Thicket* (colour plate 6), though it is painted with a pre-Raphaelite attention to detail, Shishkin frequently presents his viewer with a seemingly random, severely cropped but casual composition of the forest underbelly, its dead and fallen branches, the areas seldom penetrated by light. The moss-covered rocky interior appears as an unearthly but tranquil landscape, untouched and unspoiled by man, and the strong emphasis on vertical composition occasioned by the subject is heightened by cramming the picture plane, resulting in an unidealised and claustrophobic scene. The play of light is beautifully conceived but never the sole purpose of the canvas. It never obscures or transcends the material detail.

Frequently the use of haphazard arrangements – of dead trees, fallen or slanting, of gnarled moss-covered stumps and overgrown foregrounds – denies the viewer entrance to the scene, something academic landscape facilitated. Trees are asymmetrically arranged as opposed to the academic organisation of nature, but are pleasing nevertheless. A generation before this it would have been unthinkable to offer such disarmingly unpretentious images of dead and decaying interiors for exhibition. And though Shishkin's reputation was founded chiefly on large, highly finished canvases that seem intended for public rather than domestic spaces, his studies show an engrossment with natural phenomena, not only grand vistas and imposing interiors, but simple, unaffected patches of nature made worthy of independent appreciation. Shishkin studied the natural sciences seriously, seeking a precise artistic comprehension of Russian nature (his father was an amateur archaeologist and folklorist) and in his painstaking attention to light, tone and detail, it seems as if he was trying to reconstruct nature piecemeal in a style that might best be described as 'veristic'.

Shishkin was one of those rare artists who seemed to show no diminution of ability. His subject matter and style remained largely unchanged, his life-long passion for Russian scenery inexhaustible. His contribution to Russian landscape was one of clarity of vision, an exacting dispassionate realism, although nationalistic emotions accrued to his epic visions of the Russian forests. Whilst some, including Kramskoy, regarded Shishkin's output as over-burdened with detail, his uncontrived, purely native landscapes were certainly a vast improvement on the artificial arrangements of nature found in classical and romantic works and Kramskoy willingly acknowledged this contribution, stating: 'He is by himself a school ... a milestone in the evolution of the Russian landscape.'[10]

The observable differences of approach and style in the works of Savrasov and Shishkin illustrate the aesthetic and technical pluralism within landscape art that was less obvious in genre, where purpose and intent were given greater scrutiny. In each of the major practitioners of landscape painting a diversity of stylistic concern is made manifest precisely due to the absence of literary distractions. Pivotal in this respect, marking the transition between the founding realists and the next generation of more overtly aesthetically driven painters is Fedor Vasilev, a tragic figure who died aged twenty-three, but who packed his short and precocious life with a prodigious output and was considered by many of his peers as the most gifted painter of his generation. Vasilev was a protégé of Kramskoy's, whom he met at the artist's *Artel* and through whom he was introduced to Tretyakov who became a major patron, and Kramskoy saw in him an abundance of the versatility and flexibility he found lacking in Shishkin's more perfect technique and precise vision. Vasilev was an enthusiast for outdoor painting and was amongst those who took part in the journey down the Volga in 1870 from which came Repin's *Burlaki* (figure 3). Though never formally a member of the Wanderers he signed the Society's draft statutes as a gesture of support whilst still a student, a bold act which could have caused his expulsion from the Academy.

Vasilev was an admirer of the Barbizon school, which he studied from the Kushelëv-Bezborodko Collection housed within the Academy and which contained works by Delacroix, Courbet, Rousseau, Dupré, Diaz de la Peña, Decamps, Millet, Corot and Troyon amongst many. From such sources and his own proclivity towards outdoor painting he developed a preoccupation with landscapes of strong, emotional moods and a frequently sketchy technique, but never abandoned an essential naturalism. His more laconic scenes hint at the abundant promise his

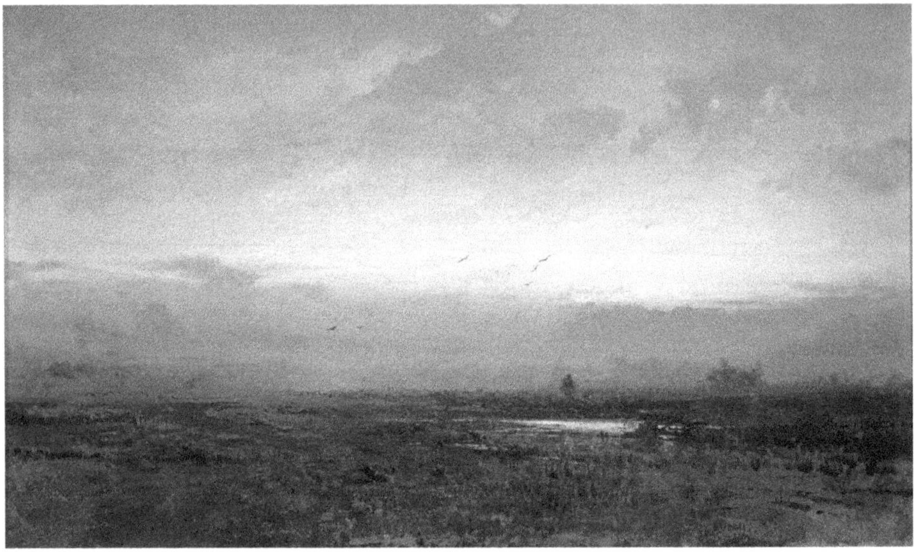

29 Fedor Vasilev, *Morning*, 1872–73, 58 x 96.5 cm

contemporaries saw with regards to an experimental direction. *Morning* (figure 29) is a remarkably simple work, seemingly without composition, the flat, open land merging with a dull sky, the mists just beginning to lift from the wet marshland, the grass in places still white with dew. Vasilev tests the limits of public acceptability with this unedifying tract of Russian bog land, a canvas by contemporary standards empty and without subject yet invested with an almost mystical treatment. His mood seems to match perfectly that of his patron Tretyakov who told the landscape painter Apollinary Goravsky: 'I need neither richness in nature nor effective use of light: no miracles. Give me a murky puddle, so long as it contains truth and poetry. There is poetry to be found in everything'.[11]

Vasilev's contribution to Russian landscape far exceeded his short career. He is recognised in Russia as one of the masters of the genre, depicting the Russian countryside with an overriding concern for artistic and aesthetic considerations, for impromptu effects of light and tone. In many ways his work appears to predict a promise that was later fulfilled by Isaak Levitan, regarded by many as the unrivalled talent of the Russian landscape school, an artist who provided Russian landscape painting with yet further diversification and, depending on one's viewpoint, progression.

From an impoverished Jewish background, orphaned early, Levitan attended the Moscow School of Arts under Savrasov and Polenov, the latter strongly influencing his preference for *plein air* painting and encouraging him to study contemporary French art. As a student abroad Polenov had been receptive to foreign art trends and in 1875 had journeyed to Normandy with Repin and other student friends to sketch and study the landscape. He specialised in genre works and particularly biblical themes, but was also highly regarded as a landscape artist. A progressively minded practitioner and teacher, Polenov was exercised chiefly by painterly problems and noted for a lack of didacticism. He maintained close links with young artists, fostering many of the more aesthetically minded talents of the next generation, often in the face of opposition from more conservative realists.[12]

Levitan developed under Polenov showing also an admiration for the Barbizon School, and studying *factura*, the actual method by which a painting is constructed – the use of paint and brushstrokes. He was particularly attracted to Corot's work though he largely eschewed the use of human figures, but almost always retained elements of human presence such as buildings and sought, like Vasilev, whose work he admired, to evoke human emotions from the moods of his landscapes. Unlike other artists he travelled widely abroad and was acquainted with French art. Initially he was unimpressed with contemporary French painting, especially Impressionism, and though he remained undecided about its merits he was later more intrigued about it, particularly the work of Monet.[13]

Though ever the consummate technician, Levitan's mode of practice is difficult to pin down. His treatment of subject is frequently light and lyrical, sometimes more brooding and elegiac, sometimes epic in its aspirations, his finish varying from tight and compact, to loose and sketchy. Indeed, when in 1879 Tretyakov purchased Levitan's *Autumn Day. Sokolniki* directly from the Moscow School of Arts' student show critics berated his selected of a 'daub', an 'unfinished sketch'.[14] At times Levitan concerned himself with seemingly random, unimportant themes, in a casual, sketch-like manner, affirming their independence as worthy subjects: a section of fencing and shrubbery, a patch of melting snow, or a small segment of forest. At other times fusions of landscape and human habitation evoke tenuous narratives. Frequently effects of light and colour are the true subject of his works, the emphasis on painting rather than subject rendered with impressionistic verve. Though he never embraced the broken or shimmering surfaces of late Impressionist landscapes, Levitan flirted with both experimental and traditional methods of painting, as if vacillating between the rendition of a fleeting moment, executed in a sketchy manner, or perfecting a specific, well-defined image.

Consistently, however, he professed an aspiration to evoke psychological responses from natural scenery, to paint landscapes complementary to the philosophical preoccupations of Russian realism – a project informed by his interest in Schopenhauer. The strains of this ambitious undertaking frequently saw his work imbued with momentous or despondent overtones that seem informed by Schopenhauer's pessimistic vision that humanity is shaped by the unconscious forces of nature. In this mode Levitan produced many works that evoke nature's almost unapproachable superiority, its eternal aspect towering oppressively over the evanescence of human life. Levitan felt these mortal limitations keenly, writing in 1887 to his close friend Chekhov: 'Can anything be more tragic than to feel the infinite beauty of your surroundings, to read nature's innermost secrets and, conscious of your own helplessness, to be incapable of expressing these powerful emotions?'[15]

This impulse towards an emotional catharsis underpins one of his most bleak, melancholic, but evocative landscapes, *The Vladimirka Road* (1892, GTG) showing on a relatively small canvas a vast, epic sweep of sky and land. The title is key as it transforms an otherwise proficient work into a major statement of intent. To a contemporary Russian audience this would have been a most atmospheric and haunting work, the road being the route by which convicts were forcibly marched to Siberian exile. The human misery which the land would have witnessed over generations seems to hang in the air, a prime example of Levitan exploiting a compatibility of landscape and human emotion with only the title providing the initial charge to what follows.

It would be unfair, however, to characterise Levitan as a psychologically inspired gloomy fatalist. His works are more diverse and as frequently in celebration of nature as they are in awe. *Spring Flood* (colour plate 7) shows a mature style that combines pleasing subject matter with compositional dexterity and inventiveness. Here Levitan emphasises the slender, ethereal nature of the bare white birches, reflected in the flood waters. Again, a human element is not abandoned; the boat and a small deluged hut give mute testimony to our presence, but aesthetic concerns are much to the fore as the trees and their reflection create an almost abstract quality of tranquil suspended forms, the laws of nature subverted and rendered groundless in this temporarily floating world.

Levitan died aged only forty, developing towards a more decorative simplification of form whilst still stressing the eternal aspect of nature and its supremacy over man. although, like most landscape productions of the Wanderers, his output might occasionally stir patriotic feelings, such nationalistic tendencies were alien to him. Within the Wanderers he was the most international in outlook even if his subject matter remained resolutely Russian. He travelled through Berlin, Munich, Vienna, Paris, Italy and Switzerland imbibing modern influences whilst retaining an allegiance to native subject matter. He was wooed by Diaghilev's *Mir iskusstva* from 1898 and exhibited at the Munich Sezession without breaking his ties to the Wanderers, a difficult cultural balancing act which few achieved. More than any of his contemporaries Levitan displayed his concern with light, colour and subtlety of mood as ends in themselves, for the process of painting beyond its ability to recreate convincingly the physical world.

Standing somewhat outside of all conventions and apart from his contemporaries is Arkhip Kuindzhi. A glorious exception to the standardisation of artistic production, the maverick Kuindzhi was of Greek origin, born in the Crimea and trained originally as a photographic re-toucher. Rejected by the Academy he remained essentially a self-taught artist but was fostered by Kramskoy, who offered encouragement and advice. He first exhibited with the Wanderers in 1874 gaining immediate success and notoriety for his unconventionality. *After the Storm* (figure 30) is typical of the concerns that dominated Kuindzhi's work: a delight in unorthodox colour, beautiful but unearthly landscapes, the commonplace made mysterious, almost alien, but poetically pleasing. The forms of nature are simplified, being totally dissimilar to Shishkin's precise documentation, everything geometrically sculpted by light rather than drawn. Mood and colour are strained to produce theatrical contrasts of light, but the essentially artificial nature of the work evokes wonderfully the passing storm. Such works have given rise to the tag 'the luminous school', though perhaps 'day glow' might be a more fitting epithet for the brilliance of Kuindzhi's colours, which were reputedly the result of his own closely guarded technical experiments. Similarly it has been asserted that Kuindzhi worked from memory without recourse to sketches, his works therefore devoid of detail and his compositions pure invention.[16]

Certainly Kuindzhi celebrated his individuality. At a time when the concept of the one-man show was a rarity his most celebrated work, *Moonlit Night on the Dnieper* (1880, GRM), was exhibited as a solitary canvas set against a black curtain under artificial lighting to showcase its deviancy. This painting, which still defies adequate reproduction, so successfully captured an effect of glimmering phosphorescent moonlight on clouds, water and the plains of southern Russia that apocryphal accounts had visitors to the exhibition caught trying to look behind the canvas, convinced it was artificially lit. As a radical experiment in technical trouble-shooting Kramskoy marvelled:

> I have known this picture for a long time, and seen it at all hours of the day, and in every kind of light, and I can safely say that the first time I looked at it I could not get rid of the physical feeling that my eyes were dazzled, as though by real moonlight, and every time I have seen it since, I have the same sensation[17]

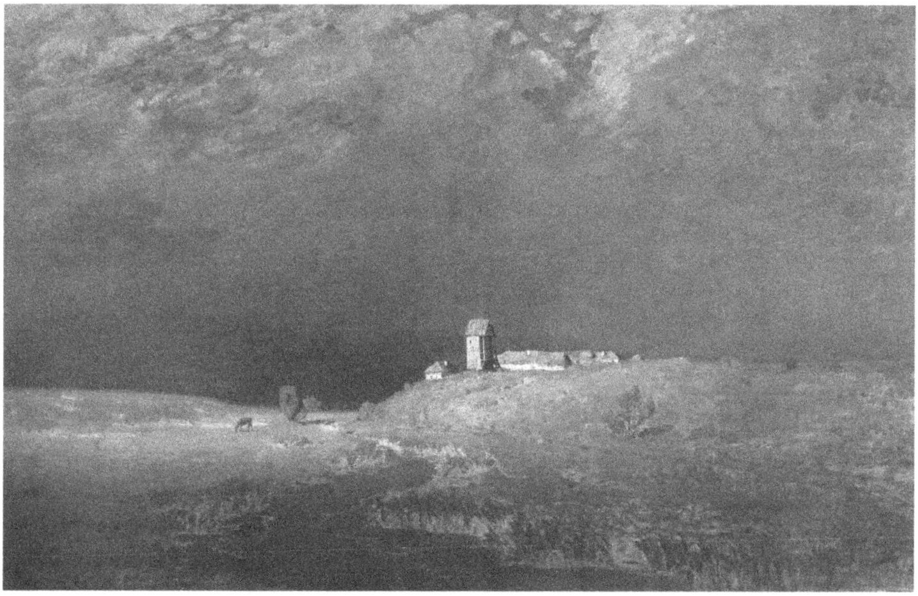

30 Arkhip Kuindzhi, *After the Storm*, 1879, 102 x 159 cm

Kuindzhi's career was dogged by controversy, though refreshingly these were of an aesthetic rather than socio-political nature, a point which refutes accusations that as a school the Wanderers were indifferent to style, though elements within the Society and the wider artistic community were exercised by any disregard of accepted conventions. Certainly Kuindzhi's unorthodox use of simplified forms and bold colours divided his realist colleagues. Mikhail Klodt accused him of ignoring the rules governing the gradual transition of colours between tones and of exhibiting 'impressions' rather than finished landscapes. Kramskoy was undecided; impressed but wary of a degeneration into superficial effects, whilst Yaroshenko, who admired Kuindzhi's talent, put Klodt's remarks down to jealousy.[18] But the rancour precipitated Kuindzhi's resignation from the Wanderers and after 1882 he ceased to exhibit, though between 1894 and 1897 he taught briefly at the then reformed Imperial Academy.

Kuindzhi's more personal works allowed him even greater freedom of experimentation and wilder liberties with colour. Though his influence was subdued by not exhibiting he continued to show to fellow painters and began to gather about him a group of young artists who formed a loose school. His works consistently showed simplification of forms, theatrical choices of subject and an idiosyncratic use of colour applied roughly. Kuindzhi advertised his fascination with the act of painting as well as his love of subject in a flamboyant, eye-catching manner. Frequently he painted the same scene in varying seasons, observing widely different states of light and colour without changing the motif. His importance to Russian landscape painting and to Russian art generally was pervasive in many areas. The drama of his works, the intensity and purity of his colour (if at times unnatural), his bizarre light effects, the simple, almost abstract nature of his designs, and the overtly technical and aesthetic concerns of his art directly influenced the art of his young followers, paving the way for the geometric, decorative elements of modern Russian art. Kuindzhi made the audacious nature of Impressionism seem almost tame in his precursing of the lurid colour schemes and distortions of form that fed symbolist and even avant-garde trends. Perhaps more than any other artist his influence was felt on late nineteenth- and early twentieth-century Russian art in the widest sense.

The landscape of mediation

Of all genres in Russian art landscape mutated the most and ossified the least. Its popularity and accessibility promoted its acceptance in terms of public approbation, critical approval and a healthy market base. Simultaneously, though surely unwittingly, it became an ideological and stylistic bridge between the conservatives and liberals, the traditionalists and the modernists. The nationalist, patriotic spirit of native landscapes, sometimes latent, sometimes overt, and a lack of socio-political content, meant it had something to offer both sides of the political divide, uniting critics and public of differing persuasions. Levitan's *The Vladimirka Road* is as close as landscape came to political comment, and then only by association.

Landscape nevertheless had other applications within the realist school. The most gifted genre painters used it emotively to parallel or enhance the psychological states of their subjects. Perov frequently utilised landscape to convince the audience of the cheerless authenticity of his scenes though it remained ancillary to his concerns; the brutalised existence of the peasantry. This is not, however, to diminish its importance. Deployed in this manner the land is not a passive backdrop but a carefully structured and integrated component making its own intervention, whether to harmonise with the figures in a desolate or oppressive manner, or to act as a foil, as with the insufferable conditions experienced by Repin's barge-haulers or Ivanov's migrant peasants. The land is as important an element as the participants and as carefully selected and arranged – a crucial and strategic gambit.

Landscape painting was also politicised in terms of the spectator and patronage. Its very existence presumes a spectator with sufficient wealth and leisure to be able to view the land as a source of contemplation, rather than a site of work. It is, however, extremely rare to find an image which structures the land purely as an object of reflection. Usually, of course, we are the spectator and our presence is taken for granted. The landscape is offered up for our consumption in the form of the painting, but spectatorship within the frame, on the part of the figures depicted, is not a feature of the Russian school. Polenov's *The Overgrown Pond* (1879, GTG) is singular in showing a portion of park land observed by a female figure sitting in a nearby arbour, an explicit imaging of the landscape being enjoyed as a leisured pastime.

But it is also relatively unusual to find mature Wanderers' landscapes filled with 'staffage' and structured as a working environment, the place of physical labour. Occasionally reapers and mowers put in an appearance but their toil is rarely exacting in the manner of Yaroshenko's *The Stoker* (figure 8) or Kasatkin's miners. The paradox which confronted artists accused of avoiding social issues and painting empty or 'pointless' scenes was that the inclusion of figures prompted a presumed critical tendency, forcing a transition whereupon the work converted to genre or 'modern history'. Adding figures effectively disqualified the work as landscape, at which juncture the populated image might be subjected to an examination of social conditions, the working masses, physical labour, agrarian hardships, and so on, regardless of the artists' intentions.

Perhaps the best example of the landscape as place of work is Konstantin Savitksy's *Repair Work on the Railway* (1874, GTG) a canvas filled with toiling labourers and modern telegraph wires which doubtless provides a reliable record of the industrial transformation of the land, but which hardly qualifies for consideration under the rubric 'landscape'. Hence the quote in *The Cause* that 'by itself landscape is pointless' emphasises the 'by itself'. This is logical given an ideology that asks art to go beyond the decorative or descriptive, but within that confine the land was nevertheless an important factor in shaping a critical, realist view of contemporary society. It was a powerful and malleable cultural tool the potential of which the Wanderers fully exploited.

From a contemporary discourse, however, it was unusual for artists to question the prevalent view of Russian landscape painting as being devoid of ideas and attuned solely to a national audience and an internal ideological discourse. The painter Aleksei Bogolyubov challenged such prejudices:

> My opinions are very extreme. I do not belong in any way to artists here [that is, in Russia]. They all cry that the idea must come above everything else in a painting. But what is this idea? What sort of idea in their understanding is there, for example, in a landscape? ... They [progressive Russian artists] demand only proclamations of some sort of social views, of some sort of Russian art. But what is Russian art? It does not and cannot exist. What there is, is a pan-European art – yes! I have argued with Stasov about this on countless occasions. I ask why, for example, Turgenev and Dostoevsky are being read in translation everywhere nowadays? Because they have a true art which affects every man, and not just some jingoistic Russian sense. The same is true of painting. Everybody, not just a Russian, must be able to admire a painting.[19]

Though this was an uncommon view landscape painting did affect a range of artistic and cultural interventions. Stylistically and emotionally it broke from the schematic conventions of classical and romantic models to produce fresher, brighter, more natural and most importantly *native* views in a variety of stylistic treatments. Latterly the painterly aestheticism of Levitan and the distortions of colour and form of Kuindzhi provided a springboard for the evolving strands of modernism. In all of its facets landscape painting was one of the major and enduring achievements of the Wanderers which carried the society forward and motivated it aesthetically when the edifice of a national school threatened to be lost entirely under the weight of political expediency.

In so doing it greatly promoted the acceptability and popularity of the realist school, yet unwittingly its lack of contentious subject matter and its nationalistic appeal paved the way for an eventual rapprochement with the forces of officialdom. The roots of this were early exposed when in 1872, after the first Wanderers exhibition, the Empress ordered a copy of Savrasov's *The Rooks Have Returned*; the same year Mikhail Klodt accepted a teaching post at the Imperial Academy, nearly twenty years before its reform. Even the progressively Francophile Benois became prone to shed his modernity and give vent to nationalistic sentiments when asserting the indigenous character of the seemingly cosmopolitan Levitan, proclaiming him 'neither a Barbizon, nor a Dutchman, nor an Impressionist, nor is he all of these put together. Levitan is a Russian artist'.[20] Dostoevsky was one of many conservative critics who, whilst castigating tendentious narratives, found much to admire and encourage in Russian landscapes. In part the success of the genre was due to the substantial patronage available, but apolitical artists also found refuge in landscape painting at a time when one's ideological motives were under close scrutiny. Their actions, however, ensured the society's reputation as an agent of liberal thought was further compromised and the celebration of things Russian continued unabated.

8

The Slavic Revival

The nationalist impulses that informed the Wanderers' production, and were in turn nurtured by aspects of the society's practice, fed also into a wider revival of interest in indigenous cultures. Addressing the nation's history and imaging the Motherland were areas of potential conservatism that might be perceived as promoting a romantic or nostalgic national discourse. Despite the contingencies of critical analogies in history painting or stylistic diversity and experimentation in landscape painting, these were deliberations easily interpreted as a desire to represent and promote Slavic-based ideals and cultural models, which in turn implied a rejection of Western paradigms.

Such tendencies were not new. The Slavophile–Westerniser debates ranged throughout the nineteenth century under various guises, and by the time the Wanderers had matured into a vital and dominant cultural force efforts to study, record and preserve the national heritage were long established. The reign of Nicholas I witnessed extensive archaeological researches into icon painting and its techniques, wooden architecture, folk tales, folk music and other manifestations of Slavic culture. During this period and into the reign of Aleksandr II (1855–81) archaeological societies were established in St Petersburg in 1846 and in Moscow in 1864. State-funded research into Russia's under-investigated art history resulted in 1852 in the publication of six sumptuously coloured folio volumes of *Antiquities of the Russian Empire*.

Whilst these symptoms of the desire to investigate and preserve the Russian heritage were overt and benign, a more insidious strain of nationalism broke out with purposeful vigour during the reign of Aleksandr III (1881–94). A man of legendary conservatism whose lack of intellect was acknowledged by even his staunchest supporters, Aleksandr was a blunt, domineering autocrat who adhered strictly to the divinely appointed status of the Tsar and whose reactionary rule was characterised by harsh judicial reforms, the assumption of summary powers of arrest, deportations, tighter press restrictions and the introduction of trials by military courts. But he was also a wily and pragmatic opponent. He supported industrial development, upheld the Orthodoxy and set about a thorough 'Russification' of political life, which included the court adopting the Russian language in place of French and German.

Aleksandr was also instrumental in advancing a native, religious and Slavic-inspired culture to similarly 'Russify' the art scene. Ethnocentricity became the keynote as Russian models began to replace imported styles of architecture and design. In pursuance of a nationalist agenda Aleksandr favoured the robust, nationally engaged realism of the Wanderers to the exclusivity and foreignness of the classical heritage and academic style. His efforts to bring the best realist painters under his patronage and guidance were assisted by the ambiguities inherent in the Wanderers' ethos, its output and its financial base, as well as extraneous political developments which were astutely capitalised upon. For example, the intelligentsia's extensive respect for the peasantry, which fed the idealism of the Populist cause, had been entangled from early on with the veneration of national culture and might be subverted to loyalist ends. Similarly, the obscuring of political and cultural differences engendered by the Russo-Turkish War of the late 1870s, and the patriotic nationalism that attended it, were issues the Tsar was able to exploit. Intervention on behalf of the oppressed Slavic 'brethren' had been supported by left and right, and broadly by many of the Wanderers, to the extent that the popularity of the Society was increasingly regarded as posited on a national discourse.

Merchant patronage was also influential in its preference for ethnocentric subject matter, images of the pre-Petrine Russia from whose lineage they drew identity. In many respects the 'nationalisation' of the Wanderers was under way early on, and was a process in which the Society colluded. The Slavic Revival of the 1870s grew with these influences, and with the birth and development of the Wanderers, resulting in an eclectic use of Old Russian stylistic devices, the 'Neo-Slavic' as it was sometimes described, in art, architecture, design, the decorative arts and the theatre. The Church of the Resurrection, for instance, built between 1883 and 1897 over the place of Aleksandr II's assassination, was executed in a sixteenth-century form in keeping with the revivalist ethos of many 'contemporary' state projects.

The Slavic Revival as a phenomenon encompassed all areas of cultural output, as well as such diverse fields as politics, economics, history and philology, but within the visual arts it was never specifically allied to the Wanderers. It did, however, draw some of its principle practitioners into related fields and further from the founding ethos of the society. Under its aegis Surikov devoted his life to reconstructions of Old Russia whilst others delved further into the realms of myth, legend, fantasy and romantic spirituality. Two major influences that informed the Slavic Revival, and intriguingly illustrate how nationalism might act as a coefficient between the new world of mercantile finance and the old world of aristocratic privilege, came from the work produced on the estates of the industrialist Savva Mamontov at Abramtsevo and of Princess Tenisheva at Talashkino.

Forward to the past: Abramtsevo and Talashkino

Situated about forty kilometres north-east of Moscow the estate of Abramtsevo, owned by Mamontov and his wife Elizaveta, was the catalyst to propelling an indigenous artistic renewal to the cultural fore. Mamontov was a leading railway magnate, whilst Elizaveta came from a family with factory interests in silk-weaving. The estate was purchased in 1870 (the year of the first Wanderers' exhibition) and under their progressive patronage, guided by principles not dissimilar to those of William Morris and the Arts and Crafts movement, an artistic colony was established that approached the revival and patronage of then dying Russian art forms from the pragmatic perspectives of production and marketing.

Mamontov was a man of diverse practical interests including music, sculpture, theatre direction and drama. Elizaveta's prominent and industrious influence diversified into artistic, ecclesiastical and social areas including the collection of peasant folk art and the revival of its production methods, the study and revival of the Orthodox liturgy, late Roman and early Church architecture, as well as the establishment of a school on the estate which took in local peasant children, at which she taught. More broadly the estate fostered and patronised the production of a wide range of folk arts including icons, wood-carving, embroidery, children's toys and ordinary household utensils. This was not, however, a purely romantic venture, and with characteristic business acumen Mamontov used his commercial contacts to further his activities. His brother Anatoley publicised the estate's achievements

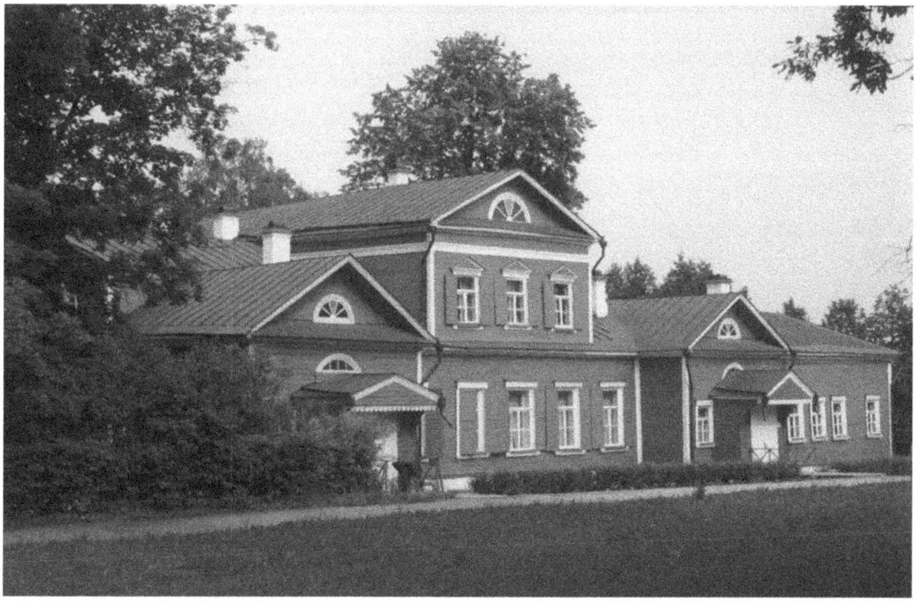

31 The Mamontov house, Abramtsevo, c.1790

through his influential printing house whilst Anatoley's wife distributed Abramtsevo artefacts through her Moscow toy store.[1]

But the estate was also the site of religious activity and a genuine spiritual revivalism. Geographically it is adjacent to the Old Russian spiritual centres of the 'Golden Ring', a circle of ancient Russian cities and towns that encircle the north-east of Moscow, including Vladimir, Suzdal, Yaroslavl, Rostov and the Trinity Monastery of St Sergius (the terminus for Mamontov's Moscow railway line). The traditional wooden estate house (figure 31) where Gogol reputedly wrote his masterpiece *Dead Souls* had previously belonged to Sergei Aksakov, the spiritual father of the Slavophile movement, to whom Elizaveta Mamontova dedicated a room preserved as during the writer's lifetime. This was seen as a suitable location from which to engender a revival of the indigenous Russian arts, which were in dire need of preservation. As the artist Ivan Bilibin noted: 'Russian folk art is dying; it has nearly died. The currents of modern life sweep it away, and only in a few places, deep in the most remote areas, do its last feeble sparks still smolder.'[2]

The irony was that whilst the Mamontovs' estate was seeking a cure to this cultural demise, their industrial interests were also the cause. After emancipation, large commercial interests drew the peasant labour force into urban factories which simultaneously usurped their established means of production as the cottage industries and craft workshops of traditional domestic arts, even icons, were overtaken by methods of mass production.[3] In addition to a patronage that came from the industrial urbanisers implicit in the erosion of the native arts, there was also the paradox that the artists who worked on the estate were academically trained professionals who in varying degrees of dedication were effectively 'dabbling' in these traditional crafts. The nucleus of the Abramtsevo colony at various times included Vasily Polenov and his sister Elena, Viktor and Apollinary Vasnetsov, Antokolsky, Repin, Nesterov, Serov and Mikhail Vrubel. Surikov was also an occasional contributor to their communal creations. Here Repin made studies for *Religious Procession in the Province of Kursk* (colour plate 1) found his inspiration for *The Zaporozhye Cossacks* (figure 27) and painted *They Did Not Expect Him* (colour plate 2), setting his drama in the estate house. Nesterov used the surrounding landscape in *The Vision of the Boy Bartholomew* (colour plate 8) and Serov's portrait of Mamontov's daughter Vera, *Girl with Peaches* (figure 36) was completed in the main house.

The communality of Abramtsevo extended to artists' families participating in revivalist projects, amateur dramatics and operatic productions, so much so that amongst the many new buildings erected on the estate were a sculpture studio and artists' living quarters. Activities were pursued with characteristic enthusiasm, family members assisting in all aspects of architectural decoration, even taking a hand in ornamental carving on the scaffolding. Mamontov's son, Andrei, was an accomplished furniture designer whilst Maria Yakunchikova, Polenov's wife, ran wood-carving and embroidery workshops on the estate, assisted by Elena Polenova. Polenova trained as an historian but under Abramtsevo's influence became a noted theatrical designer and illustrator incorporating folk forms into her work. She began by carving wooden toys on the estate and was instrumental in fostering the study and collection of carved wooden ornamentation, textiles and utensils. This provided work and training for the local population, but in so far as research was pursued on traditional designs and working methods, and the workshop produced items which could be marketed commercially through Mamontov's business outlets, the organisation and training of the workshops, as well as the distribution of the Abramtsevo 'product', were under the supervision of an educated elite.

Revivalist building was also a major feature of artistic activity as the main house was augmented with a range of Neo-Slavic designs. In 1871, following a cholera epidemic, Viktor Hartmann (whose works are the subject of Musorgsky's *Pictures at an Exhibition*) designed a peasant hospital which served the surrounding peasant population, and in 1873 Ivan Ropet designed a traditional communal bath-house. On Mamontova's initiative a school house was later added incorporating a carpentry workshop. Some architectural projects were conceived in a spirit of fun, such as Viktor Vasnetsov's tiny wooden peasant *izba* mounted on chicken's feet (from the traditional Russian fairy-tale of the witch Baba Yaga) which served as a play house for the Mamontov children. Others were more ambitious, particularly the project for the design and erection of the small Church of the Saviour 1880–82 (figure 32). This building might be said to mark the beginning proper of the Neo-Slavic in architecture since, whilst previous endeavours were marked by the enthusiastic but indiscriminate use of folk motifs and patterns applied to hybrid designs, the Church of the Saviour was the outcome of sincere and sustained research and a purer use of a revivalist style based on the Church of the Saviour at Nereditsa near Novgorod (1198). Input was provided by the art historian Andrei Prakhov, the architect Mikhail Samarin and chiefly by Polenov and Viktor Vasnetsov, all of whom had interests in Russian medieval ecclesiastical architecture. Polenov supplied the initial design and contributed scientific and archaeological knowledge utilising documentation inherited from his father, a pioneer archaeologist with a wide knowledge of medieval Russian painting and architecture. Group excursions were taken to study authentic Slavic architecture around the immediate vicinity of the Golden Ring and further afield to Novgorod and Pskov.

In the light of these visits Vasnetsov modified Polenov's design to incorporate more buttresses and shifted the front elevation to a slightly asymmetrical single-domed building. In addition he decorated windows, painted icons, and designed and laid the floral mosaic floor. In keeping with the communal approach to the project Polenov designed the iconostasis and was assisted in painting the icons and ornamentation by Repin, Mamontova and the Vasnetsov brothers. Mamontova, Polenova and Yakunchikova embroidered vestments and Antokolsky contributed sculptural work with the help of Mamontov and his son Andrei. In 1882 the church was consecrated and used for family services, weddings and burials. It still functions today.

The Church of the Saviour marked a serious communal venture underpinned by

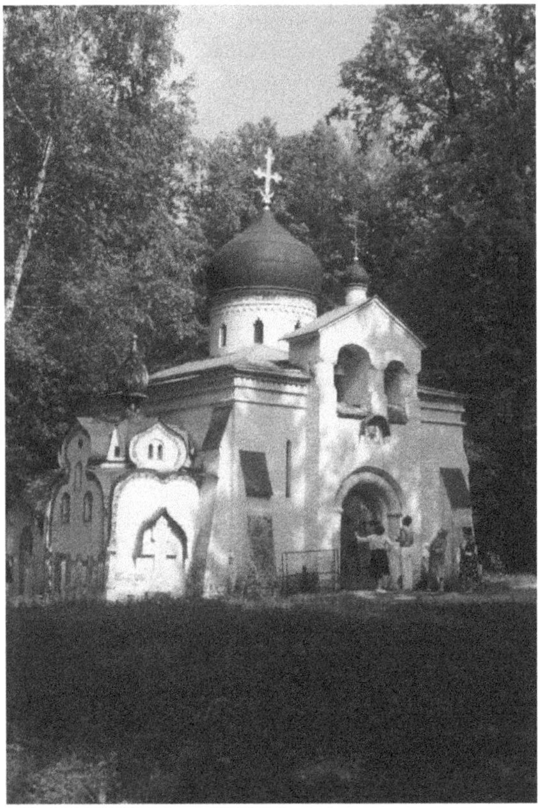

32 Vasily Polenov & Viktor Vasnetsov, *Church of the Saviour*, Abramtsevo, 1880–82.

religious conviction and historicising cultural aspirations to revive a true Russian style. Polenov said of the significance of Abramtsevo: 'It was the lot of this small ordinary-looking place to witness a life which was to play a valuable part in the history of Russian culture, and to become the cradle of a movement for reviving the national spirit in Russian art'.[4] Whilst this is true of the important influence the colony exerted on national life, the combination of enthusiasm and disparate aims, as well as varied levels of commitment (Repin never again worked in these fields and seems to have been indulging in a vacation pastime) somewhat dissipated its focus. Mamontov, for instance, though a willing participant at every level, was more devoted to the theatre and in 1885 established his private opera company, which utilised the talents of Viktor Vasnetsov and Polenov (still, it should be remembered, leading members of the Wanderers) who designed costumes and sets incorporating archaising folk motifs. It met with moderate success before being relaunched in 1896 to enjoy international acclaim, now using younger artists from Diaghilev's *Mir iskusstva* stable. Konstantin Stanislavsky, the father figure of the method school of acting, first worked at Mamontov's private theatre, providing an unlikely link with twentieth-century cinematic modernity.

Matters came to an abrupt halt in 1899 when Mamontov was arrested for misappropriation of funds. He was acquitted in July 1900 but declared insolvent, his patronage effectively at an end. He died in 1918 but his legacy proved of great influence to Russian art, traditional and modern. The Abramtsevo colony was of huge importance to the study, preservation and promotion of the traditional Russian arts, as well as an influential force in the flowering of Russian modernity; first through Art Nouveau applications, or the *style moderne* as it was known in Russia, and developing further in the synthesising of the arts which Diaghilev so spectacularly brought to fruition. In many respects his work can be seen as a continuation or development of the Mamontovs' objectives, albeit with different emphases.

Those objectives also informed the ambitious project of the colony at Talashkino established by the last of the great aristocratic patrons, Princess Maria Tenisheva (1867–1928).[5] A seemingly improbable saviour of the indigenous folk arts, Tenisheva was an accomplished artist also interested in wider questions of educational reform. Wealthy in her own right, she married Prince Tenishev in 1892, the owner of large resources in railways and foundries, who gifted her the estate near Smolensk and gave her free reign in its organisation and cultural development. Tenisheva dismissed with scorn the life of fashionable society, a role preordained for her class and gender, and set herself instead the formidable task of propagating a complete Russian cultural revival, particularly in the peasant arts. Functioning between the early 1890s and 1917, Talashkino attracted the best of a younger generation of talent including Vrubel, Konstantin Korovin, Nikolai Roerikh, Aleksandr Golovin and Sergei Malyutin, as well as the young Stravinsky. Like Abramtsevo, Talashkino was established as an artistic colony for diverse activities and artistic enterprises including theatrical productions, a major church project and various constructions in a Neo-Slavic style. Roerikh, an artist with theosophical Eastern leanings, later to contribute costume designs to the infamous 1913 production of Stravinsky's *Rite of Spring*, completed interior frescoes for the Church of the Holy Spirit as well as a dramatic mosaic façade comprising a huge, wide-eyed and forbidding face of the Saviour. Tenisheva also ran a peasant school, teaching agriculture and handicrafts, and later established workshops for embroidery and woodwork as well as a ceramics studio overseen by Elena Prakhova, the designer daughter of the art historian Andrei.

Malyutin, a member of the Abramtsevo colony, directed much of the building work on the estate and was a proficient designer of furniture in the heavier *style moderne* that marked Talashkino wares. Tenisheva herself was a competent painter and designer who successfully marketed her products through her own Moscow store as well as showcasing the estate's wares at the 1900 Paris Exposition. Amongst her many ventures aimed at artistic diversification and unhindered participation was the Tenisheva Studio, established in 1893 in St Petersburg for students who fell short of the Academy's educational requirements. This was directed by Repin between 1895 and 1898, who taught free of charge and boasted that he never refused a student. Its ethos of informality and lack of bureaucracy made it very popular and it remained open until 1904. A provincial counterpart was established in Smolensk between 1896 and 1904. Tenisheva also supported *Mir iskusstva* but was largely exploited by Diaghilev, who saw her principally as an income stream (in a cartoon of 1900 she was depicted as a cow being milked by the impresario!).

Tenisheva was, however, a diverse and committed patron whose dedication, energy and talents were skilfully deployed. Her abiding legacy was the establishment in 1898 of the Museum of Russian Antiquities and Folk Art at Talashkino, which grew to a collection of some ten thousand pieces and was eventually rehoused in 1905 in Smolensk. This included antique artefacts, old domestic embroideries, woodcarvings and metalwork collected throughout the provinces. Her personal interest was the history and technique of enamelling, on which she wrote a doctoral thesis in 1916 for the Moscow Archaeological Institute.

Like Abramtsevo, the momentum of Talashkino again foundered, though in this instance due to wider political developments. Rising unrest occasioned labour disputes at the estate's workshops and in 1906 Tenisheva left for Paris where she continued her work and where she eventually died. Though often given less credit than the Mamontovs for influencing the direction of Russian visual and decorative culture, Tenisheva was not merely a follower of the Abramtsevo experiment. Talashkino wares were distinctively of a more modern character and more eclectically diverse. Roerikh's work on the Church of the Saviour was likened to Tibetan and Thai influences, whilst Malyutin's decoration for the estate's Teremok, traditionally the place of female seclusion, was an extravagant gesture adapting peasant forms to modern decorative sensibilities.

The strength of the Slavic Revival encompassed all these diverse activities and to the dismay of many liberals the romance of Old Russia became incorporated into the wider cultural sphere, where Aleksandr III's effective management of the situation proved him to be a more astute manipulator than his 'peasant Tsar' image suggested. State patronage was increased by over 250 per cent to augment the state's buying power and funds were consistently channelled to public commissions of a Neo-Slavic design or reworkings of old Muscovite styles.[6] Cathedrals, churches, civic buildings, banks, shops and railway stations, all adopted revivalist styles. Preceding Aleksandr's coronation the Kremlin's Faceted Chamber, built in 1491 as a throne room and now the Tsar's audience chamber and state banqueting room, was stripped of its velvet hangings and redecorated with religio-historic frescoes in a Byzantine iconic style which incorporated aspects of perspective and naturalism in the figures, marking them out as contemporary adaptations of traditional models. At the far end of the Tsar's reign the Slavic impulse remained dominant in the style of the Moscow City Duma erected in 1892. Aleksandr maintained a consistent track record in these areas, supporting the inception of the Imperial Russian Historic Society as early as 1866, backing a variety of restoration projects throughout his life, and inaugurating the Historical Museum in Moscow in 1883 – housed in a suitably nationalist structure. Aleksandr's tastes and aspirations in many ways matched those of the *nouveau riche* industrialists who in seeking to assert their Slavic heritage built their luxurious town houses and sumptuous apartments in revivalist styles. In doing so Aleksandr was in part continuing a trend that had started with much earlier attempts to express a national identity. Aleksandr Ton's Cathedral of Christ the Redeemer in Moscow, for instance, was begun in 1839 in the reign of Nicholas I as the first effort to cast a major ecclesiastical monument in a new Russian style, but it was completed in 1889 under Aleksandr as part of a much wider and more forceful promulgation of his own loyalist agenda.

Stasov scornfully dismissed the whole Slavophilia vogue and its ill-defined unfocused nature as 'neither new, nor national, nor even a style'.[7] But whilst the Slavic Revival drew adherents of disparate proclivities and talents into an often incoherent wholesale exploitation of medieval and folk art forms, its popularity and influence was unquestionably pervasive and very quickly infiltrated the fine arts. In painting, the splendour and turbulence of Russian history became interwoven with scenes of a semi-mythological nature, engendered by and in turn promoting a mood of national revival, a sense of pride in the hitherto disparaged native arts. Case studies in this instance are Viktor Vasnetsov (1848–1927) and Mikhail Nesterov (1862–1942) whose careers were subverted by these trends from realist inclinations to Slavic romanticism.

Out of this world: Viktor Vasnetsov and Mikhail Nesterov

Like Surikov, Vasnetsov's background was at variance with many of his contemporaries.[8] The son of a Siberian village priest he came from a patriarchal milieu where strong folk traditions were still much alive. He entered a seminary before joining the Academy in 1868 and a decade later became a member of the Wanderers. His early works are prototypical of the Wanderers' approach to genre; factual, no-nonsense views of everyday life amongst the lower classes. Characteristic of these are *Moving House* (1874, GTG), a Perov-like treatment of an indigent elderly couple carrying their meagre belongings through a desolate winter cityscape, and *Tea Drinking in the Tavern* (1874, Kharkov State Museum of Fine Art), a wonderful parade of peasant types in an engagingly authentic dilapidated interior.

In 1878, the year Vasnetsov joined the Wanderers, he, like Surikov, conceived a growing passion for Old Moscow and Russia's medieval past, fuelled largely by his work at Abramtsevo, though in turn Vasnetsov did much to popularise the Slavic Revival and these twin strains fed off each other with oscillating vigour. Putting aside his modern genre works Vasnetsov embarked on a series of large, decorative scenes from Russia's distant, semi-mythical past, later moving into the realms of fairy stories and pure fantasy which garnered praise from those parts of the intelligentsia infected by Slavophile tendencies. In his review of the Wanderers' 1876 exhibition Andrei Prakhov, who worked with Vasnetsov at Abramtsevo, sanctioned the artist's new-found subject matter as an important contribution to the development of a Russian school of painting.[9]

More typically on the left, Stasov described his art as weak and fanciful, or at times simply ignored its existence. *After Prince Igor's Battle with the Polovtsy* (1880, GTG)

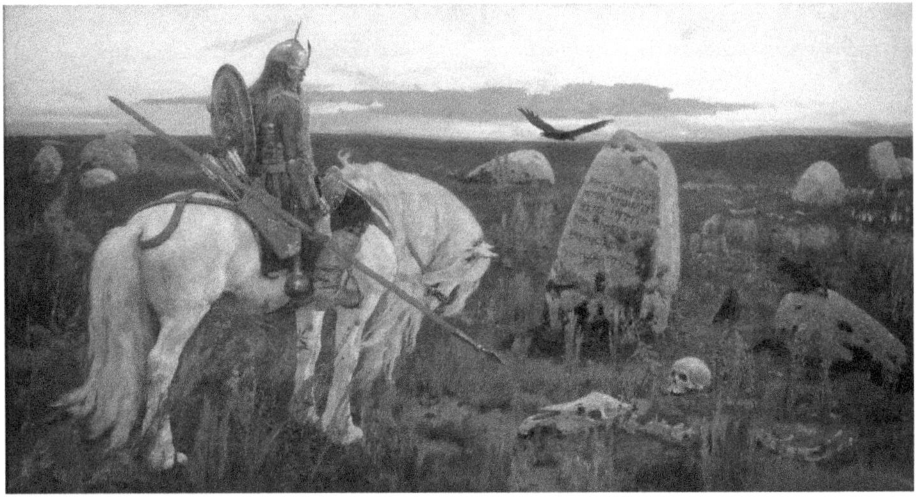

33 Viktor Vasnetsov, *Warrior at the Crossroads*, 1883, 167 x 299 cm

based on the great twelfth-century epic *The Lay of Igor's Host*, was Vasnetsov's first retreat from modern life subjects into 'historical' painting – as historical for instance as Victorian images of King Arthur's Camelot, in that the legends are presumed to have a basis in fact. One of four large panels commissioned by Mamontov for the central offices of the Moscow terminus of his Don Railway, then under construction, it depicts on an epic scale (205 × 390 cm) the warrior defenders of the Motherland fallen on the field of battle set in a broad, bleak landscape dwarfed by a vast sky. The others in the series included *The Magic Carpet* (1880, Nizhny Novgorod Art Museum) *Three Tsarevnas of the Underground Kingdom* (1881, GTG) and *Warrior at the Crossroads* (figure 33).

Although rejected by the railway's board and subsequently acquired by Mamontov, the works show shared concerns in the development of Vasnetsov's style and approach. All are essentially mannered, artificial images making use of monumental, concrete figures, and utilising non-naturalistic colour schemes, flat compositions and decorative surfaces where recession and depth are frequently evoked only by the foreshortening of figures or elements of landscape. *Prince Igor's Battle* foreshadowed critical debates that would attend much of Vasnetsov's output. Though Repin admired it Stasov was contemptuous, pointedly ignoring it at the society's exhibition of 1880 and only belatedly giving it an unfavourable review when using it as a tool with which to castigate Vasnetsov's entire artistic direction. Myasoedov and Yaroshenko threatened to resign if it was exhibited, though this proved hollow and it was not only shown but immediately acquired by Tretyakov.[10]

Warrior at the Crossroads takes Vasnetsov's work into more arcane and philosophical territory. An elegiac and melancholic piece of painting it shares pretensions akin to Kramskoy's *Christ in the Wilderness* (figure 14), being essentially a meditation on a universal theme, perhaps allied to the present (though 'podtekst' seems wholly alien to Vasnetsov's approach) but certainly of a didactic nature. The medieval warrior, like Kramskoy's Christ, addresses a moment of moral decision. One of the paths which he must chose is easy, the other, of which the runic stone gives dire warning, is hard and fraught with danger, but is the path which legend dictates must be followed. The work is a comment on courage, nobility, personal commitment and the willingness to suffer in the pursuit of one's convictions. The theosophical pretensions of the canvas are heightened by the deployment of a mystic, symbolic landscape conceived in luridly dramatic, unnatural colours in which lie the macabre skeletal remains of a previous, unsuccessful quest. The mind boggles at this bizarre scene accompanying Don Railway board members in their business deliberations, yet it works as a salon piece, aspiring to a greater depth of intellectual engagement than any of Vasnetsov's previous works and stepping outside of the fantastic recreation of myth-history towards the first stirrings of Russian symbolism; which serves to underscore the misgivings of the adherents of the realist school.

Vasnetsov's career developed, however, along more prosaic lines as the painterly illustrator of Russian legend and possibly the Society's most popular artist. His monumental decorative commissions brought him great fame whilst his prolific images of Russian folklore were reproduced throughout his lifetime and hung in many ordinary homes, most significantly *The Bogatyrs* (1898, GTG), depicting the legendary heroes of the *Byliny*, the epic cycle of folk tales. So ingrained were many of Vasnetsov's images in modern Russian culture that they were frequently accorded the dubious honour of appropriation by commercial advertising. The Weiner Brewery in Atrakhan adapted *Warrior at the Crossroads* to sell its produce, substituting the knight's lance for a large corkscrew and the runic stone for a bottle of its liqueur![11]

Vasnetsov is a good example of an artist whose divergence from mainstream realism greatly exercised not only his contemporaries but later taxed Soviet art historians. In a paradoxical manner his work is not dissimilar to the paradigm of Soviet Realism in that it encompasses mass aspiration through the medium of popular culture and seeks to image romantically what should be, rather than what is, a form of 'true lies'. But where Soviet aspiration gave shape to a 'coming into being' Vasnetsov looked wistfully to a 'what might have been' based on traditional religious values which humanist contemporaries and subsequent Soviet art history found difficult to absorb. In general terms commentators most consistently stressed the nationalism and patriotism inherent in those works depicting the heroic mythology of a warrior nation, but Vasnetsov also made many forays into the realms of pure fantasy.[12] Whilst this was not wholly unprecedented – at the first Wanderers' exhibition Kramskoy had shown his *Rusalki* (1871, GTG), an image of water spirits taken from Gogol's *May Night*, and in music folk myths and fairy-tales had long been exploited – such images were not seen consistently at

Wanderers exhibitions before Vasnetsov and were far removed from the Society's founding ethos. But they were hung. The titles of Vasnetsov's mature and often large-scale works suffice to indicate his direction: *Ivan Tsarevich Riding the Grey Wolf* (1889, GTG), *Snow White* (1899, GTG), *Sleeping Beauty* (1900–26) and *The Princess Who Never Smiled* (1914–16, both Vasnetsov Museum, Moscow).

Of course it could be argued that fairy stories are of serious concern in that they psychologically address important underlying issues of sex and gender, good and evil, fear and love, and in another context modern readings might yield much from these images. Particularly disturbing in this respect is *A Song of Joy and Sorrow* (1896, GTG) showing Sirin and Alkonost, birds of good and evil omen, widely familiar through peasant *lubki*, made frighteningly palpable by grafting convincingly real female heads onto animal bodies to produce an image worthy of a circus freak show. This seems to beg a Freudian reading, but Vasnetsov's take on Russian fantasy is more consistently of an illustrative nature, giving a contemporary shape and new interpretations to well-worn narratives; to make the familiar fresh and alive again.

Vasnetsov is also rare amongst the Wanderers in that he was active in all fields of visual production. For Abramtsevo he made architectural designs and executed all manner of decorative schemes. He designed the Neo-Slavic main façade for Tretyakov's gallery and in 1894 designed and built his own house in a fairy-tale style (which now sits incongruously amidst a drab high-rise estate) complete with a wooden tower and revivalist interiors that incorporate a range of inventive medieval-inspired furnishings. He was also widely active in stage decoration, sets and costumes, and particularly book illustration where his flair for simplified forms, elaborate decoration, and the ornamental use of heavily stylised Old Slavonic calligraphy proved very popular – indeed many of his illustrated books are still in print today. A major strand of his career was spent in the production of monumental decorations such as the Stone Age frescoes for Moscow's Historical Museum in 1880, a 25-metre-long expressionistic imagining of the nation's Neolithic past. These took two years to complete, following which Vasnetsov was awarded his most prestigious and lengthy commission, to decorate St Vladimir's Cathedral in Kiev.

St Vladimir's was under construction between 1862 and 1896, for ten of which years, 1885–96, Vasnetsov laboured on an estimated half an acre of wall producing fifteen large fresco scenes, thirty separate full-length figures and a vast array of ornamentation in the shape of flora and fauna woven into intricate polychromatic configurations. His devoutly Orthodox faith, coupled with his expertise of medieval ornamentation and illumination demonstrated on the Church of the Saviour at Abramtsevo, were deciding factors in the state choosing him over Vrubel, who some thought more apposite. Vasnetsov threw himself into the commission by touring major Christian monuments in Italy – Rome, Venice and Ravenna – as well as Russia, examining particularly frescoes and mosaics, settling eventually on a primarily Byzantine influence adapted to a modern sensibility (figure 34).

The mix of contemporary naturalism, ancient iconic elements and overt

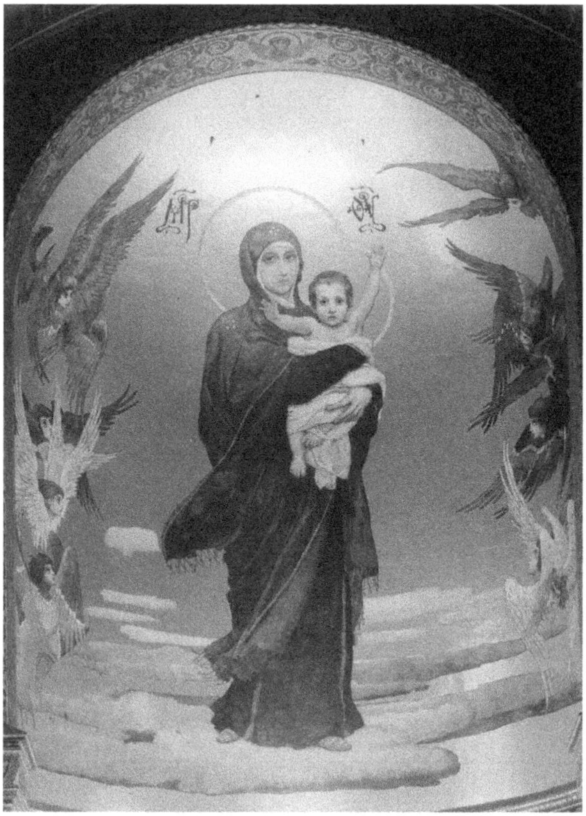

34 Viktor Vasnetsov, *The Mother of God with the Infant Christ*, apse of St Vladimir's Cathedral, Kiev, 1895.

nationalism that resulted was hailed by some as the epitome of the long-sought Russian style. Vasnetsov's Virgin, which fills the huge apse of St Vladimir's, has the traditional large eyes and straight nose of the Byzantine tradition, but is modelled in a rounded chiaroscuro and based on a Slavic ethnography. She stands astride three-dimensional but curiously simplified clouds amidst fantastic but modern interpretations of the habitual seraphs, the highest order of the nine-fold celestial hierarchy, gifted with love and associated with light and purity. The infant Christ is a naturally vital figure, a real child stretching and waving its arms as it reaches to the viewer, a marked contrast to the usually bland and passive Italian models. Even before work was completed the genesis of this massive undertaking had already passed into legend, Vasnetsov supposedly being inspired to compose the Virgin and Child after the rudimentary form of a stain which appeared unaccountably on the undecorated wall.

Augmenting these Slavic spiritualisms the key note of the decorations are nationalistic; Orthodox saints and mystical subjects vie with portraits of church fathers such as Nestor the Chronicler or powerful princes such as Aleksandr Nevsky. Large historical scenes also feature, such as *The Baptism of Vladimir* showing the

Christianisation of Russia in 988 by Grand Prince Vladimir, the event which the cathedral itself commemorates.

The Byzantine-Slavic nature of Vasnetsov's labours met with great approbation from the public and many critics, but it did not always find favour with those Orthodox believers uneasy with the mix of iconic tradition and the style and technique of contemporary naturalism. An affluent visitor recalled stopping a group of peasants in the Cathedral to congratulate them on how proud they must be with their splendid new building and its marvellous paintings. Somewhat abashed one replied: 'Yes, they are, no doubt, wonderful and beautiful, but we like the old icons best.' Much taken aback by such ingratitude the gentleman enquired what it was they found wanting in Vasnetsov's works. With total conviction and refreshing naivety the answer came back: 'They have too much life in them.'[13] It appears that the *muzhik* was innately alive to a lesson in art which many accomplished and educated artists were longer in the learning, that there is a fundamental conflict of interests between a naturalistic style and a spiritual content, between presentation and evocation. The constraints of verisimilitude counteract the sacred, for which the outward form is merely a cipher for the inward content, its other-worldliness. Too much life obscures the spirit and too much spirit the life, leaving Vasnetsov's work in a precarious aesthetic limbo.

Vasnetsov pursued his animus for fantasy images throughout his career, even into the early Soviet period, his style becoming more colourful, linear and graphic in character, his compositions tighter and more claustrophobic, often akin to medieval art. His work was described in its own time as a manifestation of neo-idealism, though it was undoubtedly appreciated at a grass-roots level as a popular imaging of nationalist sentiments. It grew from the Slavic Revival of the early 1870s, but coincided with Aleksandr III's more forceful promotion of a powerful, heroic Russian culture, itself instigating a religious revival which further endeared Vasnetsov to a wider public. In terms of personal proclivities Vasnetsov was more of a religious than nationalistic temperament, but the two were deeply intertwined. Feeding off and into this interlacing of nationalist strivings his reputation became immense.

Though now associated primarily with the Wanderers, Vasnetsov straddles several cultural territories. Even the aesthete artists of the 1890s much admired his colourful, decorative and non-tendentious productions and in 1898 the first edition of the modernist journal *Mir iskusstva* was devoted to his work. This certainly reflects the fact that his art, though narrative-illustrative, is fundamentally at odds with a realist school, its fantasy element frequently the cause of anxiety on the part of liberal voices who disparaged his departure from contemporary subjects. As images based on mass, popular culture, however, these works were difficult to dismiss. In lauding 'the people' the Russian intelligentsia had boxed itself into an ideological corner wherein it seemed contradictory to decry works based on an indigenous, non-elitist way of life. Vasnetsov, however, saw no conflict, favouring plurality and inclusiveness: 'I have always been convinced that genre and historical pictures, fairy tales, songs, folk epics and dramas, all reflect the entire inner and outer make-up of a nation, with its past and present, and perhaps even its future ... It is a poor nation that does not remember, value and love its history.'[14]

Vasnetsov's work eventually proved less controversial than did the precedent it represented in terms of a remove from contemporaneity towards not only nationalism, but also an engagement with the metaphysical. The paintings of Mikhail Nesterov, a pupil of Perov's at the Moscow School of Arts who assisted Vasnetsov's work on St Vladimir's Cathedral, moved the Society even further from its founding ethos. A deeply religious individual who occasionally retreated to seminaries in search of creative solace, Nesterov progressed from naturalistic works of folk and ecclesiastical subjects, to evolve a purposefully naïve, archaising style, mingling history, spirituality, idealism and mysticism in his pietistic visions of Russian saints and holy people. His themes speak of humility and delicate frailty, rather than the robust vigour of Vasnetsov's warrior heroes, and whilst some, including Kramskoy, regretted his choice and treatment of subjects, Nesterov was undaunted by such criticisms. Like many of the second generation of Wanderers he came from less humble origins – in this case a cultured merchant family – and was untroubled by creative insecurities.

Tretyakov became a major purchaser of Nesterov's ecclesiastical subjects and continued to patronise his eponymous visions of saints, hermits, monks and nuns. In addition to executing many church murals Nesterov produced a series of independent works anchored by his reverence for monasticism, which he saw as central to Russian Orthodoxy. He revered the Old Believers as custodians of an ancient inheritance which he celebrated in such works as *The Youth of Saint Sergius* (1892–97, GTG), *Tsarevich Dmitry the Martyr* (1899, GRM), *Taking the Veil* (1897–98, GRM) and *The Vision of the Boy Bartholomew* (colour plate 8). In the latter work Nesterov utilises a specific landscape surrounding Abramtsevo, with idealisation and mysticism in the treatment of the saintly boy and his supernatural companion. This was part of a cycle of works chronicling the life of St Sergius of Radonezh, a greatly revered monk of the fourteenth century who founded the Trinity Monastery of St Sergius close to Abramtsevo. Nesterov illustrates the tradition that the adolescent Sergius, then a shepherd boy known by his lay name Bartholomew, met a holy man who gave him communion bread and a blessing, granting him wisdom and knowledge, before urging him to do God's work. The young Bartholomew is fittingly portrayed as thin, frail, large-eyed and sallow, like an iconic saint. The lyrical landscape complements the aura of serenity whilst the faceless holy man is a numinous figure, inducing an air of surreal fantasy. Whilst the inclusion of such works proved controversial (in 1890 Myasoedov unsuccessfully demanded that it be removed from the Wanderers show and that Tretyakov should renege on its purchase), his many, similarly ethereal, paintings became regular features of Wanderers' exhibitions.[15]

The breadth of Nesterov's subject matter encompassed not just religious motifs, but nationalist sentiments embedded in landscapes, historical scenes, portraits of national figures and occasionally ambitiously abstracted conceptualisations of the spirit of place and time such as *The Land of Russia (The People's Soul)* (1914–16, GTG). This curiously static, unlocated image of mass aspiration is embodied in a large, synthetic crowd scene composed of famous figures such as Tolstoy and Dostoevsky, as well as generalised images of the Church, a tsar, a beggar and a youth, peasants and intellectuals, symbolising the nation's spiritual progress. Though it was not wholly convincing, Nesterov exhibited here an experimental ambition in attempting to give form to a spiritual communion.

Such progressive aspects of Nesterov's work problematised its critical reception. His detractors appear equivocal; confused by the fusion of tradition and modernity and not always consistent as to which they found more objectionable. That modernity and tradition in Russian art became generally enmeshed at the close of the century is evident in Nesterov's approach. His paintings are brightly coloured and simply composed, using flat, decorative designs and simple compositions that frequently abandon illusionist space, turning the world into a two-dimensional back-drop. His figures are purposely stiff and stylised as in iconic art, but rendered in an archaising style that is unmistakably modern. Nesterov was widely admired by modernist trends in the 1890s, his works contributing to, and being influenced by, the emerging Russian *style moderne.* Despite his seemingly antiquated subject matter, he like Surikov was welcomed by the *Mir iskusstva* aesthetes for his 'betrayal of the old traditions'.[16] The correlation of tradition and modernity can be observed in the appropriation of Nesterov's works. *The Vision of the Boy Bartholomew* is quoted by Andrei Tarkovsky in his films *Solaris* (1972) and *The Mirror* (1974) and in a recent exhibition theming art and religion in Russia, Nesterov (along with Vasnetsov) was viewed comparatively with Malevich, Kandinsky, Goncharova and Non-Conformist art of the 1960s–1990s as evidence as of a cultural continuity.[17]

In a concluding piece of irony Nesterov lived deep into the communist period, when spirituality in art was no longer required. He adapted and survived by painting incisive portraits of the Soviet intelligentsia, but the decisive influence of his work had already made its impact during the 1890s in its uneasy questioning of the Wanderers' public image. His output seems the epitome of a spiritual idealism, striving for purity and serenity, as opposed to the corporeal realism of the founding realists, exposing earthly iniquity and disunity. Though informed by a genuine spirituality and bolstered by the momentum of the Slavic Revival that was both compromising and promoting the Russian school of art, Nesterov was also symptomatic of a broader cultural schism, one of a growing number of young artists who failed to find creative fulfilment with the Wanderers and who felt keenly the restrictions of the society's original civic-minded values. The issues engendered by the Slavic Revival and its conservative agenda undoubtedly hastened the decline of the Wanderers hegemony and helped destroy its socio-political image, but this was not a passive capitulation to cultural change. The Society's members, who included Vasnetsov, Nesterov and many of the participants at Abramtsevo and Talashkino, were complicit in this process as fervent advocates of artistic diversification. Others, however, viewing with alarm the Society's incursions into the heritage industry, embarked on a course of cultural obstructionism in an attempt to reassert its founding ethos and establish stability. The resulting tensions proved to be undermining and eventually irreconcilable.

9

Adapted allegiances

The vexed issues of nationalism, conservatism and traditionalism that coexisted with the more radical and progressive tendencies of the Wanderers' ethos and output occasioned a multiplicity of creative tensions that served merely to illustrate further that the realist school in Russia was less the product of methodical and structured theorising, but more frequently that of disjointed cultural initiatives. Opposing and contradictory energies, political and artistic, proactive and reactive, seemed to collide randomly like particles in an accelerator, the results of which, though frequently prompted by intent, were prone to variable and unpredictable outcomes.

Aleksandr III's opportunistic but concerted attempts to compromise the Wanderers' avant-garde status, which were abetted by the Society's lack of a unified cultural agenda – its inability to 'stay on message' (chiefly because it had no consistent message to promote) – are indicative of this. The state undoubtedly pursued a concerted programme during the 1880s aimed at bringing the Wanderers under Imperial influence, to be repackaged as a national school carrying the royal seal of approval. The nationalist aspirations of the Slavic Revival were subsumed, or at least compromised, by loyalist sentiments and as noted state funding for the arts was greatly increased at this time. Imperial purchases, such as the record price paid for Repin's *Zaporozhye Cossacks* (figure 27) soon outstripped all competitors. What resulted, however, was not the orderly take-over bid envisaged by the state, but a confused and ineffective merger of irreconcilable interests.

It is customary to observe a decline in the Wanderers' critical ethos from the late 1880s through the 1890s, but also in the quality and commitment of their work. Where previously the Society had been a cultural outsider appealing to a non-traditional patronage base, under Aleksandr III it was embraced by the wealthiest benefaction imaginable. The temptation to produce mundane and noncontentious commercial work, or rousing nationalist encomiums, seems all too predictable, and doubtless some artists took the line of least resistance and maximum career benefit. The inducement was further enhanced by plans to create a new museum which, unlike the Hermitage, would be devoted exclusively to Russian art. Though inaugurated posthumously by Nicholas II in March 1898 as the Russian Museum of Emperor Aleksandr III (later the State Russian Museum), the project was greeted with much approval by those, including Stasov, who saw it as the fulfilment of the Wanderers' mission; an official recognition of the Society as the apogee of a native canon.

The Society's presumption that the new museum would narrate a story of Russian art climaxing with its own brand of contemporary realism was not fanciful. In tandem with these initiatives and concurrent with the broad spectrum of neo-nationalist commissions favoured by the state, plans were forthcoming for the long overdue reform of the Imperial Academy, in which the opinions and involvement of the Wanderers' chief practitioners were heavily canvassed. Indeed, by the time the Russian Museum of Aleksandr III opened, many of the Wanderers' key members had moved to the reformed Academy. Press attacks on the realists, particularly those emanating from the Imperial Academy's glossy journal *The Messenger of Fine Arts*, to which even Stasov was invited to contribute, gradually abated and attempts to find common cause in nationalist subject matter prepared the ground for reconciliation, though largely on Aleksandr's conditions. In short, Aleksandr adopted a variety of approaches in his quest to subvert the Wanderers' critical and democratic image towards a more traditionalist trademark.

None of these gambits was particularly subtle or new. Aleksandr cajoled or flattered the realists into a state of compromise, but was also adept in his cultural

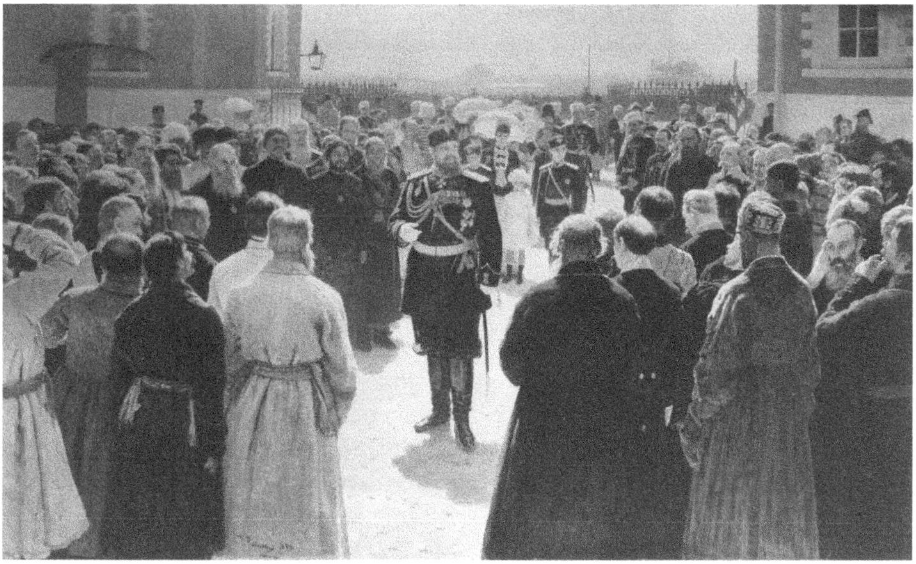

35 Ilya Repin, *Aleksandr III Receives the District Headmen in the Courtyard of the Petrovsky Palace in Moscow*, 1886, 293 x 490 cm

strategy. It has been noted, for instance, that he fostered a change of attitude amongst artists reluctant to accept official commissions.[1] Saying 'no' to the Crown was an exceptionally delicate matter, but in 1883 Kramskoy accepted a commission to paint the Tsar's coronation and in turn Repin painted Nicholas II on two occasions as well as sketching a canvas of the Tsar's wedding. With Vladimir Makovsky and Viktor Vasnetsov, he also contributed celebratory designs to Nicholas' coronation album. Repin had been early if reluctantly drawn into the sphere of official painting with a huge patriotic canvas *Aleksandr III Receives the District Headmen in the Courtyard of the Petrovsky Palace in Moscow* (figure 35) depicting the newly crowned Tsar proclaiming the unchallengeable nature of the autocracy. The reactionary speech called for already limited peasant participation in local government to be abolished, the Tsar exhorting the headmen to follow instead the benign leadership of the aristocracy. Ironically, the commission came to Repin at the time he was working on *Ivan the Terrible* (figure 25), a symbolic exorcising of the contemporary horrors perpetrated by Aleksandr's regime. With Machiavellian cunning Aleksandr arranged the commission as part of the deal to lift the ban on *Ivan the Terrible*, along with the work's exhibition at the fourteenth Wanderer's show – the first such exhibition attended by the Tsar following the change to the censorship laws occasioned by Repin's seditious historical painting. But the decision to embroil Repin in a grandiose public commission predates that controversy and shows the Tsar's early determination to compromise the Wanderers' most notorious talent.

Repin toyed with plans to adapt the commission to a reworking of *Religious Procession in the Province of Kursk* (colour plate 1) contrasting the drab headmen with the ostentatious wealth of the Court and the imperial magnificence of the new Tsar, but despite haggling he was compelled to paint the Tsar as the focus of concern.[2] In Repin's defence it should be noted that having accepted the commission he was compelled to paint the peasantry from the rear (which in part he bravely ignored) but when the work was finally exhibited it seemed a clear lapse from radicalism on his part and a major cultural coup for Aleksandr.

Internal conflicts

It is hardly coincidental that Aleksandr's most concerted efforts to bring the Wanderers in line with his self-serving nationalism capitalised on internal disputes that were threatening to fragment the Society. Throughout the 1880s the aspirations of many young painters such as Serov, Vrubel and Korovin had been frustrated by the Wanderers. They came largely from better-educated and more prosperous backgrounds than the 'men of the sixties' and, though not necessarily disparaging of that generation, were less preoccupied with art's social tendencies and more interested in formal concerns; or at least the necessity for artistic freedom. In these areas they found scant appreciation from the Wanderers of whom only Repin consistently fostered experimental attitudes. From 1882 Serov and Vrubel received informal tutelage at Repin's house, chiefly in the more spontaneous medium of watercolour

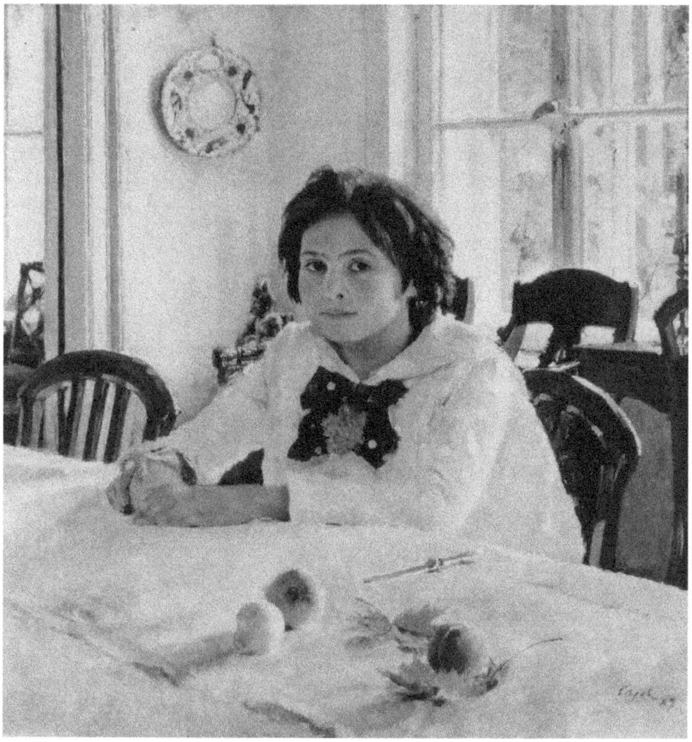

36 Valentin Serov, *Girl with Peaches*, 1887, 91 x 85 cm

at which the older artist acknowledged their influence on him. Serov in particular was close to Repin and lived with the artist's family for periods following the early death of his father, the distinguished composer Aleksandr Serov. The younger Serov's gentry background and refined outlook illustrate some of the salient differences between the established and upcoming talents. The artist's mother was also a composer and concert pianist and by comparison with Repin's background, that of a state peasant, Serov was an urbane, sophisticated and cultured individual lacking any of the social inadequacies felt by the early realists.

An early example of these concerns, painted when Serov was barely twenty-two, is the extraordinarily assured *Girl with Peaches* (figure 36). The subtle sense of light that seems to radiate from the interior and the girl's skin shows a prodigious talent consciously engaged in painting what appealed to his aesthetic sensibilities, an approach irreconcilable with that of the Wanderers. Although the sitter is known to us, Serov avoids naming her since likeness is not his primary concern. The influence of Repin's *plein airism* is evident, particularly the choice of a sunlit domestic interior sited on the Abramtsevo estate, facets similar to *They Did Not Expect Him*. But Serov works without literary concerns, the subject merely a pretext for painting for its own sake. Serov was a gifted and sincere portraitist who stressed the elegance as well as the aloofness of his often aristocratic and society sitters, nor did he show any twinges of social conscience when asked to paint royalty. He was an incisive and controlled painter but explored also the artistic potential of his sitters beyond the imperative for an accurate documentary record. He was always willing to experiment in his art, but even such understated challenges to the status quo caused hostility, Vladimir Makovsky once infamously likening Tretyakov's acquisition of Serov's *Girl in Sunlight* (1888, GTG) to infecting the merchant's collection with syphilis.[3] The level of aesthetic debate could indeed be basic at times.

Greater hostility greeted Mikhail Vrubel, the most unorthodox talent of his generation, whose background was also at variance with many of the Wanderers. He graduated in law but then decided to follow an artistic career, entering the Academy in 1880 on Repin's recommendation. Vrubel was an intellectual, widely read in art history, literature, philosophy and the classics, as well as being a scholar of Latin and a polyglot (from Makovsky's perspective he might as well have come from another planet). But Vrubel's life was dogged by controversy and lack of official recognition. As a student he was acquainted early on with the hostility his work would attract when his designs for the restoration and repainting of the twelfth-century St Cyril's Cathedral in Kiev were rejected. His fusion of Byzantine ornamentation and modern, overtly symbolist stylisations constituted a series of strange visions considered unfit for the building.

Although Vrubel was a great devotee of the decorative arts, as witnessed by his work at Abramtsevo and Talashkino where he mixed European and Neo-Slavic styles and sources, the characteristic mark of his mature paintings was an arcane but intelligible symbolism. In a series of works on the theme of the demon he sought a layering of meanings, spiritual and metaphysical, totally alien to the Wanderers' accessible, earthly narrative.[4] Fed by the manic-depressive illness that would later confine him to working only during periods of lucidity, his obsessive imagery addressed fundamental concepts of good and evil, and with the demon series the corruption of perfection. His work perplexed and enraged many, but Vrubel is now regarded as a great influence on evolving modernist trends and a link between tradition and the avant-garde through his attention to decoration, symbolism, experimentation with the paint surface, disregard of proportion, distortion of perspective and fragmentation of form. Unlike the Wanderers, who sought to make their art intelligible to a general audience, elucidated through Russian subject matter, Vrubel held that art was intrinsically an intellectual pursuit linked to spiritual fulfilment. These discrepancies are encapsulated in microcosm in the relationship between Repin and Vrubel. The older artist fostered Vrubel's talent, even advising him to paint independently of the academic curriculum, a progressive outlook much appreciated by the apprentice:

> He has made a great impression upon me: how clear and simple are his views of artistic problems and his methods of preparation for them – so sincere and so little like the idle chatter (which generally engages us so much and which so spoils us and our lives): this, after all, is rigorously and brilliantly reflected in his work.[5]

Soon after, however, Vrubel found himself at odds with the literary pretensions and social commentary of Repin's *Religious Procession in the Province of Kursk*:

> artists cannot exist without the recognition of the public, but once recognised, the artist does not have to become a slave to the public; he has his own original special business in which he is the better judge. He should respect his work and not destroy its significance to the point that it becomes a tool of journalism. That would be to swindle the public ... for me this is roughly what Repin's painting evokes.[6]

Vrubel's views are not wholly typical of his generation; he was equally scathing of the shallow and pretentious intellectualism of much modern art and regarded Western Europe as in decline from the Renaissance, to which he saw himself as heir. What is indicative of this episode is that whilst more traditional forces within the Wanderers reacted with predictable negativity towards the prospect of change, even such a liberal member as Repin, who was nurturing much of the younger talent, failed to anticipate such a brazen signal that the ethos of political and social awareness that originally drove him was now considered moribund.

That a schism didn't appear much earlier was due more to practicalities. The plurality of modernist trends that was to mark the late 1890s and early twentieth century was yet to come. For the time being artists existing outside of the creative monopoly enjoyed by the Academy and the Wanderers had little choice but to join one or the other, or to seek their reformation. Some, like Nesterov, made accommodation with the realist school, though not without controversy. Others found infiltration much harder. Only after many years and with the repeated insistence of Repin was Serov eventually admitted as a member; Korovin exhibited for nearly a decade without being enrolled and Vrubel was consistently halted at the jury stage.

The original Wanderers, particularly hard-liners such as Myasoedov, Pryanishnikov and Yaroshenko, proved increasingly reluctant to admit new members or to countenance all but the most conventional forms of realism. The Society's response to the eternal challenge of the new was as depressingly predictable as it was intractable; it closed ranks. This strategy proved pivotal to the Wanderers' decline as the secessionists, once united in their desire for artistic freedom, ossified into a proscriptive closed shop. The more astute members were aware of this and as early as 1886 Kramskoy talked of resigning since, in his view, the Society had become *de facto* a second Academy.[7] But just as the original secessionists were forced to think long and hard before leaving the Academy, so young artists in the late 1880s to early 1890s acknowledged that the Wanderers constituted the most important shop window for new talent, and, until the age of burgeoning exhibition space and entrepreneurial shows matured, they continued to seek membership. In the face of continual rebuttals, however, the Society was petitioned in early 1890 by a faction of young Muscovite artists, headed by Sergei Ivanov, to increase its jury to take account of non-members who had nevertheless been regular contributors. The reactionary response to this modest request illustrates the anxiety of the beleaguered realists; the Society's statutes were amended, reverting its administration to the founder members of 1870.[8] By this move even prominent members were disbarred from the board and Repin, in company with Viktor Vasnetsov, resigned. Repin's dissatisfaction with the Wanderers was in fact long-standing, which doubtless inclined him to view Aleksandr's overtures of reconciliation opportunistically. He had resigned from the Wanderers once before, in 1887, complaining to Konstantin Savitsky of their being 'a bureau of state functionaries' no better than the Academy from which he had escaped.[9] His second resignation was to last a full eight years, during which time the Wanderers lost the prestige of numbering the nation's most famous painter as one of its own, a loss which proved the Imperial Academy's gain.

Sleeping with the enemy

In the light of this damaging debacle, the Wanderers issued a statement in May 1892 setting out the criteria whereby pictures would be vetted for exhibition. Where previously the Society's self-censorship was informal and nebulous, mounting to little more than a tacit acceptance that certain subjects were incompatible with their ambitions (classical scenes and nudes for instance) this document was both proscriptive and exclusive. It stated unequivocally that whilst works would not be constrained by genre, they should be realist-narrative in character and that painting for its own sake would be excluded. Portraits should address the 'typical' whilst still-life subjects and figure studies were heavily discouraged.[10]

This stance further estranged the younger generation of painters but also precipitated a decline in technical if not artistic standards. The young Leonid Pasternak noted around this time:

> I was amazed ... how weak in drawing were even distinguished artists (excluding of course masters of form and drawing like Repin, Polenov, Serov and V. Vasnetsov). Neither form nor draughtsmanship, but only subject, i.e. 'a story about something', was then the chief concern of Wanderers' works. Our generation strove for, and eventually achieved, the freedom to work and exhibit using any techniques, and not just oil, as the Wanderers demanded. I remember that watercolours were then not accepted for Wanderers exhibitions at all.[11]

Eventually the disaffected painters, including Ivanov, Serov, Vrubel and Nesterov, would be forced into a schism, establishing the Union of Russian Artists in 1903 as a body specifically espousing the freedom of expression and lack of bureaucracy the Wanderers denied them. For now, however, it was the Tsar who again seized the initiative and profited from the discord. As the Wanderers pursued their internecine feud Count Ivan Tolstoy, Aleksandr's newly appointed Academy head, was already wooing the Society's big guns to participate in a reformed and revitalised national institution.[12] Repin, who had increasingly voiced his concerns about the need to improve the standard of artistic instruction, was elected with Polenov,

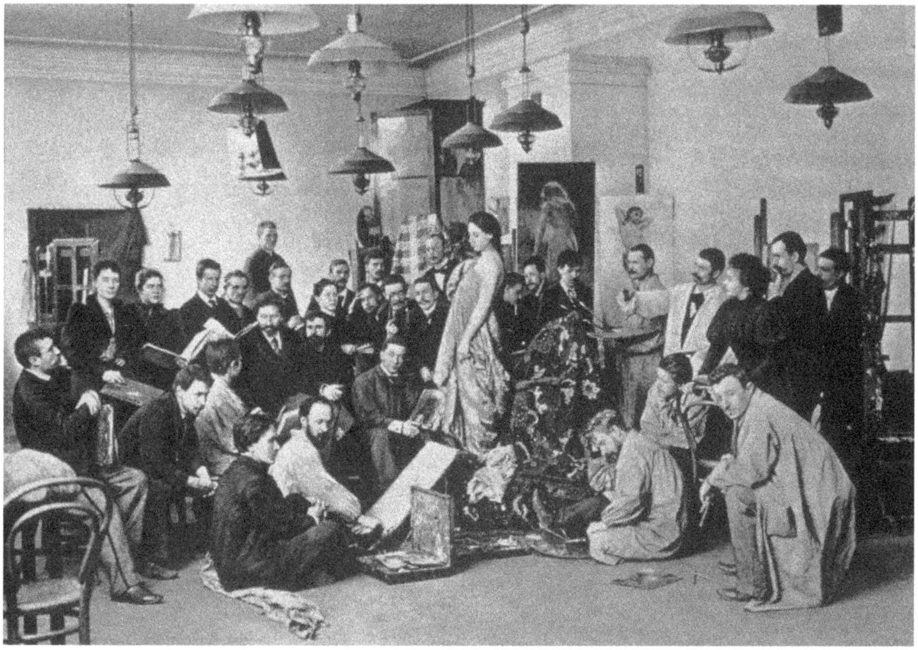

37 Ilya Repin and his pupils at the Academy of Arts, photograph, 1898.

Kuindzhi, Myasoedov and Savitsky to the Government Commission considering the means and methods of reform, proposals of which were published in 1891. In September of 1894 the Wanderers can truly be said to have fragmented as Repin, Kuindzhi, Shishkin and Nikolai Kuznetsov were joined by the previously intransigent Myasoedov and Vladimir Makovsky in accepting professorships at the august (but reformed) institution. Twelve others joined the eighty-strong Assembly which governed the Academy, but Polenov, who had advocated an end to the Court domination, was excluded and remained at the Moscow School. Yaroshenko declined, as did Surikov, who was averse to the life of an art official, despite strenuous pleading for him to join.

In defence of the defectors it seems sufficient merely to point again to the reactionary and restrictive character of the Wanderers at this time. Those who joined the reformed Academy doubtlessly sought to effect genuine change through the assumption of teaching posts and a seat on an Assembly that managed the vast apparatus of the state's arts educational system. Repin and Viktor Vasnetsov had resigned from the Wanderers three years earlier, so could hardly be regarded as deserting them. Vladimir Makovsky and Myasoedov, however, were staunch supporters of the critical-realist ethos and must, presumably, have regarded their posts as the most advantageous from which to infiltrate the system and disseminate their views.

The result, however, was not a take-over but an untidy merger with the Tsar as controlling share-holder. The Academy did not become the autonomous institution that some had hoped; the Presidency remained in the hands of the Imperial family and teaching staff continued to be appointed (and dismissed) from above, rather than elected by their peers (as illustrated by Kuindzhi's instant dismissal in 1897 when he lent his support to a student strike).[13] But teaching methods were transformed, being switched to greater deployment of practical studio instruction in place of classroom theorising. Students were free to select their own themes, to submit work for continuous assessment, as and when they saw fit, and to choose in which classes they wished to study. Repin's class, the first in Russia (possibly in Europe?) to pioneer the use of the nude female model for both male and female students, was particularly popular in respect of this 'open-door' policy and was frequently congested (figure 37).[14] In addition, the convoluted civil-service rankings which so readily identified artists as state minions were now dropped in favour of a simple diploma which entitled the holder to claim the tenth grade when seeking state employment.

Stasov, who belatedly divined that the Tsar's motives were neither benign nor disinterested, was total in his condemnation of the defectors whom he accused of betraying the realist cause for mercenary motives of position and rank. In refuting these allegations Repin eloquently summarised the dilemma that had forced the division:

> The Wanderers long ago formed itself into a *Sanhedrin* (a council) of founders; the equality of members was destroyed long since – *which is precisely why I left the Society.* It constantly pressurises the young and, significantly, is already divorced from new opinions and tastes. It does not even hide its authoritarian tone towards the young members and exhibitors but exercises its power over them, its subordinates, with great aplomb.[15]

Decline?

The principal criticism levelled at the Wanderers was not merely that of reneging on their stance as artistic rebels, but of compromising their art to such an extent that their work became increasingly indistinguishable from the Academy in terms of subject and treatment; the realists mellowed and the Academy diversified into contemporary native genre scenes. Clearly, however, the move of some of the leading realists to the reformed Academy was more potent as symbol than fact: it seemed to signal the compromise, if not the end, of the aspiration for creative freedom and an autonomous school of Russian art.

The prestige of the artists who took up posts at the reformed Academy certainly dealt a death-blow to the Wanderers' potency as a viable cultural opposition, but the 'defection' was both extensive and enthusiastic, a telling commentary on the internal disaffections that occasioned the Wanderers' disintegration. The realisation of a liberally minded school of Russian art working outside of academic strictures was certainly a major achievement, and in seeking to bring the Wanderers within Imperial controls, patronising their work, and revitalising the Academy with realist practices and subjects, the state had conceded the superiority and popularity of the Wanderers' product by its desire to arrogate it. The objective of 'free' art was, in any event, a chimera well understood by the more astute artists who remained consistently subject to official censorship, a hostile loyal press, the interventions of intrusive patrons and the pressures of conservative public mores. Negotiating all of these factors was of considerable hindrance to creative freedom but many painters accepted their presence and directed their energies more pragmatically to circumventing rather than combating them. If a considerable portion of the nation's talent divined that its interests were best served from within a reformed Academy than a feuding Society of an increasingly intransigent ethos, the decision was probably more a practical and ethical one than a statement of ideological defection. Although it did not eventually materialise, the opportunity to appropriate the Academy and make it an extension of the realist school must then have seemed valid and feasible.

It is also contestable as to whether there was a real decline in the quality or probity of the Wanderers output during the 1890s. Certainly the Society lost some of its best-known practitioners, although many retained exhibiting rights and did not completely sever their connections. The prevalence of more stock subjects, such as the ragged peasant children of Bogdanov-Belsky, has occasioned the charge that the Wanderers 'deteriorated into sorrowfully sentimental formulas about rural life, and the Courbet-like objectivity disappeared'.[16] Notwithstanding that French pretensions to impartiality were never characteristic of the Russian school, or the problematic definition of sentimentality, the prevalence of ever more imagery of humdrum proletariat existence was influenced not only by market forces, but also by artistic development. The realist school had by now developed its own characteristic motifs where previously the first generation of painters had charted new territory, seeking as well as inventing the prototypes of national life that inexorably became the Society's stock in trade.

A careful scrutiny of the Wanderers' output during these years will, as with most schools, reveal a range of formulaic images derived from common paradigms. The 'decline', however, was not wholesale and there exists a body of fascinating and progressive responses by artists seeking to revitalise the Society or to reposition it. Vasily Baksheyev's *The Prose of Life* (figure 38) is a fine example of a work seemingly out of step with a narrow conceptualisation of realism; a detached, impassive but carefully staged view of the stultifying tedium of provincial life, a pendant to Chekhov's plays of intellectual malaise, and a slice of rural ennui totally removed from the crisis and confrontation of earlier Wanderers works. The domestic setting is not dissimilar to Repin's *They Did Not Expect Him* but where Repin's protagonists are engaged in a multiplicity of anxious possibilities structured around a tense interaction, Baksheyev's apathetic characters remain studiously divorced from one another avoiding eye contact. And yet like Chekhov, Baksheyev is eloquent in this subtle delineation of languor and estrangement. The refined use of strong but harmonious coloration filtered through interior light is also a welcome advance from the dull, sometimes monochromatic palettes of more didactic artists and shows an attempt to address aesthetic potentials as well as novel subject matter.

The work of Abram Arkhipov also evidences diversification and progression (figure 39). In a series of works addressing the life of the rural Russian peasant, Arkhipov enriched the society's exhibitions with what became known as the 'eventless genre' – seemingly a cultural oxymoron – realism without literary concerns or social sermonising. Within these apparently detached observations of a random character, Arkhipov is overtly concerned with aesthetic questions emphasised in his use of a rough and sketchy application allied to casual and unobtrusive compositions. In *Before Mass*, for instance, if one draws a line from the bottom-left corner of the canvas to the top-right, half of the painting is effectively empty. The 'reality' of his works is achieved not through detail, but the use of sharp tonal contrasts,

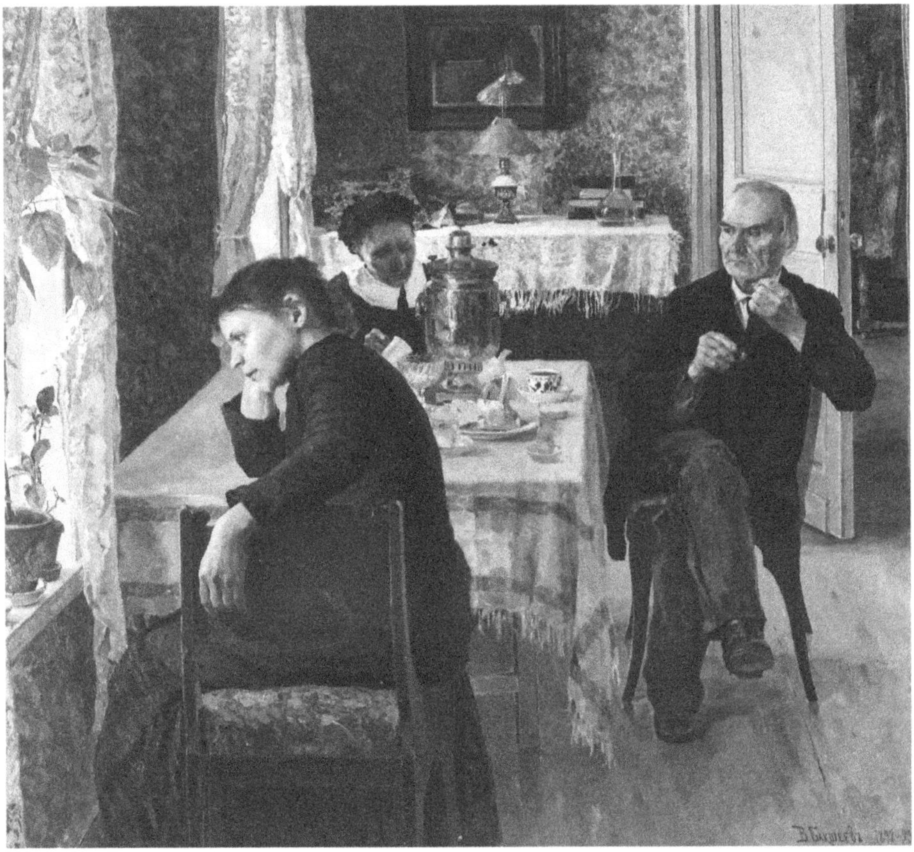

38 Vasily Baksheyev, *The Prose of Life*, 1892–93, 68 x 73 cm

often bright sunlight to evoke solidity. Unlike Serov, however, his subject matter never became a pretext for painting but remained consistently focussed on the mundane existence of the *muzhik*, creating an intriguing adaptation of modern aesthetics to established themes.

The same is true of Kasatkin's *Poor People Collecting Coal in an Abandoned Pit* (figure 7) which marries a hard-hitting but sympathetic image of indigent fortitude – a quintessential piece of critical realism – with a modern aesthetic. Though the composition is more rhetorically structured to sustain a narrative, the handling of paint is loose and applied broadly, again suggesting rather than delineating palpability. Kasatkin, who remained one of the most uncompromising exponents of critical realism even into the Soviet period, belies the assertion that the critical ethos departed from the Wanderers after the defection to the Academy. Certainly it ceased to be the factor which characterised the school, but it remained prevalent. As noted earlier, Arkhipov and Ivanov both tackled the theme of convicts on the road to exile. Ivanov's *Death of a Migrant Peasant* (figure 6) is a powerful image by the leader of the unsuccessful petition to liberalise the Wanderers – one in a line of works that remained true to the Society's critical roots in tackling such diverse issues as peasant hardships, prison life and social unrest. Even at the turn of the century Kasatkin continued to pursue politically engaged subject matter in works such as *In the Corridor of the Circuit Court* (1897, GTG), showing a prisoner under armed guard comforting his distraught wife. Admittedly by this time scenes of political repression were scarce and there is an appeal to pathos here which in part mitigates the power of the image, but though sentimental in one respect, these subjects remained inherently controversial and provide continuity with the first generation of Wanderers' talent. The figures of the armed guards, with their bayonets fixed, evoke a genuine combination of menace and callous, unemotional indifference to the suffering of the prisoner and his partner.[17]

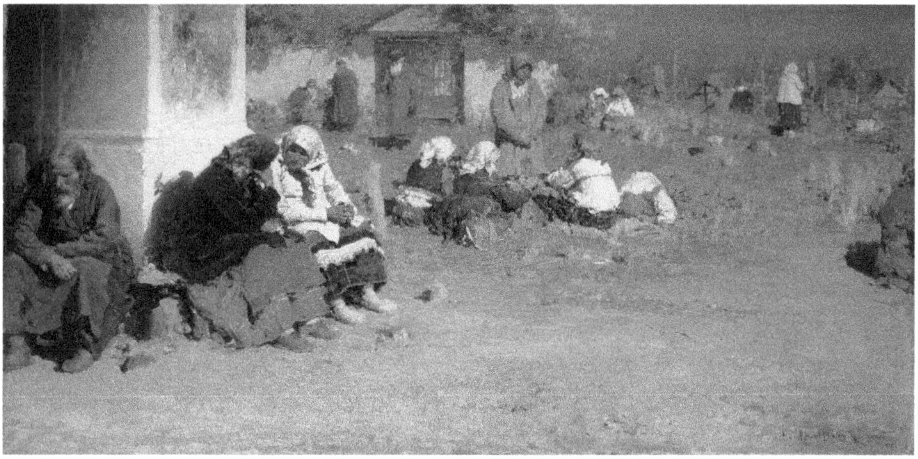

39 Abram Arkhipov, *Before Mass*, 1892, 58 x 114 cm

Ironically, the most uncompromising continuation of the critical-realist spirit during the 1890s and beyond came from Vladimir Makovsky, doyen of the radical political canvas, but, it should be remembered, one of those who transferred to the reformed Academy in 1894. His cultural activism was unaffected by this change, confirmation it seems that he, like others, saw the Academy as an opportune platform from which to broadcast their realist principles. In two highly controversial canvases Makovsky showed that none of his energies had been dissipated. *At the Vagankovsky Cemetery. Burying the Victims of Khodynka* (1896–1901, The Museum of Russian Political History, St Petersburg) resulted from a tragic event when, on 18 May 1896, during celebrations for Nicholas II's coronation, two thousand people were crushed to death as they gathered to receive traditional royal gifts. Administrative incompetence was blamed and scenting controversy Makovsky, more like a war journalist than a fine artist, hurried to the makeshift cemetery where the bodies were laid out. He filled two sketch books with grisly imagery, and this first-hand testimony was worked into an explicit canvas showing the dead on the cold, barren field, as distressed relatives search amongst the corpses for loved ones. Recalling his motives Makovsky cited morality and ethics foremost, rather than artistic considerations, evoking shades of the 1860s utilitarianism: 'I could not consider myself an artist if I did not visually embody the profoundly staggering impression made upon me.'[18] Naturally the work was not considered fit for exhibition although it was eventually shown at the World Exhibition in London 1910, and then in Rome, against the wishes of the Russian authorities. The work acquired a reputation within artistic circles even as it remained concealed; Makovsky even repulsed Court attempts to purchase the work for the immense sum of 45,000 roubles. Doubtless he knew it would be buried or destroyed.

Makovsky was also amongst the few artists who seriously addressed the massacre of 'Bloody Sunday' when in January 1905 a loyal and peaceful demonstration was brutally cut down by the Tsar's troops. Polenov and Serov considered resigning from the Academy but in the event only Serov, who had witnessed the killings, did so.[19] His bold and ethical resignation remained a unique gesture, which he followed by painting a small but laconic work *Soldiers, Brave Fellows, Where Now is Your Glory?* (1905, GRM) showing a crowd being born down upon by sabre-wielding troops. In November of 1905 Repin also resigned from the Academy, not directly as a result of the shootings, but it seems not coincidental that his dissatisfaction with the institution came to a head that year. In general, however, whether at the Academy or within the Wanderers' ranks, the realists kept their heads down.

Makovsky's reaction was to paint a large canvas, *9 January 1905 on Vasilevsky Island* (1905, The State Central Museum of Contemporary Russian History, St Petersburg) depicting the reactions of the crowd – civilians, students, workers – as the troops open fire and the first dead, young and old, fall to the ground staining the snow with their blood. A central motif of a man tearing open his shirt to present his chest to the bullets strikes a note of almost Soviet realist melodrama, but the tragedy of the remaining participants as they struggle to escape or defend their young, is addressed with genuine pathos.[20] This was very much a private painting, shown only to close friends and worked on secretly, and it was not seen publicly until 1922, two years after Makovsky's death. He nevertheless felt the need to exorcise his horror in such forceful visual terms, an act typical of realist practices that informed earlier scenes of revolutionary activity. Makovsky's cultural interventions must be regarded as brave and earnest since he could hardly expect kudos from works which could not be publicly displayed, but on the contrary the very existence of which could and did embroil him in controversies which threatened to destroy his position and rank. As ever in Russian culture there was little to be gained by speaking out but much to be lost. It would be true to say, however, that despite the continuation of a critical-realist legacy, after the defections to the reformed Academy, the Society became increasingly associated in the popular consciousness with an artistic rear-guard. In this respect the works of Kasatkin and Ivanov were not regarded as typical of their output, but by now burgeoning modernist trends in the arts were reshaping the cultural landscape beyond the control of the state or the Wanderers, and beyond the geographical boundaries of Russia, and both camps were looking increasingly out of step with progressive developments.

A transition which further tainted the realists with traditionalism and retrogressiveness has been observed in their so-called 'embourgeoisement', the process of exchanging independence for high rank, lavish lifestyles and prosperous incomes, part of which found outlet in the aspiration to joining the landed gentry.[21] Several leading painters purchased rural estates, the upkeep of which demanded an income stream most easily supported by formulaic productions and official subservience. This 'gentrification' threatened to compromise artists' integrity but also confounded public expectations since many naïvely believed that the painters of radical protest would conform to a stereotype of material simplicity. Again, this must be qualified by acknowledging that the behaviour and motives of the Society's leading figures is not necessarily indicative of, or comparable with, that of the mass of painters existing under its aegis who aimed simply to make a living. But it is pertinent to note, as we saw in relation to the Wanderers' treatment of scenes from contemporary peasant life, that many of these artists had come 'up' from backgrounds of real hardship and social restriction, some even lacking their freedom until 1861. In the same manner that Repin decried Tolstoy's homilies on the purity of the peasant existence and Maksimov dismissed populist sentimentality about the people, so artists harboured few romantic delusions about poverty and sought actively to distance themselves from it by gaining social respectability. They saw no contradiction in elevating themselves socially through merit and the fruits of their labour, nor enjoying the rewards of the high prices belatedly paid for their works.

The adoption of middle-class lifestyles can also give a misleading impression. Repin's estate of 'Penaty' on the Gulf of Finland was used as a venue for gatherings of cultural luminaries, but also for activities in keeping with the reformist 1860s. These included lectures on a wide variety of social topics such as the establishment of co-operatives, organising famine relief and the promulgation of animal rights and were delivered to illustrious guests and local workers alike, as well as to parties of workers bussed in from farther afield.[22] These qualifications aside, however, the public must certainly have perceived the change in the Wanderers' image from progressive painters of plebeian stock to that of the artist 'barin' (барин) or gentleman, a respectful title addressed to one's social superiors. Neither was this image dispelled by artists accepting official commissions. Kramskoy, Repin, Polenov and Viktor Vasnetsov were just a few of the prominent names who were drawn into the employ of the Court and the aristocracy. Indeed, the reason Makovsky was on site to witness the aftermath of Khodynka was that he had come to the capital to contribute to the Tsar's coronation album.

For many the most spectacular volte-face in this respect was Repin's agreement in 1901 to mark the centenary of the establishment of the State Council, Russia's highest governing body, in a colossal canvas measuring 400 × 877 cm: *Formal Session of the State Council in Honour of Its Centenary on May 7, 1901* (1903, GRM).[23] Critical opinion was divided then as now between whether Repin depicted a collection of corrupt, tyrannical geriatrics, or the apotheosis of official magnificence. Certainly, as in many of Serov's society portraits, the sitters can appear intellectually challenged and Nicholas II is reduced to minute proportions, all but lost in a sea of uniforms. Repin's letters of this period, however, show little disquiet about the subject or its loyalist potential. Occasionally he complained of Court interference with his creative independence, or that sittings with the Tsar were too few, but in general he exhibited no moral repugnance in seeing the commission through.

Stasov (much to the delight of future Soviet commentators) chose to see the work as overtly critical, describing it as 'a collection of rascally generals, scoundrels, villains, mutilators of the country, instigators of shameless abominations and crimes, rejoicing in evil and madness'.[24] Repin was certainly no admirer of autocracy, indeed he was frequently critical of it, and he greeted Stasov's appraisal warmly. Nevertheless, this involvement with the monarchy was seized upon by conservative and avant-garde detractors as proof of Repin's complicity with the authorities and the Wanderers' ethical decline. It is not possible here to embark on a full analysis of the issues engendered by this anomalous but seemingly retrograde work, but the context of its exegesis certainly lies in personal as well as cultural impulses. Though the canvas might be thought to have surrendered the Wanderers' critical independence, Repin was actually still at the Academy and working through his own creative neuroses. At the height of his fame he had dramatically renounced the utilitarianism of the 1860s in favour of art's aesthetic autonomy and in his academic classes had initiated progressive teaching methods such as informal *plein air* classes. He gave his students the freedom and encouragement to develop their abilities, rather than a pedantic training, and forged personal links with a younger generation of talent with whom he contributed to a number of key experimental exhibitions. These aimed at showcasing aesthetically based ideas giving attention to technique over content, in particular the primacy of the sketch (which the Wanderers had banned from exhibition). The most important of these was *The Exhibition of Experiments and Sketches* of 1896–97 in St Petersburg, which he personally funded.[25]

These activities neither excuse nor explain Repin's alacrity at fulfilling one of the largest ever state commissions on so conformist a subject, but they are indicative of the complexity of frequently paradoxical factors informing artistic development in what was, politically as well as culturally, an unstable time of rapid and unpredictable change. Where previously the boundaries of official and unofficial art seemed clearly defined, confusion and instability now dissolved or undermined such certainties. Evidence of this was provided by the 'national scandal' of 1913 when *Ivan the Terrible* was slashed by a deranged icon painter causing an unprecedented public outcry. The vandalism was seen as symptomatic of a wider moral disintegration in the arts and the distressed public turned to the Wanderers as symbols of stability, upholders of standards in an art scene now housing iconoclastic modernist trends who were belligerent, disrespectful or abusive towards the established masters; some even greeted the vandalism as a service, an early form of interventionist performance art. As one journal commented: 'This disgraceful and incomprehensible action, this piece of savagery is not an isolated instance; it is a genuine sign of the times, when there are no values, no education, a total absence of moral sense.'[26]

Contemporary to the scandal were shifts in political ideologies and nomenclature surpassed only by the Gordian knot of interlinking and diverging cliques, factions and manifestos that constituted the anarchic art world of the early 1900s as a bemused public tried to accommodate Symbolism, Expressionism, Neo-primitivism, Futurism, Cubo-Futurism and Abstraction, with Non-objective art, Rayonism, Constructivism, Suprematism and so on fast approaching. But whilst it might have seemed the pinnacle of grand irony that this once-reviled canvas, regarded in 1885 as the apogee of radicalism in the visual arts, was now recognised as a national masterpiece, the symbolism of the event was ultimately more important than the fact; whether serving the Wanderers or the Academy the realists were now seen conclusively as the legitimate national school of art. The classical canon had been overturned in favour of national and contemporary subject matter, the august institution of state tutelage and artistic dissemination had been infiltrated by the rebels, the financial base of the indigenous art market had been broadened to a more inclusive condition, and the aspirations of the Society's founding members, and of Stasov in particular, to establish a modern Russian school of art had, by the early twentieth century, been realised.

That this 'victory' or consolidation of the dominance of the Wanderers' legacy might be regarded as divergent from the Society's original ethos, or that it had been achieved through different methods and in more questionable circumstances than the founding members could have imagined, mattered perhaps less than that the objective had been attained. It would take the cataclysm of revolution to topple the realists from their hegemony, and the unprecedented political omnipotence of Josef Stalin to rehabilitate them.

Conclusion

The Wanderers commenced as a movement with radical and idealistic intentions, but by the early years of the twentieth century it would be fair to acknowledge that they were regarded as artistic epigones. In part, as discussed, this was due to their enmeshment with the forces of officialdom; the rapprochement between academic and realist factions had, for many, rendered the two indistinguishable. Substantially, however, the Wanderers were simply overtaken by fashion as the Russian art scene spawned a bewildering proliferation of antagonistic experimental activity; what we now call the avant-garde. When in October 1917 the Bolsheviks seized power the new peasant and worker state initially aligned itself with modernist culture in its desire to put space between it and the past, to start afresh without any taint of tsarist influence. This is a telling commentary on the interrelatedness of the Wanderers and officialdom: much of their subject matter was still dedicatedly proletarian, but the Society as a whole was considered too compromised by its capitalist finance base and its imperial connections to serve as a model for the new world of communist egalitarianism.

During these years of heady idealism under the progressive leadership of Anatoley Lunacharsky, the Art Section of Narkompros, the Commissariat for Education, was staffed almost exclusively by avant-garde practitioners who assumed a virtual dictatorship of arts administration. The staff, which included Malevich, Tatlin, Chagal, Rodchenko and Kandinsky, oversaw the liquidation of the Academy in 1918 in favour of the Free Art Studios, which opened their doors to all without educational or artistic restrictions. Despite the good intentions of many participants, the freedom of cultural expression embodied in these and subsequent state structures under Bolshevik control never materialised and proscription on style, in favour of modernism, ruled. Traditional realism, indeed all forms of figurative art, suffered a lack of patronage at a time when the bourgeois markets had collapsed and there was no viable alternative to state funding. The triumph of the avant-garde was, however, fleeting and generally unpopular as the masses proved themselves staunchly disinclined to countenance often highly eccentric manifestations of experimental culture. Boris Koroliov's cubist design for a memorial to Mikhail Bakunin was actually demolished by the public in what must rank as a unique manifestation of proletarian aesthetics at work![1]

Neither were the products of the avant-garde appreciated by Lenin or the Bolshevik leadership and as early as 1918 more conventional and legible variations of modernist styles were chosen for Lenin's *Decree on Monumental Propaganda*. Throughout the 1920s the avant-garde were steadily ousted by the Party through a series of decrees aimed at tightening up the political probity of the arts and making them accessible to a mass audience, and by the conservative tastes and considerable buying power of the two main holders of state finances, the Red Army and the Trade Unions. By the early 1920s realism made a spontaneous re-emergence as non-objective, analytical art, ran out of steam, and was rejected by the proletariat, or was persecuted by Bolshevik ideologues. Artists returned to figurative art to depict the evolving revolution, but even so the Wanderers were not necessarily the role-model. The Society of Easel Painters (OSt), which received Lunacharsky's endorsement in its fusion of contemporary figurative art of a formally experimental nature, whilst aspiring to clarity of subject matter that would not alienate the masses, nevertheless stated amongst its express aims: 'The rejection of abstraction and *peredvizhnichestvo* [in other words, the Wanderers]'.[2]

OSt failed however to garner a power base financially or ideologically and in time the realist mantle was taken up forcefully by The Association of Artists of Revolutionary Russia (AKhRR) formed in May 1922. Manipulating the proclivities of the Red Army and Trade Unions for intelligible pictures of revolutionary events, the AKhRR manifesto was robust and unequivocal:

> We will depict the present day: the life of the Red Army, the workers, the peasants, the revolutionaries, and the heroes of labour. We will provide a true picture of events and not abstract concoctions discrediting our revolution in the face of the international proletariat ... we must reveal our artistic experiences in the monumental forms of the style of heroic realism.[3]

Despite the fact that two of the founder members, Evgeny Katsman and Viktor Perelman, had been young members of the Wanderers, 'heroic realism' was not to be confused with the Society and the AKhRR disclaimed any such descent to avoid the smear of retrogressiveness. Visually, however, it was evident from where their style and subject matter had been drawn. Although their output was politically tendentious in the service of Communism, their subject matter was contemporary and Russian, and their academic-realist style identical to that of the nineteenth century practitioners. Isaak Brodsky's iconic image of the pensive and introspective Bolshevik leader *Lenin in Smolny* (1930, GTG) is no different in style or intent from Wanderers' portraits of their intellectual mentors; indeed Brodsky was a product of Repin's tutelage. The lineage uniting the two movements was further exposed when in 1923 the AKhRR pressed Kasatkin to join them, and again three years later when a delegation of artists led by Brodsky was sent at Lunacharsky's behest to similarly incorporate Repin.[4] Like the Wanderers the AKhRR also stressed the Russianness of their subjects (frequently in comparison with the foreign and 'alien' influences of modernism) but were at best progeny of the society, lacking its critical independence or cultural subtleties.

Though the state increasingly embraced realism as the proper language for the visual arts the process was neither crude nor sudden, official sanction making itself known gradually though pronouncements of Lenin's tastes, increasingly critical reviews of formalist art, and by building on a genuine public and professional antipathy towards non-objective art forms. The official transition to Soviet Socialist Realism was not marked until 1932 when the April Decree dissolved existing artistic groups, instituting one union for each of the professions and effectively establishing the centralised political control of the arts. This was followed by the influential 1934 First All-Union Congress of Writers, which endorsed Socialist Realism as the only acceptable method of cultural production, the ratified tenets of which were to be applicable to all arts. Although the AKhRR went through structural changes and weathered the state imposing ideological corrections to its ethos, its style and subject matter became the essential paradigm for Soviet Socialist Realism and thus the Wanderers' legacy, which might have been thought to have died with the Society's last and forty-eighth exhibition in 1923, lived on.

Throughout the 1930s Stalinist interpretations of past culture became consistently more ethnocentric with the Wanderers being subjected to a series of reinterpretations, distortions and expurgations that cast them resolutely on the critical political left, whilst also holding them up stylistically as the model for aspiring artists. In October 1934 Brodsky was appointed the first rector of the All-Russian Academy of Arts overseeing a curriculum of technical proficiency allied to a staunch adherence to party ideology. In 1936 this came under the aegis of the newly established Committee on Arts, which maintained a central control on all art and research institutions, promoting a pro-Bolshevik and anti-Western stance in which the Wanderers were key in establishing early variants of the theoretical principles underpinning Soviet Realism, particularly 'Party-mindedness' (партийность) – the adherence to a given political programme, and 'Proximity to the masses' (народность) – bringing art to the masses.[5] Through exhibitions and publications, the mass dissemination of popular prints in public spaces, as well as the reintegration of artists such as Kasatkin and Nesterov into the Socialist Realist pantheon, the autochthonic nature of Soviet art was mapped via its nineteenth-century predecessors. The Wanderers collectively and individually were cast as astute disciples of the more radical of the 1860s thinkers, Chernyshevsky and Dobrolyubov in particular. In this way the Society's resuscitation and enshrinement in the nation's cultural history was secured, but in a strictly delimited manner as precursors, anticipating but never surpassing the superiority of Soviet Realism:

> The limited conception of the world possessed by most of the Itinerants [Wanderers] can be explained by their ignorance of the laws that govern the development of society. Neither were they aware of the correct, scientifically valid path that alone could lead

> to social progress in the true meaning of the word. Nevertheless, by participating in the democratic movement of their time they too fought for the cause of historical progress.[6]

This narrow political, cultural and art historical bias has continued to dog the Wanderers and has badly served a complex series of cultural issues by crudely grafting neatly packaged and politically motivated absolutes onto the subjective and inconsistent body of their heterogeneous output. That tragedy, however, was compounded by the Wanderers' own history. That the 1917 revolution overtook them and subsumed all in its path was an occurrence that affected all, but the

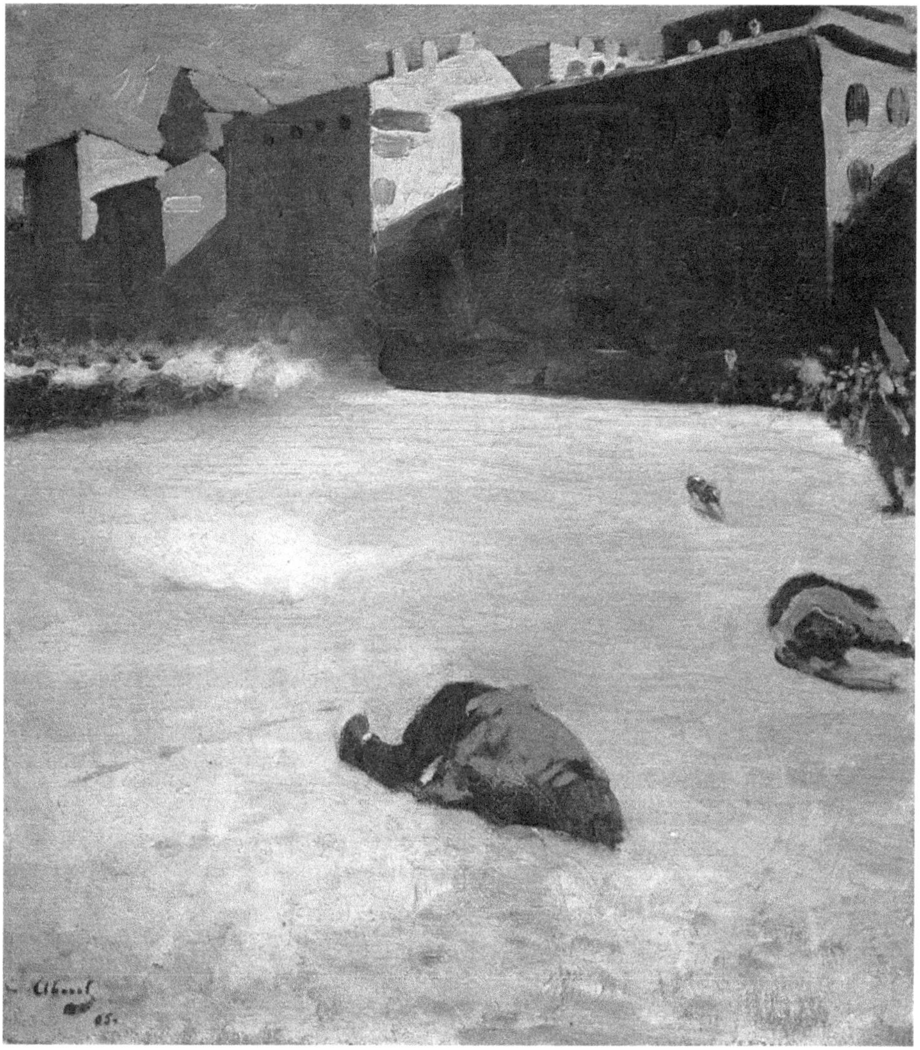

40 Sergei Ivanov, *Massacre*, 1905, 70 x 80 cm

Society had rendered itself largely obsolete before the state had occasion to break and later rebuild it. Its disintegration was assisted long before by a variety of exterior factors: the artistic searchings of a new generation of talent which conflicted with realist principles; the concerted efforts of Aleksandr III to subvert the democratic-realist nature of the Society to a non-tendentious, national school of art, celebrating Russianness and serving patriotic, eventually autocratic ends; and latterly by the forceful challenge of modernist trends antipathetic to tradition in all forms. But essentially the Wanderers self-destructed, responding intransigently to artistic diversification and appeals to accommodate new trends. This not only caused the defection of its most prominent members but alienated even those younger artists putting new blood into the flagging critical realism. Estranged to the point of schism, they formed the Union of Russian Artists in 1903 as a means to achieve freedom of expression; the very goal the Wanderers aspired to at their foundation. Sergei Ivanov's politically bold and artistically probing reaction to the events of Bloody Sunday (figure 40) is a point in question. Through deployment of a sparse composition, limited colour range and expressive technique, he vividly but laconically evokes the moment of horrific disbelief when the calm of the peaceful protest is shattered and the first demonstrators fall as the troops begin their charge. This might seem prototypical of the Wanderers' audacious critical output but it is a work painted outside the Society by an artist unable to find accommodation within its increasingly conservative strictures. The demonstrators' fall symbolically signals also the demise of the Wanderers' ethos.

In one sense, of course, Stalin's promulgation of the Wanderers was not merely on national and political grounds; he and the Party recognised its character as one attuned to public sensibilities and evincing lucid communicative skills. Whatever the criticisms one might level at the Stalinist apparatus it took the arts – or control of the arts – very seriously. But beyond the bald recognition that the Wanderers were a genuinely popular and user-friendly medium through which to channel the Bolshevik pedigree, Stalinist falsifications (and a Western readiness to ingest them) have ironically obscured the very real success of the Society and the fundamental contribution it made to national culture through its establishment of a Russian school of art where previously there was none. Through the Wanderers the identity of Russian art became inextricably linked with contemporaneity, with broad issues of nationalism, political and social commentary, and the inter-relatedness of art and the society from which it springs. To conclude with an old adage of post-modern concern, for the Wanderers there was no 'art *and* society', as if the two were separate entities ripe for comparative analyses. Their art was of its society and integral to it; it informed and was informed by a social interactivity and interdependence. That the Soviet perversion of Marxism later bowdlerised and falsified its own art history to recast the Wanderers as embryonic communists harbouring a deep-rooted hatred of capitalist exploitation, or that Soviet artists were forced to adhere to a form of bastardised figurative-narrative style derived from the Wanderers, but put to the service of an ideology that was neither critical nor realist, does not detract from the decisive interventions the Society made in reconfiguring and redefining the nature of art, the role and status of the artist, the innovative use of progressive subject matter and the exploitation of new economic potential. In these respects its legacy has withstood fluctuating trends in taste and politics to resurface in a period of plurality and inclusiveness where it might be viewed not just in its own right, as a fascinating manifestation of historically specific issues, but more widely as an absorbing case study of art's cultural contingency and negotiability.

Notes

Introduction

All translated citations are as per the published original, despite apparent inconsistencies between systems of transliteration.

1 N. Gogol, *Dead Souls*, Harmondsworth, 1981, pp. 220–1.
2 Recent exceptions, constituting just a bare mention, include R. Brettell, *Modern Art 1851–1929*, Oxford, 1999; H. Brigstock, ed., *The Oxford Companion to Western Art*, Oxford, 2001; S. Eisenman, *et al.*, *Nineteenth Century Art: A Critical History*, London, 2002.
3 И. Репин, *Далекое близкое*, Ленинград, 1982, p. 255.

Chapter 1

1 В. Порудомский, *Николай Ге*, Москва, 1970, p. 104.
2 All pre-Petrine dates are 'old style', 13 days behind the Julian calendar.
3 On Bryullov and Ivanov see R. Gray, *Russian Genre Painting in the 19th Century*, Oxford, 2000, chapter 4.
4 On the dominance of the Academy and lack of alternative training see S. Starr, 'Russian Art and Society, 1800–1850', in T. Stavrou (ed.), *Art and Culture in Nineteenth Century Russia*, Bloomington, 1983, pp. 101–3. On Grand Duchess Maria's tenure as President of the Imperial Academy of Arts, see R. Blakesley, 'A Century of Women Painters, Sculptors and Patrons from the Time of Catherine the Great', in J. Pomeroy and R. Blakesley (eds), *An Imperial Collection: Women Artists from the State Hermitage Museum*, London, 2003, pp. 72–5.
5 A. Benois, *The Russian School of Painting*, New York, 1916, p. 123. On the history of the School see Н. Дмитриева, *Московское училище живописи, ваяния, и зодчества*, Москва, 1951.
6 Starr, 'Russian Art and Society, 1800–1850', p. 91. J. Westwood, *Endurance and Endeavour. Russian History 1812–1986*, Oxford, 1988, Table 6, p. 531, records that as late as 1897, 70 per cent of the Russian population were rural peasants and 7 per cent urban peasants.

7 See Gray, *Russian Genre Painting in the 19th Century*, chapter 1.
8 This is necessarily a brief account of a more complex and protracted subject. For a fuller analysis see *Ibid.*, pp. 69–97.
9 Still the best work devoted to the artist is Т. Селинова, *Иван Петрович Аргунов*, Москва, 1973.
10 See the exhibition catalogue *В.А. Тропинин и московские художники его времени*, Москва, 1975.
11 See A. Cross, 'Ivan Ermenev and the Enigma of "The Beggars"', in M. Falchikov, C. Pike and R. Russell (eds), *Essays in Honour of Professor (Emeritus) Dennis Ward*, Nottingham, 1989, pp. 67–80. In Russian see А. Савинов, *И.А. Ерменев*, Ленинград, 1982.
12 *Мастера искусств об искусстве*, Москва, 1969, vol. 6, p. 213. Quoted in T. Alexeyeva, *Venetsianov and His School*, Leningrad, 1984, p. 10.
13 P. Roosevelt, *Life on the Russian Country Estate. A Social and Cultural History*, New Haven and London, 1995, p. 260.
14 R. Muther, *The History of Modern Painting*, London, 1896, vol. 3, p. 416.
15 On Fedotov see Д. Сарабьянов, *Павел Андреевич Федотов*, Ленинград, 1990.
16 Gray, *Russian Genre Painting in the 19th Century*, pp. 138–41 on Fedotov's associations with Hogarth.
17 And this notwithstanding that an accompanying poem which Fedotov declaimed in front of the picture was banned from publication by the censor. See А. Сомов, 'Воспоминания о П.А. Федотове' in Я. Лещинский (ed.), *Павел Андреевич Федотов: художник и поэт*, Ленинград-Москва, 1946, p. 207.
18 I largely follow but develop here from E. Valkenier, *Russian Realist Art. The State and Society. The Peredvizhniki and Their Tradition*, New York, 1989, chapters 1 and 2, which provide an excellent survey of these issues.
19 Letter to V. Stasov, 29 September 1873, in С. Гольдштейн (ed.), *Иван Николаевич Крамской. Письма, статьи в двух томах*, Москва, 1965–1966, vol. 1, p. 202. Afterwards referred to as Крамской, *Письма*.
20 О. Лясковская, *Илья Ефимович Репин*, Москва, 1953, p. 10.
21 Репин, *Далекое близкое*, p. 131.

Chapter 2

1 One lone voice, Fedor Buslaev, called for a return to Russia's Byzantine past. See Valkenier, *Russian Realist Art*, p. 203, n. 16.
2 P. Chaadaev, *First Philosophical Letter*, 1829, first published 1836. In B. Dmytryshyn (ed.), *Imperial Russia. A Source Book, 1700–1917*, Fort Worth TX, 1990, pp. 250–1.
3 В. Белинский, *Собранние сочинении, в трех томах*, Москва, 1948, vol. 3, p. 789.
4 Quoted in Gray, *Russian Genre Painting in the 19th Century*, p. 82.
5 N. Dobrolyubov, 'Provincial Sketches', in *Selected Philosophical Essays*, Moscow, 1956, p. 55. First published in *Современник*, № 12, 1857.
6 F. Dostoevsky, *The Devils*, Harmondsworth, 1987, pp. 343 and 483 respectively.
7 N. Chernyshevsky, 'The Aesthetic Relationship of Art to Reality', in *Selected Philosophical Essays*, p. 376. The thesis was first published in 1853 and appeared in abstract in 1855 in *Современник*.

8 Letter to N. Murashko, 30 November 1883, in *И. Репин. Избранные письма, в двух томах*, Москва, 1969, vol. 1, pp. 291–2. Afterwards referred to as Репин, *Письма.*

9 D. Sarabyanov, *Russian Art, From Neoclassicism to the Avant-Garde, Painting, Sculpture, Architecture*, London, 1990, p. 102.

10 Репин, *Далекое близкое*, p. 176.

11 И. Дмитриев, 'Расшаркивающееся искусство', *Искра*, № 38, 4 October 1863, pp. 521–530.

12 Репин, *Далекое близкое*, p. 176.

13 For Kramskoy's description of the events see his letter to M. Tulinov, 13 November, 1863, Крамской, *Письма,* vol. 1, pp. 9–11.

14 Letter to Stasov, 21 July 1886, *ibid.*, vol. 2, p. 252.

15 R. Auty and D. Obolensky, *An Introduction to Russian Art and Architecture*, Cambridge, 1980, p. 112; A. Bird, *A History of Russian Painting*, Oxford, 1987, p. 286.

16 Draft statutes and covering letter to the *Artel* in В. Андреев, М. Астафьева, С. Гольдштейн и Н. Приймак, *Товарищество Передвижных Художественных Выставок 1869–1899. Письма и документы*, Москва, 1987, vol. 1, pp. 51–3. Afterwards referred to as *Товарищество.* The desire to circulate their art was a natural one for a society seeking to be democratic, but must in part have been influenced by the *Artel*'s successful exhibition at the Nizhny Novgorod fair of 1865: see И. Шувалова, *Мясоедов*, Ленинград, 1971, p. 37. For Myasoedov's views see letters to Kramskoy of 2 February and 21 September 1870 in *Товарищество,* vol. 1, pp. 53–5.

17 The Statutes are reproduced in full in *Товарищество*, vol. 1, pp. 57–9.

18 For a full account of this episode see D. Jackson, 'Western Aesthetics and Russian Ethics: Repin in Paris 1873–76', *Russian Review*, 57:3, July 1998, pp. 394–409.

19 See Valkenier, *Russian Realist Art*, p. 67, especially Repin's uncharitable remark to Kramskoy about the 'quagmire ... of merchant freaks'.

20 Letter to Tretyakov, 11 June 1890, R. Christian (ed.), *Tolstoy's Letters*, London, 1978, vol. 2, pp. 460–1.

21 В. Прытков, *Любимые русские художники*, Москва, 1963, p. 54.

22 М. Антокольский, 'Заметки об искусстве' *Вестник Европы*, vol. 32, № 2, February 1897, pp. 525–6. Antokolsky writes with hindsight, though the interest for such dramatic and exotic canvases certainly existed. His enthusiasm did not however stop him pursuing a life-long concern for Russian subject matter. In 1866 Kramskoy lavished praise upon Proudhon's *Du principe de l'art et de sa destination sociale* but made no attempt to further acquaint himself with the works of Courbet: letter to S. Kramskaya, 9 July 1866, Крамской, *Письма,* vol. 1, p. 59. Kramskoy admitted a total ignorance of the Impressionists whilst in France in the mid-1870s.

23 On collecting activities see two articles by R. Gray, 'The Golitsyn and Kushelëv-Bezborodko Collections and Their Role in the Evolution of Public Art Galleries in Russia' *Oxford Slavonic Papers*, NS 31 (1998), pp. 51–67, and 'Muscovite Patrons of European Painting. The Collections of Vasily Kokorev, Dmitry Botkin and Sergei Tretyakov', *Journal of the History of Collections*, 10:12 (1988), pp. 189–98. See also G. Churak, 'Private Art Collecting in 19th Century Russia', in *The Wanderers: Masters of 19th Century Russian Painting*, exhibition catalogue, Dallas, 1990, pp. 61–80.

24 Letter to Stasov, 13 May 1876, quoted in И. Грабарь, *Репин*, Москва, 1963–1964, vol. 1, p. 159.

Chapter 3

1 Courbet, letter to a group of students, 25 December 1861, reproduced in E. Holt, *From the Classicists to the Impressionists: Art and Architecture in the Nineteenth Century*, New York, 1966, pp. 351–2.
2 *Ibid.*, p. 352.
3 Letter of July 1885, in G. Pollock, *Millet*, Oxford, 1977, p. 11.
4 Illustrations and information on each of these key works can be found in Н. Зограф (ed.), *В. Перов. Выставка произведений к 150–летию со дня рождения,* Москва, 1988.
5 Chernyshevsky, 'The Aesthetic Relation of Art to Reality', p. 375.
6 L. Nochlin, *Realism*, Harmondsworth, 1982, p. 113, states that the French population was two-thirds rural in 1871. In 1897 the peasantry still accounted for 77.1 per cent of the Russian population: Westwood, *Endurance and Endeavour*, Table 6, p. 531.
7 Letter to Repin, 13 June 1873, *М. П. Мусоргский. Письма и документы,* Москва, 1932, p. 251.
8 On this and the influence of the Russo-Turkish War see Valkenier, *Russian Realist Art*, pp. 68–73.
9 The move towards a more 'Russian' based art was not a new phenomenon, but the characteristics of Populism added a new dimension. See Gray, *Russian Genre Painting in the 19th Century*, pp. 60–1.
10 Letter to Stasov, 3 June 1872, *Письма И. Е. Репина и В. В. Стасова. Переписка*, Москва, Ленинград, 1948–1950, vol. 1, p. 37. Afterwards referred to as Репин-Стасов, *Переписка.*
11 *Товарищество*, vol. 1, pp. 60–1, 65.
12 Репин, '*Бурлаки на Волге*', *Далекое близкое*, pp. 234–5. This account, written in 1922, when the artist was seventy-eight, supplements the meagre references in letters of the time. Whilst it is fair to assume a degree of retrospective embroidery, Repin was responding to great public interest concerning its genesis. On the theme of the barge-hauler see Е. Нестерова, 'Тема бурлаков в русской живописи 1860–1870 годов', in *Илья Ефимович Репин. К 150–летию со дня рождения. Сборник статей*, С-Петербург, 1995, pp. 57–65.
13 Репин, *Далекое близкое*, p. 285. On Kanin generally see pp. 283–7.
14 В. Стасов, *Избранные сочинения*, Москва, 1952, vol. 1, p. 701.
15 В. Стасов, 'Двадцать пять лет русского искусства. Наша живопись', *Избранные сочинения*, vol. 2, p. 438.
16 Musorgsky, letter to Stasov, 13 July 1872, *М. П. Мусоргский. Письма и документы,* p. 223. Kramskoy letter to V. Polenov, 23 March, 1875, Крамской, *Письма,* vol. 1, p. 294.
17 'Apropos of the Exhibition', in B. Brasol (ed.), *F.M. Dostoievsky, the Diary of a Writer*, New York, 1954, vol. 1, p. 81.
18 В. Стасов, 'Наши итоги на всемирной выставке', *Избранные сочинения*, vol. 1, p. 344. See also 'Немецкие критики о русском художестве на венской выставке', *Ibid.*, pp. 244–5.
19 Originally published in *La France*. Quoted in Стасов, 'Наши итоги на всемирной выставке', pp. 343–4.
20 Originally published in *Indépendance Belge*, quoted in *Ibid.*, p. 344.
21 Dostoevsky, 'Apropos of the Exhibition', p. 81.

22 Quoted in В. Стасов, 'Тормозы нового русского искусства', *Избранные сочинения*, vol. 2, pp. 614–15. This is a moot point. Photographic evidence suggests the trade of barge-hauler continued long after Repin brought the workers celebrity status. See F. Ashbee and J. Lawson, *William Carrick 1827–1878*, Edinburgh, 1987, p. 27; B. Moynahan, *The Russian Century – A Photojournalistic History of Russia in the Twentieth Century*, London, 1994, pp. 14 and 15 respectively for undated images of female and male haulers. A fascinating photo published in *The Daily Telegraph*, 1 March 2001, p. 24, shows modern-day Chinese haulers and gives a graphic insight into the sheer physical endeavour required.

23 А. Давыдов, 'История и современность', *Художник*, 1969, № 8, p. 30.

24 Myasoedov left a detailed account of the characteristics embodied in his participants. See Шувалова, *Мясоедов*, pp. 59–63.

25 See H. Rubissow, *The Art of Russia*, New York, 1946, plate 50. The author provides no date or location for the work and I have been unable to trace this artist.

26 Repin, letter to I. Ostroukhov, 12 March 1883, quoted in *Товарищество*, vol. 2, p. 582, item 264, n. 1.

27 Quoted in Стасов, 'Тормозы нового русского искусства', p. 620.

28 Tolstoy's comments in H. Gifford, *Tolstoy*, Oxford, 1982, p. 67. Xenophobic review in E. Valkenier, *Ilya Repin and the World of Russian Art*, New York, 1990, p. 94.

29 See comments by the artist Mikhail Nesterov in a letter to P. Neradovsky, in М. Нестеров, *Письма*, Ленинград, 1988, p. 358. Also F. and S. Parker, *Russia on Canvas: Ilya Repin*, University Park PA, 1980, p. 67.

30 Letter to Tretyakov, 8 March 1883, *Письма И. Е. Репина. Переписка с П. М. Третьяковым. 1873–1898*, Москва-Ленинград, 1946, p. 62. Afterwards referred to as Репин-Третьяков, *Переписка*.

31 A. Chekhov, 'The House with an Attic', in *Lady with Lapdog and Other Stories*, Harmondsworth, 1981, p. 224.

32 The gravity and sincerity of the painting were a result of the artist's utilisation of childhood memories of his father's death. А. Лазуко, *Василий Максимов*, Ленинград, 1982, p. 64.

33 L. Tolstoy, *What Then Must We Do?*, London, 1950, pp. 8–15 on the phenomenon of the doss house.

34 *Товарищество*, vol. 2, pp. 462, 467, 485, 490, 515 for examples. On Kasatkin generally see Я. Минченков, *Воспоминания о Передвижниках*, Ленинград, 1980, pp. 213–33.

35 V. Garshin, 'Artists', in *From the Reminiscences of Private Ivanov and Other Stories*, London, 1988. First published in *Notes of the Fatherland*, No. 9, 1879.

36 В. Порудоминский, *Гаршин*, Москва, 1962, pp. 155–6.

37 A. Chekhov, 'Peasants', in *The Kiss and Other Stories*, Harmondsworth, 1982, p. 52. See А. Парамонов, *Иллюстрации И. Е. Репина*, Москва, 1952, pp. 151–7 on Repin's illustrations to Chekhov.

38 N. Lübbren, *Rural Artists' Colonies in Europe 1870–1910*, Manchester, 2001, p. 40.

39 J. Beavington Atkinson, *An Art Tour to Russia*, London and New York, [1873] 1986, pp. 149–51.

40 Chekhov, 'Peasants', pp. 79–80.

41 Quoted in Valkenier, *Russian Realist Art*, p. 87.

42 Letter to V. Chertkov, 29 August 1887, Репин, *Письма,* vol. 1, pp. 332–3.

43 Kramskoy's warning in 'Записка по поводу пересмотра устава Академии художеств', in Крамской, *Письма,* vol. 2, p. 294.

Chapter 4

1 Chernyshevsky, 'The Aesthetic Relation of Art to Reality', p. 369.
2 Dobrolyubov, 'Provincial Sketches', p. 55.
3 M. Шумова, *Русская живопись середины XIX века*, Москва, 1984, p. 208 and plate 131.
4 On Herzen's call see A. Герцен, 'Н.Г. Чернышевский', *Колокол*, № 186, 15 June 1864, p. 1525. For Repin's later account of Karakozov's execution see 'Казнь Каракозова', in *Далекое близкое*, pp. 197–208.
5 The ubiquity of Makovskys can be perplexing. Valkenier, *Russian Realist Art*, p. 95 confuses Vladimir with Konstantin as a banal master of the 'commonplace' at a time when Vladimir's most denunciatory works were yet to come.
6 Statistical information on arrests and social breakdown of participants can be found in Westwood, *Endurance and Endeavour*, p. 116, and H. Seton-Watson, *The Russian Empire 1801–1917*, Oxford, 1988, pp. 422–33.
7 Стасов, 'Двадцать пять лет русского искусства', p. 461. On the evolution of the canvas see E. Журавлева, 'Революционная тема в творчестве В.Е. Маковского', *Государственная Третьяковская галерея. Материалы и исследования*, Москва, 1956, vol. 1, pp. 142–4.
8 The works by Ivanov and Arkhipov are reproduced respectively in *Товарищество*, vol. 2, pp. 417, 429. The poet Nekrasov vividly describes the *étape* in his poem *Who Can Be Happy and Free in Russia?*, Oxford, 1917, p. 47. First published in Russia in 1879.
9 On the painting's evolution see И. Зильберштейн, 'К истории создания картины *Арест Пропагандиста*', in И. Зильберштейн и И. Грабарь (eds), *Художественное наследство. Репин*, 2 vols, Москва–Ленинград, 1948–49, vol. 2, pp. 337–60. Afterwards referred to as *Художественное наследство*. For the sketch of the earlier version see *Ilya Repin 1844–1930*, exhibition catalogue, Retretti, 1989, entry No. 65.
10 Repin, letter to Tretyakov, undated, 1892, in Репин-Третьяков, *Переписка*, p. 156. A. Hilton, 'The Revolutionary Theme in Russian Realism', in H. Millon and L. Nochlin (eds), *Art and Architecture in the Service of Politics*, Cambridge MA, 1978, p. 114, suggests compositional similarities with religious works by Rembrandt and facial similarities with depictions of Christ by A. Ivanov, Ge and Kramskoy.
11 Westwood, *Endurance and Endeavour*, p. 118.
12 See G. Sternin, *Ilya Repin. Paintings, Graphic Arts*, Leningrad, 1985, p. 261.
13 M. Троитский, 'Репин и народная воля', *Искусство*, № 9, 1971, p. 56. On the religious theme see Г. Поспелов, 'О понимании времени в живописи 1870–1890-х годов. Картины, посвященные судьбам личности', in *Типология русского реализма второй половины XIX века*, Москва, 1979, pp. 193–4 for various comparisons, particularly Ge's *Christ before Pilate* (1890, GTG).
14 Hilton, 'The Revolutionary Theme in Russian Realism', p. 121.
15 E. Valkenier, 'Repin's Search for the Revolutionary's Image in *They Did Not Expect Him*', *Gazette des Beaux-Arts*, vol. 91, May–June 1978, pp. 207–12, details the

successive repaintings. On the use of Garshin as model see D. Jackson, 'Garshin and Repin. Writer and Artist in a Creative Relationship', in P. Henry, V. Porudominskii and M. Girshman (eds), *Vsevolod Garshin at the Turn of the Century. An International Symposium in Three Volumes*, Oxford, 1999–2000, vol. 2, pp. 108–9.

16 Ateneumin taidemuseo, Helsinki, stock Nos: 1754.14 and 1754.15. Neither drawing, acquired from the artist in 1930, appears to have been considered by the many scholars who have written on the painting's evolution.

17 С. Васильев, 'Художественные заметки', *Московские ведомости*, 1884, May, № 128.

18 Respectively, 'Rectus', *С. –Петербургские ведомости*, 1884, № 63, and *Гражданин*, 1884, № 10, p. 2.

19 Стасов, 'Наши художественные дела', *Избранные сочинения*, vol. 3, pp. 17–18.

20 A. Benois, *Memoirs*, London, 1960, p. 110. See also R. Hare, *The Art and Artists of Russia*, London, 1965, p. 220, for another aesthetic appreciation from an author extremely contemptuous of 'purpose' painting.

21 F. Dostoevsky, *Crime and Punishment*, Harmondsworth, 1981, pp. 540–1.

22 Useful sources on the women's question include: D. Atkinson, A. Dallori and G. Lapidus (eds), *Women in Russia*, Hassocks, 1978; C. Porter, *Fathers and Daughters: Russian Women in Revolution*, London, 1976; R. Stites, *The Women's Liberation Movement in Russia: Feminism, Nihilism and Bolshevism 1860–1930*, Princeton, 1978.

23 Information on all three is contained in B. Engel and C. Rosenthal (eds), *Five Sisters: Women Against the Tsar*, London, 1975.

24 И. Зильберштейн, 'Образ передовой русской женщины', *Художественное наследство,* vol. 1, pp. 176–177. The work was formerly in the National Gallery, Prague, but has since been returned to its lawful owner under the restitution of works seized after the communist revolution of 1948.

25 Зильберштейн, 'Образ передовой русской женщины', pp. 176–7.

26 В. Фигнер, *Запечатленный труд воспоминания в двух томах*, Москва, 1964, vol. 1, p. 374.

27 See Зильберштейн, 'Образ передовой русской женщины', pp. 169–72 on Yaroshenko's portraits of female progressives; pp. 172–3 explores possible affinities between *Kursistka* and *They Did Not Expect Her.*

28 Valkenier, *Russian Realist Art*, p. 208, n. 35.

29 Stites, *The Women's Liberation Movement in Russia*, p. 105.

30 *Ibid.*, pp. 121–2.

31 Dostoevsky, *Crime and Punishment*, p. 384.

32 Various critical reactions in Зильберштейн, 'Образ передовой русской женщины', p. 170. Uspensky's comments in Hilton, 'The Revolutionary Theme in Russian Realism', p. 110.

33 Benois, *Memoirs*, pp. 100–11.

34 Respectively in Н. Минский, 'Картина и эскизы И.Е. Репина', *Северный Вестник*, 1987, № 2, February, p. 230; Грабарь, *Репин*, vol. 1, p. 248.

Chapter 5

1 А. Боткина, *П. М. Третьяков в жизни и искусстве*, Москва, 1960, p. 91.
2 Letter to Tretyakov, 8 April 1881, Репин-Третьяков, *Переписка*, p. 48.
3 Репин, *Письма*, vol. 1, p. 244.
4 Quoted in Valkenier, *Russian Realist Art*, p. 81. For a modern reading see E. Nesterova, *The Itinerants*, Bournemouth and St Petersburg, 1997, p. 152–7.
5 Letter to Kramskoy, 13 January 1878, И. Крамской, *Переписка И. Н. Крамского*, vol. 2: *Переписка с художниками*, Москва, 1954, p. 360. Afterwards referred to as Крамской, *Переписка*.
6 Valkenier, *Russian Realist Art*, p. 80.
7 Стасов, 'Портрет Мусоргского', *Избранные сочинения*, vol. 2, p. 121.
8 L. Tolstoy, *What Is Art? and Essays On Art*, Oxford, 1929, p. 123.
9 H. Troyat, *Tolstoy*, Harmondsworth, 1987, p. 492.
10 Levitan, letter to Chekhov, 26 January 1898, quoted in A. King, *Isaak Levitan. Lyrical Landscape*, London, 2004, p. 79. Repin, letter to A. Zhirkevich, 27 January 1898, in Репин, *Письма*, vol. 2, p. 138.
11 С. Толстая, *Дневники в двух томах*, Москва, 1978, vol. 2, p. 18.
12 Memoirs of both incidents respectively in Репин, 'В ясной поляне', *Далекое близкое*, pp. 399, 403–4, and A. Tolstoy, *Tolstoy. A Life of My father*, Massachusetts, 1975, p. 295.
13 Dostoevsky, *The Brothers Karamazov*, Harmondsworth, 1985, p. 147.
14 Letter to Tretyakov, 19 April 1875, quoted in Т. Курочкина, *Крамской*, Ленинград, 1989, p. 68.
15 V. Fiala, *Portrétní kresby I.J. Repina v CSR*, Prague, 1953, and Fiala's later catalogue, *Ruské kresly a akvarely v Ceskoslovenskych slirkàch*, Praha, 1968, p. 48, № 203, mistakenly identifies the sitter as Tatyana Tolstoy-Sukhotinoy, Tolstoy's eldest daughter, the owner and later seller of the work. It was purchased by a Czech collector in 1924 at a time when Tatyana was enduring post-revolutionary poverty. Unwilling to accept a guest's charitable offer of money to buy food, she sold him the drawing instead. I am grateful to Galina Pribulskaya for providing archival information on this work.
16 Valkenier, *Russian Realist Art*, p. 81.
17 Quoted in B. Groys, *The Total Art of Stalinism: Avant Garde, Aesthetic Dictatorship and Beyond*, Princeton, 1992, p. 54.
18 L. Pasternak, *The Memoirs of Leonid Pasternak*, London, 1982, p. 134.
19 Quoted in C. James, *Soviet Socialist Realism: Origins and Theory*, London, 1973, p. 84.

Chapter 6

1 Reproductions and information on Shvarts' *Vernal Train* and *Tsar Alexis Playing Chess*, together with Chistyakov's *Sofya Vitovtovna*, and Flavitsky's *Princess Tarakanova*, can be found in Шумова, *Русская живопись середины XIX века*, pp. 54, 55, 50 and 53 respectively.
2 On the reception of Ge's work see M. Салтыков-Щедрин, 'Картина Ге' *Собрание сочинений в двадцати томах*, Москва, 1968, vol. 6, pp. 148–77. See also Sarabyanov,

Russian Art, p. 126. Herzen's photographic portrait is reproduced in D. Elliott, *Photography in Russia 1840–1940*, London, 1992, p. 90.

3 Saltykov-Shchedrin's review appeared as 'Первая русская передвижная выставка', in *Отечественные записки*, 1871, № 12. It seems doubtful that Ge, who relented his pro-Petrine stance, would have agreed with this reading. See Н. Зограф, *Николай Николаевич Ге. Письма, статьи критика, воспоминания современников*, Москва, 1978, pp. 96–9. Garshin's reaction in P. Henry, *A Hamlet of his Time. Vsevolod Garshin. The Man, his Works, and his Milieu*, Oxford, 1983, p. 225.

4 Стасов, 'Художественные выставки', *Избранные сочинения*, vol. 2, pp. 7–26. Originally published in *Новое время*, 1879, 8, 14 and 15 March.

5 Westwood, *Endurance and Endeavour*, p. 62 cites this and other ludicrous examples.

6 Valkenier, *Russian Realist Art*, p. 127.

7 С. Гольдштейн, *Иван Николаевич Крамской. Жизнь и творчество*, Москва, 1965, p. 91. Henry, *A Hamlet of his Time. Vsevolod Garshin*, chapter 9, 'Garshin and the Artists', provides a wealth of critical reactions to many works by the Wanderers and their academic contemporaries.

8 Letter to Garshin, 16 February 1879. This and Garshin's Don Quixote analogy quoted in Henry, *A Hamlet of his Time. Vsevolod Garshin*, p. 184.

9 *Художественный Журнал*, March 1887, p. 187.

10 *Северный Вестник*, vol. 3, 1887, quoted in Henry, *A Hamlet of his Time. Vsevolod Garshin*, p. 188. See also Nesterova, *The Itinerants*, p. 130 on the reception of Polenov's canvas.

11 Archives of the Academy of Arts, St Petersburg, fond 25, 1, 27, 1.1.

12 See Jackson, 'Garshin and Repin. Writer and Artist in a Creative Relationship', pp. 102–11. Garshin quoted in Henry, *A Hamlet of his Time. Vsevolod Garshin*, p. 368.

13 Letter to Repin, 1 April 1885, in Christian, *Tolstoy's Letters*, vol. 2, p. 380.

14 Letter to Suvorin, 21 January 1885, Крамской, *Письма*, vol. 2, pp. 167–8.

15 Letter to Aleksandr III, 15 February 1885, quoted in *К.П. Победоносцев и его корреспонденты*, Москва, 1923, vol. 1, p. 498.

16 Ф. Ландцерт, 'По поводу картины И.Е. Репина Иван Грозный и его сын 16.XI.1581 года', *Вестник изящных искусств*, 1885, vol. 3, pp. 192–205.

17 Information contained in Центральный Государственный Исторический Архив, ф. 776, оп. 5, 1885, д. 105.

18 А. Суворин, 'Картина Репина', *Новое время*, № 3218, 12 February 1885.

19 See И. Грабарь, 'Воспоминания о художнике', in Н. & З. Радимовский, С. Гольдштейн (eds), *Василий Иванович Суриков. Письма, Воспоминания о художнике*, Ленинград, 1977, p. 264. Investigations in 1970 revealed the existence of two hanged figures on the skyline.

20 Quoted in Henry, *A Hamlet of his Time. Vsevolod Garshin*, p. 189.

21 See В. Кеменов, *Василий Суриков*, Ленинград, 1978, p. 75.

22 See Е. Сахарова, ed., *Василий Дмитриевич Поленов. Елена Дмитриевна Поленова. Хроника семьи художников*, Москва, 1964, pp. 337–8.

23 Quotations respectively in A. Benois, *The Russian School of Painting*, p. 143; И. Репин, 'Воспоминания о художнике', Суриков, *Письма*, p. 228.

24 Кеменов, *Василий Суриков*, p. 175.

25 Quoted in V. Kemenov, *Vasily Surikov*, Bournemouth, 1997, p. 19.

26 В. Чуйко, *Наблюдатель*, № 2, February 1892, pp. 58–61.

27 Д. Сарабьянов, *Русская живопись XIX века среди европейских школ*, Москва, 1980, p. 107, lists Courbet, Menzel, Repin, Surikov and Munkacsy as 'the most outstanding and consistent exponents of realism'.
28 Courbet, letter to a group of students, 25 December 1861, reproduced in Holt, *From the Classicists to the Impressionists*, p. 353.
29 В. Стасов, 'Художественные выставки 1879 года', *Избранные сочинения*, vol. 2, p. 25.

Chapter 7

1 C. Ely, *This Meager Nature. Landscape and National Identity in Imperial Russia*, DeKalb, 2002, discusses the literary development of landscape and its relationship to painting, from Western classical models to those informed by the realism of Turgenev, Tolstoy and Chekhov.
2 Ivan Turgenev, 'Singers', in *Sketches from a Hunter's Album,* Harmondsworth, 1985, pp. 162–3. First published in *The Contemporary*, №.11, 1850.
3 R. Newmarch, *The Russian Arts*, London, 1916, p. 189.
4 Репин, *Далекое-близкое*, p. 170.
5 Valkenier, *Russian Realist Art*, p. 77, quoting *Дело*, №.12, December 1871, p. 117.
6 Letter to Stasov, 10 October 1876, in Репин, *Письма*, vol. 1, pp. 180–2.
7 A. Chekhov, 'The House with an Attic (An Artist's Story)', in *Lady With Lapdog and Other Stories*, Harmondsworth, 1981, p. 217. First published in *Russian Thought*, April 1896, №. 4.
8 C. Brinton, 'Russia's Greatest Painter. Ilya Repin', *Scribner's Magazine*, vol. 40, November 1906, No. 5, p. 522. Repin's comment in a letter to M. Verevkina, 24 February 1903, Репин, *Письма*, vol. 2, p. 172.
9 See respectively A. Savinov, *Shishkin*, London, Sydney and Leningrad, 1981, p. 14; Sarabyanov, *Russian Art*, p. 160.
10 Savinov, *Shishkin*, p. 30. See Valkenier, *Russian Realist Art*, p. 78 on Kramskoy's misgivings of Shishkin's work.
11 Quoted in A. Боткина, *Павел Михайлович Третьяков в жизни и искусстве*, Москва, 1993, p. 42. For the latest work on Vasilev see Г. Чурак, *Федор Васильев*, Москва, 2000.
12 On Polenov and his influence see E. Пастон, *Василий Поленов*, Москва, 2003.
13 On the vexed question of French influence on Russian landscape painting see K. Dolinina, '"Eyes Wide Shut". Landscape Painting in Nineteenth Century Russia and France', in D. Jackson and P. Wageman (eds), *Russian Landscape*, Schoten, 2003, pp. 107–16. A survey of nineteenth-century Russian artists in France is provided by T. Mojenok, *Peintres réalistes russes en France (1860–1900)*, Paris, 2003.
14 M. Нестеров, *Давние дни*, Москва–Ленинград, 1959, pp. 118–19.
15 Quoted in T. Yurova, *Levitan*, Leningrad, 1988, p. 11.
16 Sarabyanov, *Russian Art*, p. 167.
17 Newmarch, *The Russian Arts*, p. 196.
18 Valkenier, *Russian Realist Art*, pp. 119–20.
19 A. Новитский, 'Памяти А.П. Боголюбова', *Русский архив*, vol. 1, 1897, pp. 390–1. I am grateful to Dr Rosalind Blakesley for permission to quote from her forthcoming article 'Promoting a Pan-European Art: Aleksei Bogoliubov as Artistic Mediator

between East and West', in R.P. Blakesley and S.E. Reid (eds), *Russian Art and the West: A Century of Dialogue in Painting, Architecture and the Decorative Arts*, DeKalb, Northern Illinois University Press, forthcoming.

20 Quoted in Dolinina, '"Eyes Wide Shut". Landscape Painting in Nineteenth Century Russia and France', p. 112.

Chapter 8

1 See J. Bowlt, 'Two Russian Maecenases. Savva Mamontov and Princess Tenisheva', *Apollo*, December 1973, vol. 98, No. 142, pp. 444–53. On the broader aspects of the Slavic Revival see E. Kirichenko and M. Anikst, *The Russian Style*, London, 1991. The fullest survey yet of cultural life at Abramtsevo is provided by E. Пастон, *Абрамцево искусство и жизнь*, Москва, 2003.

2 Quoted in A. Hilton, *Russian Folk Art*, Indianapolis, 1995, p. 227.

3 See D. Jackson, 'Icons in the 19th century', in S. Smyth and S. Kingston (eds), *Icons 88*, Dublin, 1988, p. 80.

4 Е. Поленова, *Абрамцево. Воспоминания*, Москва, 1922, p. 5.

5 Tenisheva's autobiography provides information on work at Talashkino as well as her studio modelled on Parisian lines: М. Тенишева, *Впечатления моей жизни*, Париж, 1933.

6 Valkenier, *Russian Realist Art*, p. 210, n. 30 details the increase in state patronage as well as the founding of the new institutions subsequently mentioned.

7 Quoted in Kirichenko and Anikst, *The Russian Style*, p. 65.

8 For the most recent works on Vasnetsov see Е. Пастон, *Виктор Васнецов*, Москва, 2001 and Е. Шилова, *Виктор Васнецов*, Москва, 2004.

9 А. Прахов, 'Художественные выставки в Петербурге', *Пчела*, № 11, April 27, 1876, p. 7.

10 Stasov's review in В. Стасов, *Статьи и заметки, не вошедшие в собранные сочинения*, Москва, 1954, vol. 2, p. 174. On Myasoedov's and Yaroshenko's threat to resign see Valkenier, *Russian Realist Art*, p. 85.

11 Reproduced in M. Anikst and E. Chernevich, *Russian Graphic Design 1880–1917*, New York, 1990, p. 95.

12 See typically N. Shanina, *Victor Vasnetsov*, Leningrad, 1979, pp. 51–7 on *Prince Igor's Battle* and pp. 103–10 on the *Bogatyrs*.

13 Newmarch, *The Russian Arts*, p. 224.

14 Quoted in В. Лобанов, *Виктор Васнецов в Москве*, Москва, 1962, p. 44.

15 Нестеров, *Давние дни*, p. 159.

16 Benois, *Memoirs*, vol. 2, p. 132.

17 On Tarkovsky see V. Lenyashin, '"Everything Gravitates Towards the Landscape." Landscape Painting in the Context of the Russian Genre System', in Jackson and Wageman (eds), *Russian Landscape*, p. 144. On Nesterov and modernity see exhibition catalogue *Kunst + Religie in Rusland*, Zwolle, 2002.

Chapter 9

1 Valkenier, *Russian Realist Art*, p. 126.
2 Letter to Tretyakov, 10 August 1884, Репин, *Письма*, vol. 1, pp. 297–8.
3 E. Valkenier, *Valentin Serov. Portraits of Russia's Silver Age*, Evanston IL, 2001, p. 48.
4 On the motif of the demon see M. Laurita, '"The Vrubel"-Demon Entanglement: The Creation of a Symbolist Myth', in *The Silver Age: Russian Literature and Culture 1881–1921*, vol. 2, 1999, pp. 1–24.
5 Letter to A. Vrubel, 6 January 1883, in M. Врубель, *Врубель. Переписка, воспоминания о художнике*, Москва, 1963, p. 56.
6 Letter to A. Vrubel, April 1883, in *Ibid.*, pp. 59–60.
7 Letter to Stasov, 21 July 1886, Крамской, *Письма*, vol. 2, pp. 251–3.
8 The young painters' petition and the Wanderers' re-framed statutes are reproduced in *Товарищество*, vol. 1, pp. 373 and 375–6 respectively.
9 Letter to Savitsky, 8 September 1887, *Репин-Стасов. Переписка*, vol. 2, pp. 237–8.
10 The full statement is reproduced in *Товарищество*, vol. 2, pp. 423–4.
11 Л. Пастернак, *Записи разных лет*, Москва, 1975, pp. 42–3.
12 On the Tsar's ambitions see A. Савинов, 'Академия Художеств и Товарищество передвижных художественных выставок', *Проблемы развития русского искусства*, Ленинград, 1972, vol. 2, pp. 42–56.
13 Valkenier, *Russian Realist Art*, p. 134.
14 This was early acknowledged in feminist art history: L. Nochlin, 'Why Have There Been No Great Women Artists?', in E. Baker and T. Hess, eds, *Art and Sexual Politics: Women's Liberation, Women Artists and Art History*, New York and London, 1973, p. 162.
15 Letter to Stasov, 11 June 1894, Репин, *Письма*, vol. 2, pp. 66–7.
16 Valkenier, *Russian Realist Art*, p. 89.
17 Reproduced in *Товарищество*, vol. 2, pp. 515.
18 'Наши художники', *Огонек*, 1911, № 49. Quoted in E. Журавлева, 'Революционная тема в творчестве B.E. Маковского', *Государственная Третьяковская галерея. Материалы и исследования*, Москва, 1956, vol. 1, p. 148. See Минченков, *Воспоминания о Передвижниках*, p. 46 on the controversy over the painting's display and acquisition.
19 The artistic climate around the 1905 revolution is dealt with in Г. Стернин, *Художественная жизнь России 1900–1910-х годов*, Москва, 1988, pp. 9–62; pp. 11–12 on the reactions of Polenov and Serov.
20 The motif of the insurgent martyr tearing open his shirt to receive the bullets is also utilised in Aleksandr Dovzhenko's 1928 film *Arsenal*.
21 See Valkenier, *Russian Realist Art*, pp. 120–3, which exposes the problematic nature of this topic. Maksimov, for example, is said to have been one of the few painters who lived 'on the verge of poverty' (p. 120) yet is later included amongst those whose work declined as he struggled to finance 'the extravaganza of country living a la nobility' (pp. 122).
22 See И. Репин, 'О Пенатах', in И. Бродский & B. Москвинов (eds), *Новое о Репине. Статьи и письма художника. Воспоминания учеников и друзей. Публикации*, Ленинград, 1969, pp. 26–7 and also a photograph of workers from the capital arriving at Penaty on pp. 176–7.

23 For a full history of the painting see И. Грабарь, 'К истории создания картины *Торжественное заседание Государственного совета 7 мая 1901 года*', in *Художественное наследство*, vol. 2, pp. 264–72. Related to this theme is D. Jackson and G. Churak, 'A Newly-Discovered Portrait of Tsar Nicholas II by Ilya Repin', *Apollo*, October 1997, vol. 146, No. 428, pp. 32–7.

24 Стасов, *Избранные сочинения*, vol. 3, p. 845.

25 See A. Hilton, 'The Exhibition of Experiments in St. Petersburg and the Independent Sketch', *Art Bulletin*, December 1988, pp. 677–98.

26 *Вечернее время*, 7 января, 1913.

Conclusion

1 On this and Lenin's plan for monumental propaganda see C. Lodder, 'Lenin's Plan for Monumental Propaganda', in M. Cullerne-Bown and B. Taylor (eds), *Art of the Soviets. Painting, Sculpture and Architecture in a One-party State, 1917–1992*, Manchester, 1993, pp. 16–32.

2 J. Bowlt, *Russian Art of the Avant-Garde. Theory & Criticism 1902–1934*, London, 1988, p. 281.

3 *Ibid.*, pp. 266–7.

4 Memoirs by delegation members are in Бродский и Москвинов, *Новое о Репине*, pp. 286–306. On Kasatkin see Valkenier, *Russian Realist Art*, p. 153.

5 M. Cullerne-Bown, *Art Under Stalin,* Oxford, 1991, p. 24.

6 A. Lebedev, *The Itinerants*, London, Sydney and Leningrad, 1982, p. 20.

Select bibliography

Entries are arranged firstly in Russian, then all other languages. As with footnotes, translated citations are as per the published original, despite apparent inconsistencies between systems of transliteration. Where relevant, square brackets denote original date of publication.

Primary sources: letters, diaries, memoirs, works of reference, etc.

Андреев, В. В., М. В. Астафьева, С. Н. Гольдштейн и Н. Л. Приймак, *Товарищество Передвижных Художественных Выставок 1869–1899. Письма и документы*, 2 vols, Москва, Искусство, 1987.

Бродский, И. А. и В. Н. Москвинов (eds), *Новое о Репине. Статьи и письма художника. Воспоминания учеников и друзей. Публикации*, Ленинград, Художник РСФСР, 1969.

Васнецов, Виктор, *Виктор Михайлович Васнецов. Письма. Дневники. Воспоминания. Документы. Суждения современников*, Москва, 1987.

Врубель, Михаил, *Врубель. Переписка, воспоминания о художнике*, Москва, 1963.

Ге, Николай, *Николай Николаевич Ге, Письма, статьи, критика, Воспоминания современников*, Москва, Искусство, 1978.

Грабарь, Игорь, В. Н. Лазарев и В. С. Кеменов (eds), *История русского искусства*, 13 vols, Москва, 1953–69.

Грабарь, Игорь, *Игорь Грабарь. Письма. 1871–1917*, Москва, 1974.

Зильберштейн, И. С. и И. Э. Грабарь (eds), *Художественное наследство. Репин*, 2 vols, Москва-Ленинград, Академия наук, 1948–49.

Крамской, Иван, *Переписка И. Н. Крамского*, 2 vols, Москва, Искусство, 1953–54.

Крамской, Иван, *Иван Николаевич Крамской. Письма, статьи в двух томах*, Москва, Искусство, 1965–66.

Мусоргский, Модест, *М. П. Мусоргский. Письма и документы*, Москва, 1932.

Нестеров, Михаил, *Давние дни*, Москва-Ленинград, 1959.

Нестеров, Михаил, *Письма. Избранное*, Ленинград, Искусство, 1988.

Перов, Василий, *В. Перов, документы, письма и рассказы, каталог произведений, библиография*, ed. А. Федоров-Давыдов, Москва, 1934.

Поленов, Василий, *Василий Дмитриевич Поленов. Письма, Дневники, Воспоминания*, Москва, 1950.

Поленов, Василий, *Василий Дмитриевич Поленов. Елена Дмитриевна Поленова. Хроника семьи художников*, ed. Е. В. Сахарова, Москва, 1964.
Репин, Илья, *Далекое близкое*, Ленинград, Художник РСФСР, [1937] 1982.
Репин, Илья, *Письма И. Е. Репина. Переписка с П. М. Третьяковым. 1873–1898*, Москва-Ленинград, Искусство, 1946.
Репин, Илья, *Письма И. Е. Репина. И. Е. Репин и В. В. Стасова. Переписка*, 3 vols, Москва-Ленинград, 1948–50, I: 1871–76, II: 1877–94, III: 1895–1906.
Репин, Илья, *И. Е. Репин и И. Н. Крамской. Переписка, 1873–1885*, Москва, 1949.
Репин, Илья, *И. Е. Репин. Письма, переписка с Л. Н. Толстым, в двух томах*, Москва-Ленинград, 1949.
Репин, Илья, *И. Е. Репин. Избранные письма, в двух томах*, Москва, 1969.
Серов, Валентин, *Валентин Серов в воспоминаниях, дневниках и переписке современников*, И. С. Зильберштейн и В. А. Самков (eds), Ленинград, Художник РСФСР, 1971.
Стасов, Владимир, *Избранное. Живопись, скульптура, графика*, 2 vols, Москва, 1950.
Стасов, Василий, *Избранные сочинения в трех томах*, Москва, 1952.
Стасов, Владимир, *Статьи и заметки, публиковавшиеся в газетах и не вошедшие в книжные издания*, 2 vols, Москва, 1952–54.
Суриков, Василий, *Василий Иванович Суриков. Письма, Воспоминания о художнике*, Радимовский, Н. А. и З. А. и С. Н. Голдштейн (eds), Ленинград, Искусство, 1977.
Толстой, Лев, *Л. Н. Толстой и художники. Толстой об искусстве. Письма, дневники, воспоминания*, Москва, 1978.
Третьяков, Павел, *Переписка П. М. Третьякова и В. В. Стасова. 1874–1897*, Москва-Ленинград, 1949.
Шишкин, Иван, *Иван Иванович Шишкин: Переписка, дневник, современники о художнике*, ed. Ирина Шувалова, Ленинград, 1978.

Benois, Alexander, *Memoirs*, tr. Moura Budberg, London, Columbus Books, 1988.
Christian, R.F. (ed.), *Tolstoy's Letters*, 2 vols, London, Athlone Press, 1978.
Christian, R.F. (ed.), *Tolstoy's Diaries*, 2 vols, New York, Scribners, 1985.
Dmytryshyn, Basil (ed.), *Imperial Russia. A Source Book, 1700–1917*, Fort Worth, Holt, Rinehart and Winston, 1990.
Dostoevsky, Fedor, 'Apropos of the Exhibition', in Boris Brasol (ed.), *F.M. Dostoievsky, the Diary of a Writer*, New York, 1954, vol. 1, pp. 79–81.
Milner, John, *A Dictionary of Russian and Soviet Artists 1420–1970*, Woodbridge, Antique Collectors' Club, 1993.
Pasternak, Leonid, *The Memoirs of Leonid Pasternak*, intr. Josephine Pasternak, tr. Jennifer Bradshaw, London, Quartet Books, 1982.
Paxton, John, *Companion to Russian History*, New York, Facts on File, 1983.
Paxton, John (ed.), *Imperial Russia. A Reference Handbook*, London, Macmillan, 2000.

Secondary sources: books, articles, catalogues, etc.

Edited exhibition catalogues are ordered by catalogue title.

Алленов, Михаил, *Русское искусство XVIII-начала XX века*, Москва, 2000.
Боткина, А. П., *Павел Михайлович Третьяков в жизни и искусстве*, Москва, 1995.

Ванслов, В., и М. Ракова (eds), *Художники Передвижники: сборник статей*, Москва, 1975.
Василий Перов. Выставка произведений к 150-летию со дня рождения. Каталог, ed., Н. Ю. Зограф, Москва, ГТГ, 1988.
Василий Иванович Суриков. К 150-летию со дня рождения. Живопись. Каталог выставки, Москва, ГТГ, 1998.
Василий Иванович Суриков. К 150-летию со дня рождения. Акварель. Каталог выставки, Москва, ГТГ, 1998.
Верещагина, А. Г., *Историческая картина в русском искусстве. Шестидесятые годы XIX века*, Москва, Искусство, 1990.
Гольдштейн, С. Н., *Иван Николаевич Крамской. Жизнь и творчество*, Москва, 1965.
Горина, Т., *Илларион Михайлович Прянишников 1840–1894*, Москва, 1958.
Государственный Русский музей: каталог, 1, Живопись; XVIII век, ed. Г. Голдовский, С-Петербург, 1998.
Государственная Третьяковская Галерея. Каталог собрания. Живопись второй половины XIX века. Том 4. Книга первая: А-М, Москва, 2001.
Грабарь, Игорь, *Репин*, 2 vols, Москва, [1937] 1963–64.
Дмитриева, Нина, *Михаил Врубель*, Ленинград, Художник РСФСР, 1990.
Зилоти, В. П., *В доме Третьякова*, Москва, Искусство, 1998.
Илья Ефимович Репин 1844–1930: к 150-летию со дня рождения, ed. Я. Брук, Москва, Красная площадь, 1994.
Илья Ефимович Репин: к 150-летию со дня рождения. Сборник статей, ed. В. Леняшин, С-Петербург, Palace Edition, 1995.
Карпова, Т. (ed.), *XIX век: целостность и процесс вопросы взаитодействия искусств,* Москва, Пинакотека, 2002.
Кеменов, Владимир, *Василий Суриков*, Ленинград, 1978.
Курочкина, Т. И., *Крамской*, Ленинград, Художник РСФСР, 1989.
Лазуко, Албина, *Виктор Васнецов*, Ленинград, Художник РСФСР, 1990.
Ландцерт, Ф. П., 'По поводу картины И. Е. Репина *Иван Грозный и его сын 16.XI.1581 года*', *Вестник изящных искусств*, 1885, III, pp. 192–205.
Леняшин, Владимир, *Валентин Серов*, Ленинград, Художник РСФСР, 1989.
Леняшин, Владимир, *Василий Перов*, Ленинград, Художник РСФСР, 1989.
Лобанов, В. М., *Виктор Васнецов в Москве*, Москва, 1962.
Лясковская, О. А., *Илья Ефимович Репин*, Москва, ГТГ, 1953.
Мальцева, Фиана, *Алексей Саврасов*, Ленинград, Художник РСФСР, 1984.
Манин, Виталий, *Русский пейзаж*, Москва, Белый город, 2000.
Манин, Виталий, *Куинджи и его школа*, Ленинград, Художник РСФСР, 1987.
Минченков, Я., *Воспоминания о Передвижниках*, Ленинград, 1980.
М. В. Нестеров 1862–1942, каталог, Москва, ГТГ, 1990.
Нестерова, Елена, 'Тема бурлаков в русской живописи 1860–1870 годов', in *Илья Ефимович Репин. К 150-летию со дня рождения. Сборник статей*, С-Петербург, 1995, pp. 57–65.
Нестерова, Елена, *Алексей Саврасов*, С-Петербург, 2002.
Парамонов, А. В., *Иллюстрации И. Е. Репина* Москва, Искусство, 1952.
Парамонов, А. В., *Передвижники*, Москва, Искусство, 1975.
Пастернак, Леонид, *Записи разных лет*, Москва, Советский жудожник, 1975.
Пастон, Элеонора, *Виктор Васнецов*, Москва, 2001.

Пастон, Элеонора, *Абрамцево искусство и жизнь*, Москва, 2003.
Пастон, Элеонора, *Василий Поленов*, Москва, 2003.
Прибульская, Г. И., 'Репин и Академия Художеств. По материалам биографи художника', in *Илья Ефимович Репин. К 150-летию со дня рождения. Сборник статей*, С-Петербург, 1995, pp. 103–10.
Ракова, М., *Русская историческая живопись середины девятнадцатого века*, Москва, Искусство, 1979.
Рогинская, Ф.А., *Передвижники*, Москва, 1993.
Рогинская, Ф.С., *Товарищество Передвижных Художественных Выставок*, Москва, Искусство, 1989.
Русские художники. Энциклопедический словарь, ed., В. Назаров, С-Петербург, Азбука, 1998.
Сарабьянов, Дмитрий, *Русская живопись XIX века среди европейских школ*, Москва, Советский жудожник, 1980.
Сарабьянов, Дмитрий, *Павел Федотов*, Ленинград, Художник РСФСР, 1985.
Секлюцкий, В. В., *Николай Александрович Ярошенко*, Ставрополь, 1963.
Стасов, Владимир, 'Портрет Мусоргского', *Избранные сочинения*, Москва, 1952, vol. 2, pp. 119–21.
Стасов, Владимир, 'По поводу лекции проф. Ландцерта о картине Репина', *Новости*, 135, 9 мая 1885, p. 1.
Стернин, Григорий, *Русская художественная культура второй половины XIX-начала XX века*, Москва, Советский жудожник, 1984.
Стернин, Григорий, 'О художественной жизни России в годы первой русской революции', in *Художественная жизнь России 1900–1910–х годов*, Москва, Искусство, 1988, pp. 9–62.
Третьяковская Галерея. Каталог живописи XVIII-начала XX века. (До 1917 года), Москва, ГТГ, 1984.
225 лет Академии художеств СССР, каталог выставки, 1757–1917, vol. 1, П. М. Сысоев intr., Москва, Изобразительное искусство, 1985.
Чурак, Галина, *Федор Васильев*, Москва, 2000.
Шилова, Екатерина, *Виктор Васнецов*, Москва, 2004.
Шумова, М.Н., 'Из истории картины И.Е. Репина *Бурлаки на Волге*', in *Илья Ефимович Репин. К 150-летию со дня рождения. Сборник статей*, С-Петербург, 1995, pp. 50–6.
Шумова, М.Н., *Русская живопись середины XIX века*, Москва, 1984.
Шувалова, Ирина, *Мясоедов*, Ленинград, 1971.
Шувалова, Ирина, *Иван Шишкин*, 1990, Ленинград, Художник РСФСР.

Alexeyeva, Tatyana, *Venetsianov and His School*, tr. Carolyn Justice and Yuri Kleiner, Leningrad, Aurora, 1984.
Allenov, Mikhail, *Moscow: Treasures and Traditions*, exhibition catalogue, Washington, Seattle Art Museum, 1990.
Alpatov, Mikhail, *Russian Impact on Art*, New York, Greenwood, 1969.
Anderson, Roger and Paul Debreczeny (eds), *Russian Narrative & Visual Art. Varieties of Seeing*, Gainesville, University Press of Florida, 1994.
Andreeva, G.B. *et al.*, *Russia's Golden Map. Masterpieces of Russian Art*, Moscow, Scanrus, 2003.

Anikst, Mikhail and Elena Chernevich, *Russian Graphic Design 1880–1917*, New York, Abbeville Press, 1990.
Auty, Robert and Dmitri Obolensky (eds), *An Introduction to Russian Art and Architecture*, Cambridge, Cambridge University Press, 1980.
Barooshian, Vahan, *V.V. Vereshchagin. Artist at War*, Gainesville, University Press of Florida, 1993.
Beavington Atkinson, John, *An Art Tour to Russia*, London and New York, Waterstone, 1986. First published 1873 as *An Art Tour to Northern Capitals of Europe*.
Benois, Alexander, *The Russian School of Painting*, London, Werner Laurie, 1916.
Bird, Alan, *A History of Russian Painting*, Oxford, Phaidon, 1987.
Bowlt, John, 'Two Russian Maecenases. Savva Mamontov and Princess Tenisheva', *Apollo*, December 1973, vol. 98, No. 142, pp. 444–53.
Bowlt, John, 'Russian Painting in the Nineteenth Century', in Theofanis Stavrou (ed.), *Art and Culture in Nineteenth-Century Russia*, Bloomington, Indiana University Press, 1983, pp. 113–39.
Bowlt, John, *Russian Art of the Avant Garde. Theory and Criticism 1902–1934*, London, Thames and Hudson, 1988.
Burrus, Christina, *Art Collectors of Russia*, London and New York, Tauris Parke Books, 1992.
Chamot, Mary, *Russian Painting and Sculpture*, Oxford, Pergamon Press, 1963.
Chernyshevsky, Nikolai, 'The Aesthetic Relation of Art to Reality', in *Selected Philosophical Essays*, Moscow, 1953, pp. 281–381. First published 1853.
Chernyshevsky, Nikolai, *What Is to Be Done?*, tr. Michael Katz, Ithaca and London, Cornell University Press, 1996.
Dmitrenko, A., *Fifty Russian Artists*, tr. Angus Roxberg, Moscow, Raduga Publishers, 1986.
Dobrolyubov, Nikolai, *Selected Philosophical Essays*, Moscow, Foreign Languages Publication House, 1956.
Eisenman, Stephen *et al.*, *Nineteenth Century Art: A Critical History*, London, Thames and Hudson, 2002.
Elliott, David, *Photography in Russia 1840–1940*, London, Thames and Hudson, 1992.
Ely, Christopher, *This Meager Nature. Landscape and National Identity in Imperial Russia*, DeKalb, Northern Illinois University Press, 2002.
Engel, Barbara, and Clifford Rosenthal (eds), *Five Sisters: Women Against the Tsar*, London, Routledge, 1975.
Fiodorov-Davydov, Alexei, *Isaac Levitan: The Mystery of Nature*, Bournemouth and St Petersburg, Parkstone-Aurora, 1995.
Frankel, Tobia, *The Russian Artist: The Creative Person in Russian Culture*, New York and London, Macmillan, 1972.
Garshin, Vsevolod, *From the Reminiscences of Private Ivanov and Other Stories*, London, Angel Books, 1988.
Gray, Camilla, *The Russian Experiment in Art, 1863–1922*, London, Thames and Hudson, 1986.
Gray, Rosalind, 'Muscovite Patrons of European Painting. The Collections of Vasily Kokorev, Dmitry Botkin and Sergei Tretyakov', *Journal of the History of Collections*, 10, No. 12 (1988), pp. 189–98.
Gray, Rosalind, 'The Golitsyn and Kushelëv-Bezborodko Collections and Their Role in the Evolution of Public Art Galleries in Russia,' *Oxford Slavonic Papers*, NS vol. 31 (1998), pp. 51–67.

Gray, Rosalind, *Russian Genre Painting in the 19th Century*, Oxford, Clarendon Press, 2000.
Great Russian Masters, exhibition catalogue, Helsinki, Ateneumin taidmuseo, 1995.
Guerman, Mikhail, *Mikhail Vrubel*, Bournemouth and St Petersburg, Parkstone-Aurora, 1996.
Gusyev, Vladimir and Yevgenia Petrova, *The Russian Museum*, St Petersburg, Palace Editions, 1998.
Hamilton, George, *The Art and Architecture of Russia*, Harmondsworth, Penguin Books, 1983.
Hare, Richard, *The Art and Artists of Russia*, London, Methuen, 1965.
Henry, Peter, *A Hamlet of his Time. Vsevolod Garshin. The Man, his Works, and his Milieu*, Oxford, Willem A. Meeuws, 1983.
Hilton, Alison, 'The Revolutionary Theme in Russian Realism', in Henry A. Millon and Linda Nochlin (eds), *Art and Architecture in the Service of Politics*, Cambridge MA, MIT Press, 1978, pp. 108–27.
Hilton, Alison, 'The Exhibition of Experiments in St. Petersburg and the Independent Sketch', *Art Bulletin*, December 1988, pp. 677–98.
Hilton, Alison, *Russian Folk Art*, Indianapolis, Indiana University Press, 1995.
Holt, Elizabeth, *From the Classicists to the Impressionists: Art and Architecture in the Nineteenth Century*, New York, New York University Press, 1966.
Ilya Repin 1844–1930, exhibition catalogue, Retretti, Painokumppanit, 1989.
Ilya Repin, Russia's secret, exhibition catalogue, Zwolle, Waanders, 2001.
Ingles, Elisabeth, *Russia's Four Seasons. Landscape and Images of Mother Russia*, Bournemouth, Parkstone, 1999.
International Exhibition, 1862, Official Catalogue of the Fine Arts Department, London, 1862.
Iovleva, Lidiya, *The Tretyakov Gallery Moscow. A Panorama of Russian and Soviet Art. Painting, Graphic Art, Sculpture*, tr. B. Meerovich, Leningrad, Aurora, 1983.
Iovleva, Lidiya, *State Tretyakov Gallery. Guidebook*, Moscow, Avant-Garde, 2000.
Isdebsky-Pritchard, Aline, *The Art of Mikhail Vrubel (1856–1910)*, Michigan, Ann Arbor, 1982.
Jackson, David, 'Western Aesthetics and Russian Ethics: Repin in Paris 1873–76', *Russian Review*, vol. 57, No. 3, July 1998, pp. 394–409.
Jackson, David, 'Garshin and Repin. Writer and Artist in a Creative Relationship', in
P. Henry, V. Porudominskii and M. Girshman (eds), *Vsevolod Garshin at the Turn of the Century*, 3 vols, Oxford, Northgate Press, 1999–2000, vol. 2, pp. 102–11.
Jackson, David, 'The Motherland. Tradition and Innovation in Russian Landscape Painting', in David Jackson and Patty Wageman (eds), *Russian Landscape*, Schoten, BAI, 2003, pp. 52–78.
Jackson, David and Galina Churak, 'A Newly-Discovered Portrait of Tsar Nicholas II by Ilya Repin', *Apollo*, October 1997, vol. 146, No. 428, pp. 32–7.
Jackson, David and Patty Wageman (eds), *Russian Landscape*, Schoten, BAI, 2003.
Jacobs, Michael, *The Good and Simple Life: Artist Colonies in Europe and America*, Oxford, Phaidon, 1985.
Kelly, Aileen, *Towards Another Shore. Russian Thinkers between Necessity and Chance*, New Haven CT, Yale University Press, 1998.
Kelly, Catriona and David Shepherd (eds), *Constructing Russian Culture in the Age of Revolution, 1881–1940*, Oxford, Oxford University Press, 1998.

Kemenov, Vladimir, *Vasily Surikov*, Bournemouth, Parkstone, 1997.
King, Averil, *Isaak Levitan. Lyrical Landscape*, London, Philip Wilson, 2004.
Kirichenko Evgenia and Mikhail Anikst, *The Russian Style*, London, Laurence King, 1991.
Kunst + Religie in Rusland, exhibition catalogue, Zwolle, Gemeentemuseum Den Haag, 2002.
Laurita, Mary, 'The Vrubel'-Demon Entanglement: The Creation of a Symbolist Myth', in *The Silver Age: Russian Literature and Culture 1881–1921*, vol. 2, 1999, pp. 1–24.
Lebedev, Andrei, *The Itinerants. Russian Realist Artists of the Late 19th and Early 20th Centuries*, London, Sydney and Leningrad, Pan Books-Aurora, 1982.
Loukomski, George, *History of Modern Russian Painting 1840–1940*, London, Hutchinson & Co, 1945.
Mojenok, Tatiana, *Peintres réalistes russes en France (1860–1900)*, Paris, Publications de la Sorbonne, 2003.
Moynahan, Brian, *The Russian Century – a Photojournalistic History of Russia in the Twentieth Century*, London, Chatto and Windus, 1994.
Muther, Richard, *The History of Modern Painting*, 3 vols, London, Henry & Co, 1895–96.
Nesterova, Elena, *The Itinerants. The Masters of Russian Realism,* Bournemouth and St Petersburg, Parkstone-Aurora, 1996.
Newmarch, Rosa, *The Russian Arts*, London, Herbert Jenkins, 1916.
Nochlin, Linda, *Realism*, Harmondsworth, Penguin Books, 1982.
Novouspensky, Nikolai, *Paintings from the Russian Museum Collection*, Leningrad, Aurora, 1975.
Parker, Fan and J. Stephen, *Russia on Canvas: Ilya Repin*, University Park PA and London, Pennsylvania State University Press, 1980.
Perrie, Maureen, *Alexander II. Emancipation and Reform in Russia 1855–1881*, London, The Historical Association, 1993.
Petrov, Vesevelod, *Russian Art Nouveau: The Diaghilev Group of Russian Artists*, Bournemouth and St Petersburg, Parkstone-Aurora, 1998.
Pipes, Richard, *Russia Under the Old Regime*, Harmondsworth, Penguin Books, 1984.
Pomeroy, Jordana and Rosalind Blakesley (eds), *An Imperial Collection: Women Artists from the State Hermitage Museum*, London, Merrell Publishers, 2003.
Raeff, Marc, *Russian Intellectual History*, New York, Harcourt, Brace & World, 1966.
Roosevelt, Priscilla, *Life on the Russian Country Estate. A Social and Cultural History*, New Haven and London, Yale University Press, 1995.
Rosenblum, Robert and Hugh Janson, *Art of the Nineteenth Century: Painting and Sculpture*, London, Thames and Hudson, 1984.
Rubissow, Helen, *The Art of Russia*, New York, Philosophical Library, 1946.
Rusakova, Alla, *Mikhail Nesterov*, Leningrad, Aurora, 1990.
Russia, The Land, The People. Russian painting, 1850–1910, exhibition catalogue, Washington, DC, Smithsonian Institution, 1986.
Russian and Soviet Painting, exhibition catalogue, New York, Metropolitan Museum of Art, 1977.
Rzhevsky, Nicholas (ed.), *The Cambridge Companion to Modern Russian Culture*, Cambridge, Cambridge University Press, 2001.
Salmina-Haskell, Larissa, *Russian Paintings and Drawings*, Oxford, Ashmolean Museum, 1990.

Salmond, Wendy, *Arts and Crafts in Late Imperial Russia*, Cambridge, Cambridge University Press, 1996.
Sarabyanov, Dmitry, *Russian Art. From Neoclassicism to the Avant-Garde. Painting, Sculpture, Architecture*, London, Thames and Hudson, 1990.
Sarabyanov, Dmitri, *Valentin Serov*, Bournemouth and St Petersburg, Parkstone-Aurora, 1996.
Savinov, Alexei, and Alexei Fyodorov-Davydov, *Shishkin*, London, Sydney and Leningrad, Pan Books-Aurora, 1981.
Seton-Watson, Hugh, *The Russian Empire 1801–1917*, Oxford, Oxford University Press, 1988.
Shanina, N., *Victor Vasnetsov*, Leningrad, Aurora, 1979.
Shuvalova, Irina, *Ivan Shishkin: Artist of the Russian Forest*, Bournemouth, Parkstone, 1995.
Stavrou, Theofanis (ed.), *Art and Culture in Nineteenth-Century Russia*, Bloomington, Indiana University Press, 1983
Sternin, Grigory, *Ilya Repin: Painting, Graphic Arts*, Leningrad, Aurora, 1985.
Sternin, Grigory, *Ilya Efimovitch Repin: Painter of Russian History*, Bournemouth, Parkstone, 1996.
Stites, Richard, *The Women's Liberation Movement in Russia: Feminism, Nihilism and Bolshevism 1860–1930*, Princeton, NJ, Princeton University Press, 1978.
Tolstoy, Leo, *What Is Art? and Essays On Art*, tr. L. and A. Maude, Oxford, Oxford University Press, 1929.
Tolstoy, Leo, *What Then Must We Do?*, tr. A. Maude, Oxford, Oxford University Press, 1950.
Twilight of the Tsars. Russian Art at the Turn of the Century, exhibition catalogue, London, South Bank Centre, 1991.
Valkenier, Elizabeth Kridl, 'The Peredvizhniki and the Spirit of the 1860s' *Russian Review*, vol. 34, part 3, July 1975, pp. 247–65.
Valkenier, Elizabeth Kridl, 'Politics in Russian Art: The Case of Repin', *Russian Review*, vol. 37, part 1, January 1978, pp. 14–29.
Valkenier, Elizabeth Kridl, 'Repin's Search for the Revolutionary's Image in *They Did Not Expect Him*', *Gazette des Beaux-Arts*, vol. 91, May–June 1978, pp. 207–12.
Valkenier, Elizabeth Kridl, 'The Intelligentsia and Art', in Theofanis Stavrou (ed.), *Art and Culture in Nineteenth-Century Russia*, Bloomington, Indiana University Press, 1983, pp. 153–71.
Valkenier, Elizabeth Kridl, *Russian Realist Art. The State and Society. The Peredvizhniki and Their Tradition*, New York, Columbia University Press, 1989.
Valkenier, Elizabeth Kridl, *Ilya Repin and the World of Russian Art*, New York, Columbia University Press, 1990.
Valkenier, Elizabeth Kridl, *Valentin Serov. Portraits of Russia's Silver Age*, Evanston, IL, Northwestern University Press, 2001.
The Wanderers: Masters of 19th Century Russian Painting, exhibition catalogue, Dallas, University of Texas Press, 1990.
Westwood, J.N., *Endurance and Endeavour. Russian History 1812–1986*, Oxford, Oxford University Press, 1988.
Yurova, Tamara, *Levitan*, Leningrad, Aurora, 1988.

Index

Notes: Page numbers and ranges in italics include one or more relevant illustrations. 'Pl.' and 'Pls' refer to colour plates.

Abramtsevo 134, *135–9*, 140, 141, 144, 147, 148, 154
aesthеticism 23, 24, 113, 116, 164–5
Aksakov, Sergei 136
Aleksandr II 133
  assassination 59, 64, 68, 69, 80, 105, 108, 134
Aleksandr III 107, 114, 115, 118, 133–4, 140–1, 146, 150–2, 156, 170
All-Russian Academy of Arts 168
Antiquities of the Russian Empire 133
Antokolsky, Mark 29, 32, 136, 137
archaeological research 133
Argunov, Ivan 13–14
  Portrait of a Russian Woman in Peasant Costume 13
Arkhipov, Abram 160–1
  At the Etape 62
  Before Mass 160, *161*
art collections 30–1, 33, 78–9, 80, 84, 125
Art Nouveau (*style moderne*) 139, 148
Artel (co-operative) 26–7, 28, 29, 57, 58, 59, 60, 98, 125
artistic compromise 17, 151–2, 158
Arts and Crafts movement 135
Association of Artists of Revolutionary Russia (AKhRR) 167–8
autocracy, academic 10–12
autonomy, artistic 6, 28
avant-garde artists 166–7

Baksheyev, Vasily 159–60
  Prose of Life, The 159, *160*
Bakunin, Mikhail 65, 167
  Revolutionary Catechism, The 65
Barbizon school 125, 127
Bastien-Lepage, Jules 113
Baudelaire, Charles 116
Bee, The 106
Belinsky, Vissarion 22, 23, 42, 83
Benois, Aleksandr 12, 70, 76, 113, 115, 132
Bilibin, Ivan 136
'Bloody Sunday' 162–3
Bogdanov, Ivan
  Novice, The 52–3
  Reckoning Up 53
Bogdanov-Belsky, Nikolai 159
  At the School Door 52
Bogolyubov, Aleksei 132
Bonch-Bruyevich, Vladimir 76
book illustration 144
Borovikovsky, Vladimir Lukich 78
Brodsky, Isaak 167–8
  Lenin in Smolny 167

Bronnikov, Fedor
Field of the Damned. Place of Execution in Ancient Rome, The 104–5
Bruni, Fedor 38–9, 97, 98, 120
Brazen Serpent, The 10
Bryullov, Karl 9–10, 16, 31, 78, 97
Last Day of Pompeii, The 9
Byliny 143
Byzantine art 7, 140, 145, 146, 154

Cathedral of Christ the Redeemer, Moscow 141
Catherine the Great 9
Cause, The 122, 131
censorship, state 16, 17, 18–19, 22, 23, 57, 58, 64, 68, 74–5, 100, 101–5
Chaadev, Petr 21–2, 57
Chagal, Marc 166
Chardin, Jean-Baptiste-Siméon 15
Chekhov, Anton 47, 55, 68, 127, 159
'House with an Attic: An Artist's Story', 'The' 123
'Peasants' 53–4
Chekhov, Nikolai 123
Chernyshevsky, Nikolai 22, 23–4, 25, 26, 29, 36, 42, 57, 59, 69, 86, 168
Aesthetic Relationship of Art to Reality, The 23, 86
What Is to be Done? 23, 26, 74, 101
Chertkova, Anna 74
child labour 35
Chistyakov, Pavel 98
Church of the Holy Spirit, Talashkino 139
Church of the Resurrection, St Petersburg 134
Church of the Saviour, Abramtsevo *137–8*, 140, 144
Claresi, Jules 40
classicism 100, 134
commercialism 150–1
Committee on Arts 168
compromise, artistic 17, 151–2, 158
Contemporary, The 79
Corot, Jean-Baptiste-Camille 33, 125, 127
Cossacks 110, *113–14*, 115
Courbet, Gustave 29, 33, 34, 36, 100, 117, 125
Burial at Ornans 34
Return from the Conference 35

death 25, 45, *47–8*
Decamps, Alexandre-Gabrielle 125
Degas, Edgar 113
De Hooch, Pieter 15
Delacroix, Eugene 33, 125
Delaroche, Paul 32
Diaghilev, Sergei 114–15, 116, 128, 138, 139, 140
Diaz de la Peña, Narcise-Virgile 125
Dmitryev, I. 24
Dobrolyubov, Nikolai 22, 23, 24, 27, 57, 64, 83, 168
domestic dramas *53–4*, 67–70, Pl.2
Dostoevsky, Fedor 17, 23, 39, 40, 48, *79*, 80, 81, 91, 102, 103, 132, 148
Devils, The 23, 66
drunkenness *25*, 35, 53–4
Dukhobors 112

Elizabeth, Empress 9
'embourgoisement' 163–4
Ermenev, Ivan 35
Beggars 14
Blind Men Singing 14
ethnocentricity 134, 168
exhibitions 44, 102
Exhibition of Early Russian Art 7
Exhibition of Experiments and Sketches, The 164–5
Munich Sezession 128
one-man 129
Paris Universal Exhibition 40, 83, 117
Russian Landscape 4–5
Vienna World Exhibition 39
Wanderers (Society of Travelling Art Exhibits) 6, 7, 28, 29, 30, 41–2, 78–9,

84–5, 89, 99, 100, 106, 111, 122, 128, 144, 147, 148, 155, 168
World Exhibition, London 162

fantasy 143–4, 146
family portraits *92–5*, 136, *153*
Fedotov, Pavel 14, 16–17, 46
Major's Courtship, The 17
Newly Decorated Knight, A (also exhibited as *After the Party*) 16–17
Fet, Afanasy 96
Figner, Vera 71, 72, 73, 76, 113
figurative art 167
First All-Union Congress of Writers 168
Flavitsky, Konstantin
Princess Tarakanova in the Petropavlosk Fortress at the Time of the Flood 98
folk art 133, 135, 136–40
folklore 142, 143–4, 146–7
Free Art Studios 166
freedom
creative 26, 57, 130, 164
personal 9
French Revolution 34

Garshin, Vsevolod 37, 51–2, 69, 99, 103, 106, 112, 122–3
'Artists' 51–2, 122–3
'Nadezhda Nikolaevna' 76
Ge, Nikolai 6–7, 27–8, 78, 85, 88, 98–100, 116
Last Supper, The 98–9, 102
Peter the Great Interrogating Tsarevich Aleksei at Peterhof 99–100
Portrait of Leo Tolstoy 88
What is Truth? 30
genre painting 14, 15, 17, 18, 32, 34–5
Gerôme, Jean-Léon 32
Goethe, Wolfgang von 85
Gogol, Nikolai 1, 2, 5, 17
Dead Souls 136
May Night 143
Taras Bulba 115
Golovin, Aleksandr 139
Goncharova, Natalia 148
Goravsky, Apollinary 126
Gorbachov, Mikhail 4
Gorky, Maksim 55, 96
Granet, François-Marius 15
Grazhdanin 39, 70

Hartmann, Viktor 137
Hermitage 15, 16, 33, 120, 151
heroic realism 167
heroism 102–3, 142–3
Herzen, Aleksandr 27, 59, 78, 98
Hildenbandt, Varvara Ikskul von 95
Historical Museum, Moscow 140, 144
history painting 34, 42, *97–118*, Pl.4
Hogarth, William 16, 17

iconic art 7–8, 140
idealism 85–6
Imperial Academy of Arts 6, 7, 9, 10–11, 12, 14, 15, 16, 18, 27, 28, 33, 38, 58, 97, 100, 108, 109, 114, 125, 128, 130, 132, 141, 151, *157*, 156–9, 162, 166
administration 11–12
discipline 10–11
honours system 10, 11–12, 26
Society of Art Exhibits 28
student secession 22, 24, 26–7, 58
Imperial Russian Historic Society 140
Impressionism 3, 29, 127, 130
intelligentsia
portraits of *79–90*, 92, 96, 148
Russian 7, 8–9, 29
Soviet 148
Ivan the Terrible 110
see also Repin, Ilya, *Ivan the Terrible and His Son Ivan. 16 November 1581*
Ivanov, Aleksandr 113, 114
Christ Appearing to the People 10, 102
Ivanov, Sergei 52, 116, 131, 155, 156, 161, 163
Death of a Migrant Peasant 47–8, 161
Etape. One Did Not Survive 62
Massacre 169

Kamenev, Lev 27
Kandinsky, Wassily 148, 166
Karakozov, Dmitry 59, 62
Kasatkin, Nikolai *48–50*, 52, 57, 92, 131, 161, 163, 168
In the Corridor of the Circuit Court 161
Miners. The Shift 49
Poor People Collecting Coal in an Abandoned Pit *49–50*, 161
Katkov, Mikhail 80–1, 83
Katsman, Evgeny 167
Khliudov, Gerasim 30
Kiprensky, Orest 78
Klodt, Mikhail 130, 132
Kokorev, Vasily 30
Koroliov, Boris 167
Korovin, Konstantin 139, 152, 155
Korovin, Sergei 58, 103–4
Before Punishment in the Volost Administration 58, 103–4, *105*
Korzukhin, Aleksei
Drunken Father's Family, The 53
Kovalevsky, P.M. 81
Kramskoy, Ivan 19, 26, 27, 28, 29, 32, 38, 39, 50, 55, 80, 84–5, 88, 90–2, 100, 107, 115, 125, 128, 130, 147, 152, 155, 164
Bee Keeper 92
Christ in the Wilderness *66*, 67, 82, 102–3, 117, 143
Contemplator, The 91
Miller, The 90, 92
Mina Moiseyev 90
Mocking. 'Hail King of the Jews!' 103
Nekrasov at the Time of His Last Poems 83
Peasant Holding a Bridle (Mina Moiseyev) 91–2, Pl.3
Peasant Ignaty Pirogov. Model at the Academy of Arts, The 91
Portrait of a Peasant 91
Portrait of an Unknown Woman 95
Portrait of Leo Tolstoy 88
Portrait of Sofya Kramskoya, the Artist's Daughter *93–4*
Rusalki 143
Woman with an Umbrella 95
Woodsman, The 91, 92
Kramskoya, Sofya *93–4*
Kremlin, Faceted Chamber 140
Kuindzhi, Arkhip 123, 128–30, 132, 157, 158
After the Storm *128–9*
Moonlit Night on the Dnieper 129
Kushelëv-Bezborodko, Prince 33, 125
Kuznetsov, Nikolai 157
Inspecting His Estate 42–3
Kuznetsov, P.I. 110

landscape painting *119–32*, Pls 5,6
Lay of Igor's Host, The 142
Ledakov, Anton 40
Lenin, Vladimir Illich 88, 167, 168
Decree on Monumental Propaganda 167
Levitan, Isaak 17, 19–20, 87, 123, 126, 127–8, 132
Autumn Day. Sokolniki 123, 127
Spring Flood 128, Pl.7
Vladimirka Road, The 128, 130
Levitsky, Sergei 78, 98
Losenko, Anton
Vladimir and Rogneda 97
Lunacharsky, Anatoley 166, 167

Maikov, Vasily 79
Makovsky, Aleksandra 60
Makovsky, Konstantin 60
Makovsky, Nikolai 60
Makovsky, Vladimir 59, 60–2, 76, 77, 152, 153, 157, 162–3, 164
9 January 1905 on Vasilevsky Island 162
Acquitted Woman, The 71
Arrival of the Village Teacher, The 72
At the Etape 62
At the Vagankovsky Cemetery. Burying the Victims of Khodynka 162
Doss-House, A 48
No Entry 53

On the Boulevard 48, 53
Prisoner 67
Sentenced *61–2*, 103
Vecherinka (*Evening Gathering*) *60–1*, 75
Maksimov, Vasily 55, 163
Sick Husband, The *46–7*
Malevich, Kasimir 86, 148, 166
Malyutin, Sergei 139, 140
Mamontov, Anatoley 135–6
Mamontov, Andrei 136, 137
Mamontov, Savva 134, 135, 137, 138–9, 142
Mamontova, Elizaveta 135, 136, 137
Mamontova, Vera 136
Manet, Edouard 29, 34, 113
Maria, Grand Duchess 11, 12
Marxism 3, 96, 170
Meisonnier, Jean-Louis-Ernest 32
'Men of the Sixties' *see Raznochintsy*
Meshchersky, Prince V.P. 70
Messenger of Fine Arts, The 151
Mickiewicz, Adam 83
Mikhailovich, Aleksei 111
Millet, Jean-François 33, 125
Angelus, The 46
Man with a Hoe 34
Minsky, Nikolai 76
'Last Confession', 'The' 66–7
Mir iskusstva 114–15, 116, 128, 138, 140, 146, 148
modernism 116, 122, 155, 166
Moiseyev, Mina 90, 91–2, Pl.3
Monet, Claude 127
Morozova, Boyarina 111–13
Morris, William 135
Moscow Archaeological Institute 140
Moscow City Duma 140
Moscow School of Arts 12, 14, 19–20, 38, 48, 60, 123, 126, 127, 147, 157
Motherland 119–20, 133
see also landscape painting
Museum of Russian Antiquities and Folk Art 140
Musorgsky, Modest 37, 39, *83–4*
Pictures at an Exhibition 137
muzhik see peasants
Myasoedov, Grigory 27, 28, 41–2, 142, 147, 155, 157
Drought, The 45
Grandfather of the Russian Navy, The 41–2
Reading the Emancipation Manifesto 42, 92
Zemstvo Dines, The *41–2*, 57

narod see peasants
Narodnaya Volya ('The People's Will') 59, 64, 66–7, 71, 105–6
National Gallery, London 4
national heritage 37, 109, 112
see also nationalism; peasants, integrity; Populism
national identity 21, 120
see also Slavic Revival; Slavophile–Westerner question
nationalism 31, 33, 118, 132, 145–6, 150–1, 152
see also Slavic Revival; Slavophile–Westerner question
naturalism 15, 16, 18, 110, 117, 120–1, 125–6
nature *see* landscape painting
Nechaev, Sergei 65–6, 71
Nekrasov, Nikolai 69, 78, 79, 83
Neoclassicism 97
Nesterov, Mikhail 118, 136, 147–8, 155, 156, 168
Land of Russia (The People's Soul), The 148
Taking the Veil 147
Tsarevich Dmitry the Martyr 147
Vision of the Boy Bartholomew, The 136, 147, Pl.8
Youth of Saint Serius, The 147
Nestor the Chronicler 145
Nevsky, Aleksandr 145
New Times 80
Nicholas I 9, 10–12, 13, 22, 133, 141
Nicholas II 151, 152, 162, 164

nihilism 74–5
Non-Conformist art 148
Novosti 108

objectivity 40–1, 54, 90–1, 100, 117
Otrovsky, Aleksandr 17, 78, 79

Pasternak, Leonid 156
patronage 12–13, 14, 17, 26, 28, 30–1, 109, 110, 122, 125
peasants 14, 15, 16, *32*, 34–5, 36, *38–48*, *50*, 54–6, 90–2, *160–1*, Pls 1,3
  integrity 36–7, 41, 44, 90–2, 96, 119–20
  social status 40, 41, 43
  urban life *48–52*
  see also serfdom
Pecht, Friedrich 39
People's Will *see Narodnaya Volya*
Perelman, Viktor 167
Perov, Vasily 25, 27, 31–2, 35, 38, 39, 45, 46, 78, 81–2, 121, 122, 131
  Arrival of a District Police Officer at an Investigation, The 58
  Drowned Woman 35
  Easter Procession *25*, 35, 57
  Fomushka sych ('Owl-faced Tommy') 90
  Last Inn by the Town Gate, The 35
  Last Journey, The 35
  Pilgrim in a Field. On the Way to Eternal Bliss 45
  Portrait of Fedor Dostoevsky *79*, 102
  Torture of the Boyarina Morozova, The 108
  Troika 35
Perovskaya, Sofya 71, 75, 113
Peter the Great 7, 8–9, 21, *99–100*, 110, 111, 116
Petrashevsky circle 17
photo-realism 92
Pirogov, Ignaty 91, 92
Pisarev, Dmitry 22, 64
  Destruction of Aesthetics, The 23
Pissarro, Camille 113
Pobedonostsev, Konstantin 107, 108, 109
'podtekst' *see* subtext
Polenov, Vasily 104, 126–7, 136–7, 138, 157, 162, 164
  Christ and the Woman Taken in Adultery 104
  Overgrown Pond, The 131
Polenova, Elena 136, 137
political themes *60–77*
Populism 36–7, 55, 59, *60–4*, 102–3, 104, 109, 113, 134
portraiture *78–96*, 148, 156
Potemkin, Prince 13
Poussin, Nicolas 120
poverty 14, *25*, 35, *49*, 92
Prakhov, Adrian 106, 137, 139, 141
Prakhova, Elena 139
prison/prisoners 25, *26*, 58, *61–4*, *65*, 66–7, 71–2, 73, 76, 103, *105*, 161
prostitution 25, 52
Proudhon, Pierre Joseph 29, 36, 100
  Du principe de l'art et de sa destination sociale 116
Pryanishnikov, Fedor 30
Pryanishnikov, Illarion 27, 155
  Burned Out 38
  Peasants Driving Home 38
  Procession of the Cross, The 45
  Saviour's Day in the North, The 45
Pukirev, Vasily
  Unequal Marriage, The 25
Pushkin, Aleksandr 78

Raznochintsy ('Men of the Sixties') 22, 23, 24, 57, 152
realism 44–5
  French 36, 41, 100, 117
  Russian 1, 2, 4, 5, 7, 9, 10, 14, 16, 17–18, 19, 20, 21, 24, 34, 35, 36, 38, 70, 96, 99, 101, 102, 114–15, 116–18, 122, 127, 131, 132, 134, 143, 146, 148, 151, 156, 158, 159, 160, 165, 167–8
Redgrave, Richard
  Outcast, The 52
Regnault, Henri

Execution without Trial Under the Moorish Kings of Granada 108
religio-historical subjects *102–5*
religion 112, 135, 136
religious art 7–8
religious subjects *25*, 35, 43–6, 57, *66*, 67, 82, 98–9, Pl.1
Repin, Ilya 3, 4, 19, 24, 29, 33, 37, 38–41, 43–5, 53–4, 55–6, 59, 62–4, 66–70, 71–2, 76, 77, 80–1, 82–5, 87, 89–90, 92–3, 94–5, 102, 105–9, 111, 113–15, 120, 122, 126, 131, 136, 137, 138, 142, 151, 152–3, 154–5, *156–7*, 158, 162, 163–5, 167, 168
Aleksandr III Receives the District Headmen in the Courtyard of the Petrovsky Palace in Moscow *151*, 152
Archdeacon, The *82–3*
Arrest of a Propagandist *63–4*, 68, 73, 76, 103
Autumn Bouquet 95
Barge-haulers on the Volga (Burlaki) *32*, 38–41, 42, 45, 47, 48, 51, 57, 89, 125
Cautious One, A 90
Christ Raising Jairus's Daughter from the Dead 32
Drunken Father, The 53
Drunken Kiryak, The 53–4
Formal Session of the State Council in Honour of Its Centenary on May 7, 1901 164
In the Laboratory 72
In the Sunlight 95
Ivan the Terrible and His Son Ivan. 16 November 1581 67, 80, 102, *105–9*, 115, 117, 152, 165
Leo Tolstoy Barefoot (also exhibited as *Tolstoy at Prayer*) *88*, 89
Leo Tolstoy Ploughing 89
Parisian Café, A 29, 32
Peasant with an Evil Eye 90
Portrait of Aleksandra Tolstoy *94–5*
Portrait of Leo Tolstoy Seated 88
Portrait of Modest Musorgsky *83–4*
Portrait of Varvara Ikskul von Hildenbandt 95
Religious Procession 43
Religious Procession in the Province of Kursk 43–5, 46, 47, 54, 56, 83, 136, 152, 155, Pl.1
Revolutionary Woman Awaiting Execution (also exhibited as *Anguish* sometimes referred to as *Vera Figner in Prison*) 71–2
Secret Meeting, A (also exhibited as *By Lamplight* and *Meeting of the Nihilists*) 64–5, 66
Spurning Confession (also exhibited as *Spurning Confession Before Execution*) *65*, 66–7, 68
They Did Not Expect Her 68, 71
They Did Not Expect Him (Ne zhdali) 67–70, 77, 103, 136, 153, 159, Pl.2
Tolstoy at Prayer (also exhibited as *Leo Tolstoy Barefoot*) *88*, 89
Tsarevna Sofya in New Maiden Convent at the time of the Execution of the Streltsy and the Torture of All Her Servants in 1698 100–1
Under the Guard 62–3
Vera Repin Resting 93
Wide World 123
Zaporozhye Cossacks Writing a Mocking Letter to the Turkish Sultan, The *113–14*, 115, 136, 150
Repin, Nadya 95
Repin, Vera (daughter) 95, 136, *153*
Repin, Vera (wife) 93
Repin, Yury 93
revolutionary activism 57–77
Rodchenko, Aleksandr 166
'rodina' (Motherland) 119–20, 133
see also landscape painting
Roerikh, Nikolai 139, 140
Romanova, Sofya Alekseevna 100
romanticism 143
see also Slavic Revival
Ropet, Ivan 137

Rousseau, Henri 33
Russia 4, 10
cultural/political reforms 8–9, 21, 35, 38, 41, 99, 111, 117–18
Russian Museum of Emperor Aleksandr III (later State Russian Museum) 30, 150–1
'Russification' 118, 134
Russo-Turkish War 37, 134
Ryabushkin, Andrei
Tsar Mikhail Fedorovich Holding Council with the Boyars in His Royal Chamber 116

Saltykov-Shchedrin, Mikhail 37, 78, 79, 98, 99, 100
Samarin, Mikhail 137
Savitsky, Konstantin 76, 123, 156, 157
Meeting the Icon 46
Repair Work on the Railway 48, 131
Savrasov, Aleksei 27, 123–4, 125, 126
Rooks Have Returned, The 122, 124, 132, Pl.5
scholarships 31–2
Schopenhauer, Arthur 127
Selyaninov, Mikula 89
Semiradsky, Heinrich 100, 105
Torches of Christianity 104
sentimentality 36–7, 55
serfdom 9, 13, 14, 16, 19, 22, 42–3
Serov, Aleksandr 153
Serov, Valentin 136, 152–4, 155, 156, 161, 162, 164
Girl in Sunlight 154
Girl with Peaches 136, *153*
Soldiers, Brave Fellows, Where Now is Your Glory? 162
Shakespeare, William 85, 87
Sheremetev family 13
Shevchenko, Aleksandr
Landlord Exchanging Peasants for Dogs, The 43
Shevchenko, Taras 69
Shibanov, Mikhail 13–14
Celebrating the Marriage Contract 13
Shishkin, Ivan 32, 124–5, 129, 157
Morning in a Pine Forest 123
Thicket, The 124, Pl.6
Shurygin, Arseny
Arrest (also exhibited as *Contemporary Idealist, A*) 58
Shvarts, Vyacheslav 97–8, 99, 116
Scenes from the Domestic Lives of the Russian Tsars: Playing Chess 97
Vernal Train of the Tsarina on a Pilgrimage at the Time of Tsar Alexei Mikhailovich, The 97
Slavic Revival 133–49
Slavophile–Westerner question 8–9, 18, 21–2, 31, 99, 109–10, 133
social inequality *41–2*, 57–8
social satire 14, 16–18
social status 4, 9, 22, 44
artists 9, 10, 11, 13, 19–20, 24–5, 54, 60, 110, 147, 154, 163–4
merchants 13, 30
peasants 40, 41, 43
see also serfdom
Socialist Realism, Soviet 2, 168–9
Society for the Encouragement of Artists 12
Society for the Foundation of Schools of Reciprocal Training 15
Society of Art Exhibits 28
Society of Easel Painters (OSt) 167
Society of Travelling Art Exhibits *see* Wanderers (Society of Travelling Art Exhibits)
Soldatenkov, Kozma 30
Solzhenitsyn, Aleksandr
First Circle, The 96
Soroka, Grigory 16
spiritual revivalism 136–8, 147
St Petersburg Society of Artists 115
St Vladimir's Cathedral, Kiev 144–6, 147
Stalin, Josef 88, 101, 165
Stalinism 3, 4, 5, 22
Stanislavsky, Konstantin 138

Stasov, Vladimir 29–30, 31, 36, 37, 39, 40, 41, 42, 44, 45, 62, 70, 74, 80–1, 84–5, 92, 100, 101, 108, 112, 113, 117, 118, 122, 141, 142, 151, 158, 164, 165
State Russian Museum *see* Russian Museum of Emperor Aleksandr III (later State Russian Museum)
Steuben, Karl 69
Golgotha, The 69
Stravinsky, Igor 139
Rite of Spring 139
Stupin, A.V. 12
style moderne (Art Nouveau) 139, 148
subjectivity 54
subjects, artists' 13–14, 17–18, 25, 26, 27, 31
'Bloody Sunday' 162–3
child labour 35
death 25, 45, *47–8*
domestic dramas *53–4*, 67–70, Pl.2
drunkenness *25*, 35, 53–4
exile 67–70, Pl.2
family portraits *92–5*, 136, *153*
fantasy 143–4, 146
folklore 142, 143, 146–7
historical 34, 42, *97–118*, Pl.4
imperial family 152
individual misfortune 52–3
landscapes *119–32*, Pls 5,6
peasants 14, 15, 16, *32*, 34–5, 36, *38–48*, *50*, 54–6, 90–2, *160–1*, Pls 1,3
political themes *60–77*
Populism *60–4*
portraits *78–96*, 148, 156
poverty 14, *25*, 35, *49*, 92
prison/prisoners 25, *26*, 58, *61–4*, *65*, 66–7, 71–2, 73, 76, 103, *105*, 161
prostitution 25, 52
religio-historical *102–5*
religious *25*, 35, 43–6, 57, *66*, 67, 82, 98–9, Pl.1
social inequality *41–2*, 57–8
social satire 14, 16–18
terrorism *64–7*, 71–2
types *81–5*
urban life *48–52*
women *51*, 52, 68, *71–6*, *93–4*, 95
subtext 99, 101–2, 104, 123
Sukhodolsky, Petr
Midday in the Countryside 121–2
Surikov, Vasily 76, 110–13, 114, 116, 117, 118, 134, 136, 141, 148, 157
Boyarina Morazova, The 111–13, Pl.4
Morning of the Execution of the Streltsy, The 109, 110–11
Suvorin, Aleksei 80, 106, 107, 108

Taine, Hippolyte 116
Talashkino 139–40, 148, 154
Tarkovsky, Andrei
Mirror, The 148
Solaris 148
Teniers, David 15
Tenishev, Prince 139
Tenisheva Studio 139
Tenisheva, Maria, Princess 134, 139–40
Tereshchenko family 30
terrorism 59–60, *64–7*, 71–2
theatre 134, 135, 138
Tintoretto (Jacopo Robusti) 113
Titian (Tiziano Vecellio) 113
Tolstoy, Aleksandra *94–5*
Tolstoy, Ivan, Count 156
Tolstoy, Leo 30, 44, 53, 55, 74–5, *85–90*, 94, 96, 106–7, 115, 148, 163
Childhood 112
'Kreutzer Sonata', 'The' 75
Resurrection 112
What is Art? 85–7
What Then Must We Do? 48, 75
Ton, Aleksandr 141
Tretyakov, Pavel 29, 30–1, 44, 69, 78, 79, 80, 84, 111, 125, 126, 144, 147, 153
Tropinin, Vasily 14, 78
Troyon, Constant 125
Tsarist regime 3–4, 6, 7, 10, 24
Turgenev, Ivan 78, 79, 92
Sketches from a Hunter's Album 90, 119
typicality *81–5*

Ugryumov, Grigory
Yan Usmar's Feat of Strength 97
Ulanov, Ivan *82–3*
Union of Russian Artists 156
urban life *48–52*
Urusova, Princess 111, 112
Uspensky, Gleb 76
utilitarianism 22–3, 162, 164
utopianism 22, 23

Valkenier, Elizabeth 5
van Gogh, Vincent 34
Vashon (French critic) 40
Vasilev, Fedor 19, 123, 125–6
Morning 126
Vasnetsov, Apollinary 116, 136, 137
Vasnetsov, Viktor 118, 136, 137, 138, 141–7, 152, 156, 157, 164
After Prince Igor's Battle with the Polovtsy 141–2
Baptism of Vladimir, The 145–6
Bogatyrs, The 143
Ivan Tsarevich Riding the Grey Wolf 144
Magic Carpet, The 142
Mother of God with the Infant Christ, The 145
Moving House 141
Princess Who Never Smiled, The 144
Sleeping Beauty 144
Snow White 144
Song of Joy and Sorrow, A 144
Tea Drinking in the Tavern 141
Three Tsarevnas of the Underground Kingdom 142
Warrior at the Crossroads 142–3
Venetsianov, Aleksei 14–16, 22, 35, 78, 90, 120–1
Sleeping Shepherd Boy 15
Threshing Floor, The 15
Ventsel, Nikolai 64
Vereshchagin, Vasily
Burlaki 40
Vermeer, Jan 15
Veronese, Bonifacio 113
Vladimir, Grand Prince 146
Vladimir Aleksandrovich, Grand Duke 28, 38, 83, 108
Vrubel, Mikhail 136, 139, 144, 152–3, 154–5, 156

Wagner, Richard 85
Wanderers (Society of Travelling Art Exhibits)
early support 29–31
exhibitions 6, 7, 28, 29, 30, 41–2, 78–9, 84–5, 89, 99, 100, 106, 111, 122, 128, 144, 147, 148, 155, 168
formation 27–8
legacy 166–71
'nationalisation' 134
ossification 155–6
patronage 30–1
standards 156–7
Westernisation 8–9, 21, 109, 110, 111
see also Slavophile–Westerner question
Wilkie, David 17
women *51*, 52, 68, *71–6*, *93–4*, 95

Yakobi, Valery
Prisoners' Halt, The 25, *26*, 58, 76
Yakunchikova, Maria 136, 137
Yaroshenko, Nikolai 50–2, 59, 68, 73–6, 77, 142, 155
At the Litovsky Fortress 73–4, 76, 102, 111
Convict, The 62, 73, 76
Dismissed. At the Station 51, 52, 73
For Reasons Unknown 73
Kursistka 61, *72*, 73–4, 76, 77, 82
Life is Everywhere 73
Nevsky Prospekt at Night 52, 73
Progressivist, The 73
Stoker, The 50–1, 73, 131
Student 73

Zasulich, Vera 71

Lightning Source UK Ltd.
Milton Keynes UK
UKHW050230140921
390503UK00019B/288

9 780719 064357